Beyond Oligarchy

 Cornell University

Michele Ford and Thomas B. Pepinsky, editors

Beyond Oligarchy
Wealth, Power, and Contemporary Indonesian Politics

SOUTHEAST ASIA PROGRAM PUBLICATIONS
Southeast Asia Program
Cornell University
Ithaca, New York
2014

Cornell Southeast Asia Program Publications
640 Stewart Avenue, Ithaca, NY 14850-3857

Cornell Modern Indonesia Project No. 77

Printed in the United States of America

ISBN: hc 978-0-87727-326-4
ISBN: pb 978-0-87727-303-5

Cover designed by Kat Dalton
Cover photograph by Henri Ismail, reprinted with permission

TABLE OF CONTENTS

ACKNOWLEDGMENTS

The editors acknowledge the support of our colleagues and of the institutions that provided funding for the workshop on which this volume is based. In Australia, these include the International Portfolio, the Sydney Southeast Asia Centre, and the Department of Indonesian Studies at the University of Sydney, as well as the Australian Research Council. In the United States, these include the Institute for Social Sciences, the Southeast Asia Program, and the Department of Government at Cornell University.

PREFACE

In December 2012, a group of political economists, political scientists, and political sociologists gathered at the University of Sydney to consider the effects of inequalities in wealth and power on contemporary Indonesian politics.[1] The lively and critical discussion over two days centered on competing interpretations of oligarchy in Indonesian democracy by scholars representing a range of theoretical traditions. This volume is the product of those discussions.

As Jeffrey Winters noted at the workshop, "beyond oligarchy" could mean one of two things in assessments of the state of Indonesian politics. On the one hand, it could refer to a time when oligarchs were no longer politically dominant. On the other, it could refer to a framing of politics that does not focus as closely on the interests and influence of the very rich. What we mean by "beyond" is very much the latter. Like the great majority of scholars of contemporary Indonesian politics, all those present at the Sydney workshop are sensitive to the influence of material power on the politics of post-Suharto Indonesia. However, most of the participants do not explicitly work within the oligarchy framework, as proposed either by Winters or by Richard Robison and Vedi Hadiz. Instead, they emphasize other factors shaping Indonesian politics, including non-material sources of political power, the organization of oppositional forces, electoral institutions and the political incentives that they produce, and the craft and skill of Indonesia's political leaders. The debate, then, is over starting points and emphases. Is material power the fundamental driver of Indonesian politics? How should scholars approach non-material interests in the context of oligarchy?

The insights generated by scholars of oligarchy should be taken seriously. Indeed, the express purpose of the workshop was to challenge the assumption that scholars drawing on different theoretical traditions necessarily always operate within "parallel universes" when it comes to the study of politics in Southeast Asia.[2] As the workshop demonstrated, this does not have to be the case. At the same time, it is important to recognize that—extensive citation of the work of Robison and Hadiz in contemporary research on Indonesian politics notwithstanding—there had been little productive exchange among proponents of the oligarchy thesis and scholars who adopt a different perspective. As a result, the literature risks becoming mired in stale, predictable, and unproductive pronouncements, rife with caricatures and misrepresentations, on all sides. In the absence of vigorous and genuine

---

[1] The workshop was co-hosted by the Department of Indonesian Studies at the University of Sydney, the Sydney Southeast Asia Centre, and the Cornell University Southeast Asia Program. Ford's co-convenorship of the workshop and co-editorship of this volume, as well as a special issue of *Indonesia* (October 2013) that included a selection of the papers, was undertaken as part of an ARC Discovery Project grant (DP120100654).

[2] Richard Robison, "Interpreting the Politics of Southeast Asia: Debates in Parallel Universes," in *Routledge Handbook of Southeast Asian Politics*, ed. Richard Robison (London: Routledge, 2011), pp. 5–22.

exchange, there is a danger that the field could evolve into a collection of inward-looking scholarly camps whose failure to engage seriously with the important theoretical and empirical contributions of those working in other traditions lessens its collective capacity to understand and theorize Indonesian politics. The purpose of the workshop, and of this volume, is to promote such exchange.

Our experience in Sydney, and subsequently at the 2013 conference of the Association for Asian Studies (AAS) in San Diego, California, confirmed that these conversations best happen in person. Face-to-face interactions force us to take responsibility for our positions, and to respond to questions and challenges informed by different theoretical traditions in a way that written exchanges do not. The essays in this collection—the output of those face-to-face discussions—represent distinctive statements about political power and material inequality in contemporary Indonesia. By publishing them as a collection, we seek to reclaim a tradition of focused debate about Indonesian politics at a time in which major works on post-New Order Indonesia have offered very different interpretations of the essential character of Indonesian democracy.

One of the distinctive features of an earlier generation of Indonesia scholarship[3]—one which we seek to emulate—was that it not only applied existing theoretical perspectives to Indonesia, but refined theories and concepts, and generated new ones, from a close understanding of the Indonesian case. In this way, area-focused analyses can contribute to broader disciplinary developments in political science and related fields, something that all contributors to this volume agree is an essential goal. Together, these essays constitute a first step in that direction. As the organizers of the workshop and the editors of this collection of essays, we acknowledge that the impulse to carve out a distinctive theoretical space can hamper productive exchanges across traditions that recognize common points of departure. While these essays do not entirely overcome this impulse, they nevertheless collectively represent the first truly open and critical exchange on this topic since the fall of the New Order. We hope and expect that they will spark further debate on Indonesian politics over coming years.

Michele Ford and Thomas B. Pepinsky
November 28, 2013

---

[3] See, among others, Benedict Anderson and Audrey Kahin, eds., *Interpreting Indonesian Politics: Thirteen Contributions to the Debate* (Ithaca, NY: Cornell Southeast Asia Program Publications, 1982); and Karl D. Jackson and Lucian W. Pye, eds., *Political Power and Communications in Indonesia* (Berkeley, CA: University of California Press, 1978).

BEYOND OLIGARCHY?

Michele Ford and Thomas B. Pepinsky

The collapse of Indonesia's New Order has proven a critical juncture in Indonesian political studies, launching new analyses about the drivers of regime change and the character of Indonesian democracy. It has also prompted a new groundswell of theoretical reflection among Indonesianists on concepts such as representation, competition, power, and inequality. As such, the onset of Indonesia's second democratic period represents more than just a new point of departure for comparative analyses of Indonesia as a democratizing state: it also serves as a catalyst for theoretical and conceptual development. The contributions in this volume address one prominent arena that has encompassed much of the recent analysis of democratic Indonesia: material wealth and inequality, and how that relates to political power.

A focus on material wealth and political power emerges naturally from Indonesia's political history since independence. Among most academic analysts of Indonesian politics, there is broad agreement that Indonesia has undergone a democratic transition, but that political democratization has not produced an ideal-type liberal democracy as imagined by democratic theorists abroad and aspired to by many activists in Indonesia. There is also broad agreement that material interests and the relations among the holders of political and economic power are central to explaining the character of Indonesian democracy in the post-Suharto era. The analysis of material wealth and its organization is central—in various ways—to a host of other issues and concerns: accounts of corruption in democratic Indonesia that draw on insights from public choice analyses;[1] institutionalist accounts of democratic Indonesia's political economy;[2] the politics of business and economic

---

[1] Ross H. McLeod, "Soeharto's Indonesia: A Better Class of Corruption," *Agenda* 7,2 (2000): 99–112.

[2] See, for example, Thomas B. Pepinsky and Maria M. Wihardja, "Decentralizatior Economic Performance in Indonesia," *Journal of East Asian Studies* 11,3 (2011): 33⁷ Andrew MacIntyre, "Institutions and the Political Economy of Corruption ir Countries" (discussion paper, Workshop on Corruption, Stanford Univers¹˙ February 1, 2003).

reform;[3] and discussions of elections, party competition, and elite politics under the new democratic order.[4]

Yet despite wide agreement that material wealth is important for characterizing politics and political economy in democratic Indonesia, analytical focus on material power and its consequences for Indonesian democracy is most closely associated with the concept of oligarchy, and specifically with these three major scholars of Indonesian politics: Vedi Hadiz, Richard Robison, and Jeffrey Winters. Robison and Hadiz's *Reorganising Power: The Politics of Oligarchy in the Age of Markets*[5] and Winters's *Oligarchy*[6] share an approach to Indonesian politics that emphasizes the primacy of material resources as a form of both economic and political power. Relative to closely related literatures in political science, political economy, and sociology, *Reorganising Power* and *Oligarchy* are also theoretically distinctive, departing from the conceptualization of oligarchy that has emerged from the power elite and elite theory traditions.[7]

This volume contains eight contributions to the analysis of material wealth and political power in Indonesia. Our introductory chapter begins with an overview of oligarchy as a concept—and as articulated by these three prominent scholars of Indonesian politics—before turning to discuss the challenges raised by the remaining contributors, and the implications of these challenges for the study of Indonesian democracy.

OLIGARCHY: AN OVERVIEW

A core feature of analyses of Indonesia using the oligarchy framework is the claim that democratization has changed the form of Indonesian politics without eliminating oligarchic rule. Both Winters and Robison and Hadiz accept that the formal structures of electoral democracy can coexist with oligarchic rule, most often where democracy exists in minimalist or procedural terms.[8] Hadiz and Robison observe that oligarchy and procedural democracy are compatible, and find that meaningful elections have changed the *behavior* of oligarchs. Both analyses allow that democracy has had real effects on oligarchic rule, but deny that this implies that oligarchy is necessarily diminished by competitive elections. This point has important consequences for any evaluation of the quality of Indonesian democracy

---

[3] See Christian Chua, *Chinese Big Business in Indonesia: The State of Capital* (New York, NY: Routledge, 2008); and Yuri Sato, "Overview of the Seven Years' Experiment: What Changed and What Matters?" *The Developing Economies* 43,1 (2005): 3–16.

[4] See, for example, Nankyung Choi, "Democracy and Patrimonial Politics in Local Indonesia," *Indonesia* 88 (October 2009): 131–64; and Andreas Ufen, "From Aliran to Dealignment: Political Parties in Post-Suharto Indonesia," *South East Asia Research* 16,1 (2008): 5–41.

[5] Richard Robison and Vedi R. Hadiz, *Reorganising Power in Indonesia: The Politics of Oligarchy in an Age of Markets* (London: RoutledgeCurzon, 2004).

[6] Jeffrey A. Winters, *Oligarchy* (New York, NY: Cambridge University Press, 2011).

[7] See C. Wright Mills, *The Power Elite* (New York, NY: Oxford University Press, 1956); and Gaetano Mosca, *The Ruling Class,* trans. Hannah D. Kahn (New York, NY: McGraw-Hill Book Company, 1939). As Winters argues, these works are departures from the classical understandings of oligarchy that originated in the works of Plato and Aristotle.

[8] Adam Przeworski, "Minimalist Conception of Democracy: A Defense," in *Democracy's Value,* ed. Ian Shapiro and Casiano Hacker-Cordon (New York, NY: Cambridge University Press, 1999), pp. 23–55.

in the post-Suharto era. While the behaviors and strategies of oligarchs may have been modified by the imperatives of electoral democracy—and, indeed, by the introduction of additional loci of decision-making with the advent of decentralization—there is no institutional, electoral, or mobilizational "fix" to the problem of oligarchy. According to both Winters and Robison and Hadiz, the degree of political change needed to disrupt the nexus between wealth and political power in Indonesia (as elsewhere) is, in fact, no less than revolutionary.

The commonalities between *Reorganising Power* and *Oligarchy* notwithstanding, their understandings of how material inequality shapes Indonesian politics differ in several important ways. A close examination of these differences, therefore, is timely, not least because of the influence that these analyses exert. The approach offered by Robison and Hadiz in *Reorganising Power* and related work has been invoked in many interpretations of Indonesian politics since the fall of the New Order.[9] Winters, meanwhile, has used his expertise as a scholar of Indonesian political economy to produce a work that has been recognized as a signature contribution to mainstream political science.[10] As Winters's argument joins that of Robison and Hadiz in characterizing oligarchy in Indonesia, it is important to recognize that, whatever their similarities, these arguments draw on different theoretical backgrounds and have different implications for the study of Indonesian politics.

The first and central difference between the two analyses of oligarchy lies in its definition. Both theses emphasize the key concept of wealth defense. Robison and Hadiz describe oligarchy as a "system of power relations that enables the concentration of wealth and authority and its collective defence,"[11] and Winters as the "politics of wealth defense among materially endowed actors."[12] But whereas Robison and Hadiz are decidedly neo-Marxist in their positioning of oligarchy within the development of global capitalism, Winters's emphasis is more Weberian, concerned with the role and locus of coercion in the politics of wealth defense. In other words, while both Robison and Hadiz and Winters understand oligarchy differently than do analysts of oligarchy, elite domination, and related phenomena who work within the power elite tradition, they also understand it quite differently from one another. This fundamental difference has great consequences for the operationalization of wealth defense as a concept. For Hadiz and Robison, the collective nature of oligarchy is fundamental, as is the concurrence between conflicts over wealth and political authority. Winters's definition of oligarchy, by contrast,

---

[9] See, for example, Vedi Hadiz and Richard Robison, "Neo-liberal Reforms and Illiberal Consolidations: The Indonesian Paradox," *Journal of Development Studies* 41,2 (2005): 220–41; Garry Rodan and Kanishka Jayasuriya, "Capitalist Development, Regime Transitions and New Forms of Authoritarianism in Asia," *Pacific Review* 22,1 (2009): 23–47; Nankyung Choi, *Local Politics in Indonesia: Pathways to Power* (London: Routledge, 2011); and Yuki Fukuoka, "Oligarchy and Democracy in Post-Suharto Indonesia," *Political Studies Review* 11,1 (2013): 52–64.

[10] In Winters's 2011 book, Indonesia constitutes one case study in a larger comparative exploration of oligarchies ranging from the prehistoric era, through classical Greece and Rome and medieval European, to contemporary treatments of Singapore, the Philippines, and the United States.

[11] See Vedi R. Hadiz and Richard Robison, "The Political Economy of Oligarchy and the Reorganization of Power in Indonesia," this volume, pp. 35–56. It is worth noting that these authors' most recent definition differs from that which they offered in *Reorganising Power in Indonesia*.

[12] Winters, *Oligarchy*, p. 7.

does not require collective behavior by oligarchs, nor the pursuit or defense of authority: these are possible, not necessary, implications of oligarchic rule.

Various other differences follow from these different conceptualizations of oligarchy. Most obviously, *Oligarchy* and *Reorganising Power* differ in their focus. *Reorganising Power* offers a deep analysis of the Indonesian case. In it, Robison and Hadiz argue that Indonesia's oligarchy is a condition of late capitalism in the periphery. Their historical discussion reveals that it is also a relatively recent development, dating to the late New Order period:

> … the relationships between state authority and the bourgeoisie in Indonesia changed from a Bonapartist form in the early Suharto era to one that took an oligarchic form in the later New Order period. This was a state that had become the possession of its own officials and that acted to preserve its own institutional underpinnings and on behalf of major capitalist interests. Such a state was transformed to one that was defined by an increasing fusion of wealth and politico-bureaucratic power, articulated in the relationships and interminglings between the leading families of business and those of politics and the bureaucracy as they became enmeshed directly in the ownership and control of capital.[13]

This change in the relationship between wealth and political power over the course of the New Order suggests that capitalism does not always produce oligarchic rule. This approach contrasts with the comparative focus adopted by Winters, which positions oligarchy as a more general phenomenon. In Winters's analysis, oligarchy is a property of any social formation characterized by a very uneven distribution of material resources. The central message from this conceptualization is that oligarchy manifests itself differently across epochs and political contexts.[14] But insofar as capitalism produces extreme inequalities in wealth, it produces extreme inequalities in material power, and oligarchy is inevitably the result.

As applied to Indonesia, these approaches also differ in their primary unit of analysis. With his definition of oligarchy as the politics of wealth defense by materially endowed actors, Winters's analysis centers on individual actors who sometimes act collectively, but often do not. The emergence of various forms of oligarchy—warring, civil, sultanistic, and ruling—presented in *Oligarchy* is primarily determined by the different threats oligarchs face and how wealth defense is accomplished. Electoral politics is a possible channel for the exercise of power in the pursuit of wealth defense, and oligarchs may choose to support, sponsor, or even become political elites. But while "extreme material inequality necessarily produces extreme political inequality,"[15] this linkage does not require that all individual oligarchs engage in the political sphere or hold positions of direct rule, according to Winters. This contrasts with Robison and Hadiz's emphasis on the collective system of power relations in Indonesia and the evolving relationship between the state and the bourgeoisie, which—returning to their definition of oligarchy—entails the fusion of wealth accumulation and political power from the late New Order period. Neither

[13] Hadiz and Robison, "The Political Economy of Oligarchy," p. 38.

[14] Other forms of economic organization—feudalism, plantation agriculture, and many others—can also produce extreme wealth stratification, and thus oligarchy.

[15] Jeffrey A. Winters, "Oligarchy and Democracy in Indonesia," this volume, pp. 11–12.

approach ultimately privileges structure over agency, but Winters's analysis of Indonesian politics places relatively more emphasis on agency than does the analysis by Robison and Hadiz.

The identity and importance of "outsiders" as a challenge to oligarchy also differ in the two approaches. The fusion of wealth accumulation and political power and the emphasis on the systemic aspects of oligarchy in Robison and Hadiz's conceptualization imply that outsiders are those who are not members of the politico-bureaucratic elite. Winters, by contrast, distinguishes between oligarchs and actors in the social formation who are able to muster substantial power resources other than material wealth and use them to threaten oligarchs' capacity to engage in wealth defense. Thus, like other kinds of non-oligarchic power contenders, the "political elite" only coalesces and becomes legible as an analytical category when the power resources of its members are sufficient to threaten the material interests of the very wealthy, and are used for that purpose.

Both analyses invoke a similar caveat when it comes to "outsiders" who rely on mobilizational power. All three authors point to the disorganization and fragmentation of the Indonesian working class, and, indeed, of other oppositional forces.[16] Yet the implications of this fragmentation differ for the two analyses. Class relations are a central problematique for Robison and Hadiz. In the Indonesian case, they argue, the working class is disempowered to an extent that it is unable to act in pursuit of its own interests either by itself or in alliance with the liberal middle class. Winters agrees that the Indonesian working class is insufficiently powerful to challenge the material resources of the oligarchs, but would argue that the working class is but one potential vehicle for mobilizational power in Indonesia or elsewhere. In other words, where Robison and Hadiz understand working-class movements as the logical outcome of class-based exploitation, Winters chooses not to look to class but rather to mobilizational power—which may at times coincide with particular class formations—as a fundamentally different kind of power resource, which offers the possibility of explosive change but little else. This is so, he argues, because of the difficulty in sustaining a high level of mobilizational activity, but also because great material wealth can be used to purchase mobilizational and indeed other forms of power.

A final distinction between the two analyses of oligarchy lies in the scale or level of analysis. Winters's analysis uses examples from multiple jurisdictional levels of oligarchic power, but in the case of Indonesia offers little discussion of how to apply the concepts of oligarchic scale and intensity beyond Jakarta, or of how oligarchic power at different scales may interact. In some locations in the Indonesian periphery, including most obviously resource-rich regions, "national level" oligarchs have a direct interest and may seek direct influence. It is vital, however, also to pay careful attention to local oligarchs, whose existence is important to our understanding of local politics in both empirical and theoretical terms. The material resources of local oligarchs are almost always far less in absolute terms than those of the national level oligarchs. But they are focused in a particular place, and complemented by the other power resources generated as a consequence of their social and economic position in that locality. This is important theoretically for those who seek to understand the impact of material wealth on local politics and to account for the ways that the

---

[16] Edward Aspinall, "A Nation in Fragments: Patronage and Neoliberalism in Contemporary Indonesia," *Critical Asian Studies* 45,1 (2013): 27–54.

combination of power resources held by local oligarchs stacks up against the very partial deployment of the resources of much richer national oligarchs in that particular locality if we are to understand the impact of material wealth on local politics. Such discussion does not fault Winters's analysis of oligarchy—its focus on national politics is certainly reasonable given the comparative nature of his work—but being able to shift the scale down to local politics is necessary for any complete understanding of Indonesian politics.

By contrast, Hadiz and Robison address local politics in decentralized Indonesia directly. Observing that decentralization has created a new arena of political conflict, they argue that the local political-bureaucratic elite inherited from the New Order has found this arena to be productive for amassing material resources. Not surprisingly, then, those local elites use the authority conferred upon them through decentralization to defend both the wealth that they have accumulated and the opportunities to do so afforded to them by the political structures associated with decentralization. The challenge facing Hadiz and Robison's perspective on local oligarchy lies in the positioning of non-material power resources, which are acknowledged by Hadiz and Robison to be essential components of local power configurations, but not necessarily theorized.

These differences—in definition, focus, unit of analysis, treatment of outsiders, and scale—clearly delineate the two dominant understandings of oligarchy in contemporary scholarship on Indonesia. Of course, for reasons outlined above, it would be mistaken to overdraw these distinctions, for there are broad commonalities between these analyses. But critiques of Winters's conception of oligarchy are not *necessarily* critiques of Robison and Hadiz, and vice versa. Careful demarcation of the two approaches, while acknowledging their deep similarities, is necessary to comprehend how oligarchy is employed as a way of understanding the importance of concentrated material wealth in Indonesia's political economy. This careful comparison of works by these authors allows for a better assessment of the strengths and weaknesses of their general approach—focused on oligarchy—by other scholars working within and outside this tradition.

THE CONTRIBUTIONS

Winters's essay, which begins this volume, outlines the key elements of his thesis of oligarchy as it applies to post-Suharto Indonesia. In it, Winters asserts that the dramatic changes brought about by democratization are real and important, but that they neither disrupted nor diminished oligarchic power. Rather, electoral democracy has been accompanied, he argues, by a shift from a sultanistic form of oligarchy, in which Suharto effectively set the rules of the oligarchic game, to a much less constrained "electoral ruling" form of oligarchy, in which oligarchs' strategies of wealth defense include an intense focus on the political realm. Winters concludes that this shift has been wildly successful, with oligarchs having "captured and now thoroughly dominat[ing] the country's democratic institutions" (p. 20).

While agreeing with Winters's conclusion that oligarchs dominate the political institutions of democratic Indonesia, Hadiz and Robison's contribution offers a very different interpretation of the impact of Indonesia's transition to democracy on the form oligarchy takes. Where Winters identifies a dramatic shift in oligarchs' strategies of wealth defense (and consequently in oligarchic form), Hadiz and Robison argue that "the social order of the previous regime and its ascendant political forces remain intact and in charge of the state" (p. 54). Always central to their conceptualization of oligarchy, politico-bureaucratic power thus "continues to be the key determinant of how private wealth and social power is accumulated and distributed" (p. 35). Reformist individuals and new political vehicles may have emerged, but they have been quickly drawn into predatory politics, succumbing to a system shaped by an unchanging logic of oligarchy.

The six essays that follow offer analyses from scholars who bring different insights into Indonesian politics, and who represent different traditions in contemporary Indonesian political studies. The first of these is R. William Liddle's essay, which acknowledges an imbalance of material resources but advances an interpretation of Indonesian politics that prioritizes the actions of key individuals. Its main critique of the oligarchy framework in either form—either Winters's or Robison and Hadiz's—is that it prioritizes material power over other power resources, and obscures the craft that skillful politicians bring to bear in shaping the political arena. Like Winters, Liddle privileges agency. But where Winters is concerned with the cumulative effects of wealth defense by materially endowed actors, Liddle's ontology of the political centers on the individual and his or her ability to create, possess, and deploy political resources (pp. 57–58). In this way, individual actors can counteract constraints, which in the Indonesian context (as elsewhere in the modern world) necessarily include constraints imposed by those who possess great material wealth. His "theory of action" is a statement of what that analysis should become. It is equally a critique of approaches that focus on interest groups and social movements, to the extent that they privilege collective agency over the agency of the individual.

The key argument made in Thomas Pepinsky's essay is that a critical approach within the pluralist tradition offers a conceptual "toolkit" that allows us to move beyond the claims made about the intersection of material wealth and political power by proponents of the oligarchy thesis towards causal accounts of its consequences for policymaking. Pepinsky characterizes his approach as a framework of analysis rather than a theory or description of Indonesian politics, and he argues that such a framework can accommodate the key insights offered by each of the oligarchy theses while not being limited to them. At the core of his case lie two claims: that (a) critical pluralism has the capacity to produce hypotheses that can be falsified through empirical analysis; and that (b) the hypotheses it generates include, but are not limited to, hypotheses that test the link between political actions by or on behalf of those with great material wealth and the outcomes of contestations over policy. Therefore, unlike oligarchy, he contends, critical pluralism has the capacity to explain variation in policy outcomes under broadly similar structural conditions, and focuses on testing casual propositions derived from such explanations.

Marcus Mietzner takes up the pluralist critique of oligarchy in a focused discussion of political parties. Like other contributors to this volume, Mietzner does not dispute the influence of wealth in contemporary Indonesian politics. But he does challenge two key aspects of the oligarchy framework. First, he centers his analysis on the distinction between oligarchs and political elites, and distinguishes among several different types of oligarchs. In order to make this possible, Mietzner adopts a narrow definition of oligarchs, describing them as "actors whose primary power resource is the personal and direct possession of large amounts of capital" (p. 101), rather than individual actors who can deploy great wealth (Winters) or the systemic confluence of wealth and political authority (Hadiz and Robison). Following this definition of oligarchs—which makes no assumption about the purposes to which capital may be put to use—Mietzner also challenges the primacy accorded to wealth defense by theorists of oligarchy in their explications of oligarchs' motivations for engaging in electoral politics. Second, he highlights the empirical and analytical risks of ignoring counter-oligarchic actors, pointing to the influence of non-oligarchic political elites and the new generation of civil society actors-cum-politicians as evidence of "ongoing and fierce contestation between oligarchs and counter-oligarchic forces" in Indonesia's political parties (p. 100).

The theme of contestation runs through the remaining three essays. Edward Aspinall points to another important analytical gap in the oligarchy thesis, namely, the failure to acknowledge or theorize the role of mobilization and popular agency. As a consequence, he argues, scholars drawing on this framework have produced "mono-tonal characterizations of Indonesian politics" in the late New Order and Reformasi periods (p. 125). Aspinall's key contention is that such characterizations do not recognize the influence of non-elite forces in shaping either regime change or post-authoritarian politics, including through alliances with elements of the ruling elite. Importantly, those alliances do not merely signify opportunities for cooptation, but can also channel non-elite interests in the policymaking process. Aspinall is careful to acknowledge that extreme material inequality has political consequences. He also emphasizes that oppositional forces are fragmented and disorganized. He nevertheless concludes that because Indonesian politics is marked by contestation as much as it is by oligarchic domination, an analytical focus on domination alone can neither understand nor explain the history and trajectory of Indonesian politics.

One of the key social movements in contemporary Indonesia is the labor movement. Both Winters and Hadiz and Robison acknowledge that organized labor can threaten the oligarchy at particular (revolutionary) moments in time. As Winters rightly points out, the exercise of mobilizational power by subaltern actors is difficult to sustain and too easily neutralized by rent-a-mobs paid for by oligarchs. But as Teri Caraway and Michele Ford argue in their close study of trade union engagement in the political sphere, proponents of the oligarchy thesis underestimate the potency of the Indonesian labor movement's latent mobilizational power. While trade unions remain small and fragmented, they have nevertheless enjoyed a series of important policy victories in the post-Suharto years. At the core of these victories has been increasing militancy and a growing capacity to exploit inter-oligarch/elite competition in a context where significant financial resources are required for, but do not guarantee, electoral victory. Caraway and Ford conclude that the cases they present do not invalidate the oligarchy thesis, but draw attention to its fundamental limitations when it comes to explaining specific political (and policy) outcomes.

In the volume's final contribution, Michael Buehler argues that the best way to understand Indonesian politics is through an analysis of elite competition—an approach he argues is free from the weaknesses not only of the oligarchy framework but of the alternatives presented in other chapters described here. Buehler agrees with the proponents of the oligarchy thesis that Indonesia's bureaucratic and political institutions remain dominated by "old interests." He differs from Winters in his claim that these "old interests" are, in fact, political elites, not oligarchs, and from Hadiz and Robison in his recognition that the Indonesian political landscape has changed markedly despite continuity in the economic interests that predominate and the relative weakness of societal interest groups *vis-à-vis* political elites. Buehler contends that the most consequential change in Indonesian politics since democratization is that political elites are now forced to rely more on support from interest groups within society. However, elites' persistent dominance means that they continue to mediate the influence of those interest groups. In other words, opportunities for change have emerged in the "interstices created by *changing* relations among state elites," and are thus confined by the limits imposed by the actions of those elites (emphasis in original, p. 174).

As this brief overview reveals, it is inaccurate to describe the eight contributions in this collection as capturing a single debate between proponents and opponents of oligarchy in Indonesian politics. Neither do they track other familiar organizing principles in contemporary Indonesian political studies: political science versus area studies, North American versus Australian schools, basic methodological or epistemological divides (quantitative versus qualitative, rationalist versus interpretivist, or positivist versus realist, and so on).[17] Rather, the essays by Aspinall, Buehler, Caraway and Ford, Liddle, Mietzner, and Pepinsky challenge the two oligarchy approaches on their ontology of Indonesian politics (Aspinall, Buehler, Liddle), their conceptualization of oligarchs and elites (Buehler and Mietzner), their methodological orientation (Pepinsky), their focus on non-material power resources (Aspinall, Buehler, Caraway and Ford), and their explanatory capacity (all six).

Aspinall, whose work most closely draws on comparative scholars of social movements and contentious politics, shares with Hadiz and Robison the emphasis on the disorganization and fragmentation of social forces as a fundamental characteristic of Indonesian democracy. Buehler, like the oligarchy theorists, recognizes the persistent importance of "old interests" in democratic Indonesia, but differs in his understanding of their relationship with the popular sector. Caraway and Ford explicitly recognize economic inequality, but highlight the indeterminacy of oligarchs' interests with regard to labor politics, and the opportunity that indeterminacy creates for the exercise of collective power to shape political outcomes. Mietzner rejects the possibility of a distinct and cohesive politics of wealth defense by distinguishing among types of oligarchs, and probing the purposes to which they deploy their material resources. Pepinsky's emphasis on the policy objectives of political actors pairs nicely with Mietzner's, while more strongly embracing the structural constraints articulated in the oligarchy framework. His essay is also more closely aligned with the contemporary emphasis on falsifiability and causal explanation in the social sciences than are any of the other essays. Liddle's contribution, meanwhile, has a distinctive focus on agency: while other contributors are attentive to individuals and their actions, only Liddle argues that individual choices must be seen as basic drivers of broad changes in Indonesian politics.

In sum, just as the two oligarchy theses differ in critical ways, so, too, do the alternatives offered here. Accordingly, the different perspectives on material power and inequality in democratic Indonesia offered in this volume open new opportunities for engagement across established traditions in the study of

---

[17] On these divides, see Thomas B. Pepinsky, "Context and Method in Southeast Asian Politics" (revised 2013; paper first presented at the conference "Methodology in Southeast Asian Studies: Grounding Research—Mixing Methods," University of Freiburg, May 2012 (https://courses.cit.cornell.edu/tp253/docs/context_method.pdf, accessed March 3, 2014); and Thomas B. Pepinsky, "Introduction: State of Indonesian Political Studies," in *Producing Indonesia: The State of the Field of Indonesian Studies,* ed. Eric Tagliacozzo (Ithaca, NY: Cornell Southeast Asia Program Publications, 2014), pp. 233–36.

contemporary Indonesian politics. And by highlighting the ways in which different approaches to material power and Indonesian democracy can engage with one another, the contributions also delineate essential disagreements and conceptual differences that cannot be ignored. Together, the contributions to this volume constitute the first collection of state-of-the-art research conceptualizing Indonesian politics in nearly two decades. They cast new light on questions of power, inequality, and representation that have been long debated in Indonesia, and which will continue to animate scholars of democratization and inequality in the decades to come.

OLIGARCHY AND DEMOCRACY IN INDONESIA

Jeffrey A. Winters

INTRODUCTION

Of all political power resources in Indonesia, material power is by far the most concentrated, versatile, durable, and least constrained. The gap in material power across the population is among the largest in the world. Data from 2010 show that the average net worth of Indonesia's forty richest oligarchs is over 630,000 times the country's GDP per capita (in Thailand and South Korea the gap is 190,000 and 69,000 times, respectively). Although these oligarchs constitute less than 2/1,000,000ths of the population, their combined assets equal 10 percent of GDP.[1] Even if we widen the lens to include the 43,000 Indonesians with liquid financial assets of at least US$1 million, the result is still an extraordinary concentration of material power resources in very few hands.[2] Although these individuals represent barely 2/10,000ths of the population, on average they have at their disposal financial assets that are 1,220 times the annual income of the median Indonesian. Their combined assets equal fully 25 percent of GDP. Indonesia is following the classic pattern of capitalist development: as living standards at the bottom and middle of society gradually improve, a small number of ultra-wealthy citizens at the top are rapidly pulling away from the rest.

The starting point for understanding contemporary Indonesian politics is the observation that extreme material inequality necessarily produces extreme political

---

[1] For further comparisons, see Table 1 later in this article.

[2] The global wealth management industry calls these people high net-worth individuals, or HNWIs. In 2004, Indonesia had about 34,000 HNWIs with at least US$1 million in non-home financial assets, 19,000 of whom were Indonesians residing semi-permanently in Singapore. Their ranks grew to 39,000 by 2007. The average wealth of Indonesia's HNWIs in 2010 was US$4.1 million, and their combined net worth was about US$177 billion (US$93 billion of which was held offshore in Singapore). See Capgemini, "World Wealth Report," Capgemini and Merrill Lynch, Inc., 2011; and "*Forbes* 40 Richest," *Forbes*, November 23, 2011, at www.forbes.com/lists/2011/80/indonesia-billionaires-11_land.html. Gini coefficients, which are an extremely blunt measure, compare the resources of the top fifth of society against the bottom fifth. They do not capture the extremes reported here because oligarchs make up only a fraction of the top 1 percent, and their wealth is invisible when commingled with that of the entire top 20 percent.

inequality. Whether in democracies or authoritarian systems, the more unequal the distribution of wealth is, the more exaggerated the power and influence of enriched individuals becomes, and the more intensely the material gap itself colors the political motives and objectives of oligarchs. Whatever other more dispersed power resources exist across society—such as the small individual influence conferred by one-person-one-vote under Indonesia's democracy, or leverage based on mobilization and direct action by activists and labor—it is this gross asymmetry in material power that shapes, dominates, and warps the country's ordinary politics. Oligarchic theory best captures the power and politics of extreme wealth concentration in Indonesia's political economy and brings into relief its role within the country's social formation.

Wealth is the most potent and flexible of all power resources for influencing political outcomes during non-crisis periods, and those who deploy wealth power have a political impact far out of proportion to their numbers in society. Although concentrated wealth profoundly shapes politics in every country, it does so to varying degrees depending on the effectiveness of limits designed to dampen its use for direct and indirect political objectives, and on the strength mustered by other actors across the political spectrum. Material power is much less reliable during major crises, disruptive periods of upheaval and violence, and episodes of high social mobilization. In these circumstances, other power resources tend to overwhelm the political influence of wealth. Except in cases where crises lead to the destruction of oligarchs themselves—as occurred in the revolutions engulfing Russia, China, Vietnam, Cambodia, and Cuba—the disruption of the wealth power of oligarchs is rarely permanent. And as several of these cases demonstrate, even the thorough elimination of oligarchs across decades does not preclude their reemergence under conditions that once again favor the accumulation of large fortunes in private hands.

In Indonesia, the impact of material power on the country's ordinary politics is particularly exaggerated for two main reasons: there are few effective limits on the use of money for political and wealth-defense objectives, and countervailing power resources (particularly in civil society) are very weak. The claim is not that oligarchs, who are a relatively new phenomenon in Indonesia, are the only political actors worthy of scholarly attention, that they always win, or that there are not many important political matters about which oligarchs have no strong or common interest (there is no coherent oligarchic position on central control versus regional autonomy, for instance). Rather, it is that the power of oligarchs is formidable and that their influence over the country's politics is deep and distorting. Ironically, because of the myriad ways available for oligarchs to express their power within Indonesia's democracy, their role is arguably greater since Suharto's fall than before the transition. To the dismay of progressive Indonesians and their allies abroad, the wealth power of oligarchs shapes and constrains Indonesia's democracy far more than democracy constrains the power of wealth. There is nothing necessarily permanent about this oligarchic dominance. But for the present, oligarchs and oligarchy rightfully hold a central place in the analysis of Indonesian politics.

POWER RESOURCE THEORY AND OLIGARCHS

A focus on oligarchs and oligarchy is rooted in power resource theory. As articulated by Korpi, this theory starts with the distribution of power capacities across members of a political community. It argues that "we should reverse the behavioral approach and begin the study of power with power resources rather than with the exercise of power."[3] Differences in power resources, especially when they are large, affect what various actors or groups in a society can do, including what they might threaten, or merely be reasonably anticipated, to do. The forms of power that matter—how they are blended, who has power and on what scale, and how power distributions are shifting—are all difficult to assess. Contending actors must constantly evaluate their own power resources and those of others, and act accordingly.

Power resource theory recognizes that influence and leverage can be difficult to measure, and that power held is not always power used. I might possess tremendous power capacities and yet never display them because others whose interests conflict with mine already understand what I am capable of and allow me to prevail without provoking me to act. This outcome constitutes a very real manifestation of power, however silent or invisible its expression. I can also free-ride as others with similar interests fight the political battles and achieve the desired outcomes for me. Or I might benefit from prior political victories that produced policies, norms, or institutions that structurally satisfy my core political goals (at least for the present). In such circumstances, political inaction leaves no trace evidence or data points hinting at the immensity of my power or revealing how my vital political interests are being satisfied.

With its emphasis on capacities, power resource theory posits that at any given time every member of society possesses some quantum of power, ranging from very small (almost zero) to immense. If we could estimate the power capacities of each person, we could rank members of society from least to most powerful. A non-exhaustive list of key power resources includes formal political rights, official positions (both inside and outside government), coercive power, mobilizational power, and material power.[4] The first four of these, when distributed in highly exclusive or concentrated ways, are the basis of what is generally known as "elite" politics. The last one, material power, is the basis of oligarchy. All five of these power resources exist in Indonesia, and each plays a role in the country's politics. For instance, formal political rights, which range from citizenship to the opportunity for all adults to participate politically and vote in the country's various democratic contests, are important not only on election day, but also prior to elections via the polling-posturing-positioning game that takes place among parties and top political contenders (both of which are heavily populated by oligarchs). Official positions, whether as government officials or as leaders of major organizations such as parties, corporations, unions, religious organizations, and even huge soccer clubs, are an enormous power resource for the individuals who hold them because these persons can exercise the rule-based prerogatives of the entities they oversee and, by virtue of office, deploy its resources and personnel (which can include police, soldiers, and security staff). Coercive power resources refer to non-official capacities to unleash violence. A general in a country's armed forces is empowered by official position; a

---

[3] Walter Korpi, "Developments in the Theory of Power and Exchange," *Sociological Theory* 3,2 (1985): 33. For a sophisticated discussion of power resource theory and a critique of competing approaches (including pluralism), see Evelyne Huber and John D. Stephens, *Democracy and the Left: Social Policy and Inequality in Latin America* (Chicago, IL: University of Chicago Press, 2012), pp. 35–40.

[4] Jeffrey A. Winters, *Oligarchy* (Cambridge: Cambridge University Press, 2011), pp. 11–20.

warlord or mafia figure is empowered by access to means of coercion and by personal command over armed followers or underlings.

Mobilizational power refers both to the capacity of some elites to move others in politically formidable ways (as Sukarno did before becoming president, or as Gandhi or Martin Luther King, Jr. did as activists) and to the power-augmenting status of being mobilized. Hundreds of thousands (or millions) of people who are otherwise minimally empowered can, in concert, become tremendously powerful when they are organized into a union or perhaps mobilized for mass actions that disrupt the politics of the ordinary (often short-circuiting or overwhelming oligarchic power in the process). Except when well institutionalized, most manifestations of mobilizational power are episodic and very difficult to sustain due to the great personal demands mobilization places on participants.[5]

Material power, the last category, is the basis of oligarchic power. Oligarchs are actors empowered by wealth—a power resource that stands out among the other forms. It is by far the most versatile in that it is easily converted into other manifestations of power. This can range from buying offices and political–legal outcomes to hiring masses and armed militia. Wealth is unique in that it can be deployed through others for its own defense, while making few direct personal demands on oligarchs themselves. Unlike workers or demonstrators, oligarchs can sleep, play, or be far away while their wealth power is fully engaged around the clock and for decades if necessary. It is oligarchic resources that get exhausted, not oligarchs.

Throughout history, extreme concentrations of wealth have faced constant political and social challenges. Great fortunes in the hands of a few attract threats from various directions—from the non-rich, from states or powerful rulers above, or laterally from other oligarchs. The unique political challenge for oligarchs, and the basis of oligarchy, is defending against these threats.[6]

> Oligarchy does not refer to a system of rule by a particular set of actors. It describes the political processes and arrangements associated with a small number of wealthy individuals who are not only uniquely empowered by their material resources, but set apart in a manner that necessarily places them in conflict with large segments of the community (often including each other). Oligarchy centers on the political challenges of defending concentrated wealth. The oligarchies that have existed since the dawn of settled human history and that continue to exist today differ according to how those political challenges have been met.[7]

---

[5] Ideology is not a power resource in its own right that can be "held" or possessed by an individual actor. Rather, ideologies are contested and constructed ideas developed by multiple actors over time. They reflect the relative strength of other power resources—with the greatest contest since the mid-nineteenth century being between those wielding material power and the mobilizational power of workers. For a careful treatment of this contest, see Dietrich Rueschemeyer, Evelyne Huber Stephens, and John D. Stephens, *Capitalist Development and Democracy* (Chicago, IL: University of Chicago Press, 1992).

[6] This political activity by individual oligarchs has the salutary effect of defending material stratification itself, whether or not oligarchs think systemically or collude for this purpose.

[7] Winters, *Oligarchy*, p. 39.

In other words, oligarchy is defined by the politics of wealth defense, and it assumes different forms as the threats to and responses by oligarchs change. Oligarchs can stand alone and rule, or they can be embedded within authoritarian regimes and democracies. Important variations in oligarchy depend on whether oligarchs are armed or disarmed and, by extension, whether they are involved in the violence at the root of all exclusive claims and rights to property. It also matters whether oligarchs are directly engaged in rule, and, if so, whether they rule as individuals or as a group. Combinations of these factors result in four types of oligarchy: warring, ruling, sultanistic, and civil.[8] During Dutch rule there were no Indonesian oligarchs to speak of. The country evolved into a classic example of sultanistic oligarchy under Suharto. Since 1998, it has become an electoral ruling oligarchy, fusing strong elements of democracy and ruling oligarchy, but without effective institutions of law to guarantee the impersonal defense of property and wealth.

Oligarchs are distinct from elites, who exert their minority influence based on non-material power resources (the first four types elaborated above). The categories of oligarch and elite can be layered upon each other, with oligarchic power potentially leading to elite power (and vice versa). But there is no necessary overlap. Many oligarchs have only material power resources at their disposal, and many elites never amass empowering fortunes. It is also important to recognize that democracy and oligarchy are not necessarily zero-sum political phenomena, as the Indonesian case clearly shows. Oligarchs are the political product of extreme material stratification in society rather than the result of a democratic deficit. It follows that democratic transitions have no automatic effect on the power resources available to oligarchs, and thus on oligarchy.

> Democracy and oligarchy are defined by distributions of radically different kinds of power. Democracy refers to *dispersed formal political power* based on rights, procedures, and levels of popular participation. By contrast, oligarchy is defined by *concentrated material power* based on enforced claims or rights to property or wealth. The nature of the political powers that get widened or narrowed as systems become more or less democratic is distinct from the political powers that can be dispersed or concentrated materially. This is why democracy and oligarchy are remarkably compatible provided the two realms of power do not clash.[9]

Oligarchs are aware that democracy poses potential new threats, and the historical record dating back to Aristotle is filled with nervous commentary from the wealthy on how democratic power in the hands of the many could challenge stratification by taking and redistributing the wealth of the few. But such clashes have been infrequent—both because oligarchs are always present and vigilant at moments of democratic founding (thus ensuring that various wealth-defending safeguards are built into the institutions, laws, and practices of participatory polities, as James Madison and his colleagues did in the US case), and because the formidable

---

[8] For a further elaboration and theorization of these types of oligarchies, see ibid., chapter 1, and passim.

[9] Ibid., p. 11.

capacities of oligarchs to punish hyper-performing democracies are well known and tested at one's peril.

Indonesia after the fall of Suharto represents a complex but stable blend of oligarchy and democracy, with wealth-power pervading a political arrangement that tolerates and responds to popular participation. The country's political system evolved rapidly into an electoral ruling oligarchy in which holding office is increasingly linked to private wealth.[10] Indonesia is, moreover, an important example of what might be termed democracy without law. Some oligarchs are directly engaged in rule as they operate within party institutions and compete for office according to basic democratic norms. At the same time, they and others outside the ruling group engage in an obligatory process of wealth transfers among each other (*bagi-bagi*) as oligarchs and elites compete over who gets to keep the riches from the archipelago's natural and agricultural resources. Having rules and norms in the democratic political realm does not ensure oligarchs are tamed by impersonal institutions of law. Quite the contrary: law in Indonesia routinely bends to oligarchs and elites, even as it applies in a mundane (if technically flawed) manner to the vast majority of the population. Thus, Indonesia is not a lawless society. Rather, its "rule of law" problems are primarily due to the inability of the legal system to tame the ultra-powerful.

Given that oligarchy can be readily blended with democracy and other political forms, it means that oligarchic theory neither denies nor conflicts with other approaches that examine the role of actors or groups in civil society struggling to shape policy or win key political battles. There are issues about which there is no coherent oligarchic stance or interest, and there are also matters about which oligarchs care deeply and yet clash spectacularly among themselves. Meanwhile, social organization and movements from below can fluctuate significantly over time, and people-power moments can burst onto the political stage with very little warning. An acknowledgement of tremendous oligarchic power does not imply that other power resources, particularly mobilizational power and popular participation, are irrelevant. The challenge is to understand when, how, and how long they become dominant and decisive (as they briefly did in 1998).

This article traces how oligarchs incubated during Suharto's New Order quickly came to dominate Indonesia's new democracy as the regime collapsed and how their control has deepened since 1998.[11] The central argument is that from a power resource perspective, oligarchs are disproportionately influential actors within Indonesia's political economy, that they arose and gained power during Suharto's New Order, and that the transition to democracy does not constitute a significant disruption or even diminution of their power. Oligarchy itself changed dramatically with Suharto's fall—shifting from the sultanistic to the ruling form—with important consequences for how wealth defense is attempted and secured in Indonesia. But

---

[10] The wealth is already owned prior to gaining office or is quickly amassed after supporting oligarchs deploy their resources to elevate individuals to elite positions (which the newly elevated almost always use to grab enough wealth to reduce their reliance on oligarchs by becoming one themselves).

[11] In addition to Winters, *Oligarchy*, see also Richard Robison, *Indonesia: The Rise of Capital* (Sheffield: Equinox Publishing, 1986); Jeffrey A. Winters, *Power in Motion: Capital Mobility and the Indonesian State* (Ithaca, NY: Cornell University Press, 1996); and Richard Robison and Vedi Hadiz, *Reorganising Power in Indonesia: The Politics of Oligarchy in an Age of Markets* (London: Routledge Curzon, 2004).

oligarchy did not disappear. The emphasis in this piece is on how oligarchic power is manifested in contemporary Indonesia. Although oligarchs and oligarchy are not the sole focus of the country's politics, they constitute its most important element as long as ordinary citizens remain poorly organized and minimally empowered.

EMERGENCE OF OLIGARCHS IN INDONESIA

The oligarchic capture of Indonesian democracy began with a group of oligarchs who played a background role in Suharto's collapse and experienced virtually no disruptions in their ranks during the years of political transformation. But accompanying the transition from dictatorship to democracy was an equally important transition: from a sultanistic oligarchy under which the ultra-rich were tamed personally by Suharto, to a more chaotic electoral ruling oligarchy under which there are far fewer effective constraints on oligarchic power. The capacity to use wealth strategically has emerged as one of the most vital power resources in Indonesian electoral politics.

Unlike in the Philippines, where landed oligarchs took root during the nineteenth century under the Spanish, the Dutch East Indies had only elites and no oligarchs during the colonial period. Despite government programs designed to foster entrepreneurs, the Sukarno years from World War II through the late 1960s were far too chaotic economically and politically for a group of Indonesians empowered by concentrated wealth to emerge. It was during the sultanistic rule of Suharto that Indonesia's modern oligarchs first arose. He not only created the country's oligarchs practically out of nothing, but he controlled them like a mafia Godfather. No matter how big or rich you became, Suharto could break you. All issues of wealth defense, property claims, and contracts radiated out from the Don. This put a premium on the politics of proximity—being close to Suharto mattered more than anything else. The more that was at stake financially, the more vital it was to have access to the inner circles around the dictator, if not to the man himself.

Suharto began as a member of the Indonesian elite holding the formal office of general in the armed forces. But he quickly became ultra-wealthy and thus became an oligarch himself—ruling a sultanistic oligarchy as first among equals. A key element in operating such a sultanistic oligarchy is that all competing bases of independent power must be subverted. Suharto and his cronies made sure this was the case across the entire economy and bureaucracy. We know from the work of Daniel Lev that it was not Suharto who first attacked Indonesia's legal system.[12] Lev reminds us that the relatively strong and independent legal infrastructure that existed in the early 1950s was attacked first by General Nasution and President Sukarno. Suharto finished the job and made sure that the only recourse oligarchs had, and the only thing that could reliably tame them, was the dictator himself. His most significant contribution to Indonesia's crippled system of law after 1965 was to make sure it could not recover from the devastating blows it sustained during Sukarno's Guided Democracy period.

---

[12] See Daniel S. Lev, "Colonial Law and the Genesis of the Indonesian State," *Indonesia* 40 (October 1985): 57–74; Daniel S. Lev, *Legal Evolution and Political Authority in Indonesia: Selected Essays* (The Hague: Kluwer Law International, 2000); and Daniel S. Lev, "The State and Law Reform in Indonesia," in *Law Reform in Developing and Transitional States*, ed. Tim Lindsey (New York, NY: Routledge, 2007).

Indonesia's new stratum of oligarchs was built up in phases and driven initially by General Suharto's efforts to consolidate his regime once Sukarno was pushed aside. Suharto focused first on extracting national wealth that could be channeled to buy off potential competitors in the armed forces. He encouraged early business partnerships between ethnic Chinese Indonesians and the generals. By the mid-1970s, erstwhile Chinese traders emerged as oligarchs in their own right. It was in the early 1980s that Suharto paid more attention to *pribumi* Indonesians through instruments like "Team 10."[13] Later in that same decade, Suharto's children arose as the last significant group of oligarchs. Indeed, one of the most important factors that weakened Suharto's New Order was his grown children's capacity to disrupt the system of wealth defense and oligarchic taming based on the politics of proximity to the dictator. Suharto's children, whose access to their father trumped all other channels of security for oligarchs, rapidly became the most predatory and disruptive force within Indonesia's oligarchy. Suharto refused to limit or punish his children, and thus for other oligarchs it was no longer possible to turn to him to safeguard property, enforce business deals, limit predations, and manage risks (most of which were increasingly coming from the kids themselves). The New Order went from being a highly predictable and reasonably tamed oligarchy, which tends to promote investment, to being a frustrating and increasingly risky system for oligarchs to navigate within. Not only did Suharto's children engage in predatory behaviors that threatened domestic and foreign oligarchs and weakened the economy, but a broader cohort of predatory actors linked to the children grabbed a piece of the action as well.

Once it became clear that powerful figures like General Benny Murdani and even General Prabowo Subianto could pay a high price with Suharto for speaking up about the friction his children were causing, Indonesia's oligarchs knew that the reliable system of security and response based on proximity to Cendana, Suharto's private residence, had broken down. Cendana was increasingly the source of wealth threats rather than the epicenter of wealth defense. The final straw came when Suharto started grooming some of his children for political succession. This ominous development occurred in the years just prior to the onset of the financial crisis in 1997. It is not that Indonesia's elites and oligarchs (and equally frustrated foreign counterparts in places like Washington, DC, and New York) worked and plotted to bring Suharto down. Rather, they quietly but actively abandoned him as he faced what would be the final economic shock of his reign. It was readily apparent to everyone, not least the students beginning to assemble in the streets, that Suharto was exposed and politically vulnerable.

When the dust finally settled, and democracy took shape, all of the oligarchs and elites were still there. Virtually none went down with Suharto except one or two who stood by him to the end. Although oligarchic and elite continuity was nearly 100 percent, two things had changed. One was that the actors at the top had to adapt to the new democratic game. Not only did they do this with relative ease, but they were better positioned than anyone else to capture and dominate Indonesia's money-driven electoral politics. Whereas many oligarchs in the Philippines and some Latin American democracies are armed and can engage their militias against each other, for historical reasons Indonesia's oligarchs were disarmed from the start. This has

---

[13] For an extensive discussion of Team 10 (Tim Keppres 10), see Winters, *Power in Motion*, chapters 3–4.

facilitated the game of divvying up the democratic spoils among them and helped keep the competition fairly orderly. The oligarchs have the money, media empires, networks, and positions in the parties (or the resources to create new ones) that allow them to dominate the new democratic system and pursue strategies of wealth defense outside the political theater. To contend for office (or, for the ethnic Chinese, to fund indigenous Indonesians who run), oligarchs have to deploy huge sums of money, sometimes down to the village level.

The other thing that changed when the New Order ended, however, is that Indonesia went practically overnight from having Suharto to constrain oligarchs to having to rely on the country's debilitated legal infrastructure to do the job. Unfortunately for the nation, there are no longer any strong, independent, or impersonal institutions of law and enforcement to which Indonesia's most powerful actors must submit. On matters of property, wealth, economy, corruption, and criminality of all kinds, the law bends to individual oligarchs and elites rather than the reverse. This is because these actors have the material power resources at their disposal to buy and distort the legal system, from the police and prosecutors up to the judges and politicians. The multiple pathologies this creates in Indonesia have undercut the momentum of *Reformasi* and spawned dangerous longings for the predictability of an iron-fisted leader.

There has been a steady, but misplaced, undercurrent of dissatisfaction with Indonesia's democracy. Rampant corruption, elected officials who perform wretchedly, indecisive leadership, a surge in fundamentalist and sometimes violent Islamic politics,[14] and slower economic growth rates have been blamed on Indonesia's democratic transition after 1998. It is not uncommon to hear people at all levels of society express nostalgia for the order of Suharto's regime. Lt. Gen. (ret.) Kiki Syahnakri, the vice-chair of Indonesia's vocal Association of Retired Officers, opined that "from a social and cultural perspective, Indonesia is just too unwieldy for the extreme liberal democracy we've adopted."[15] When pressed on the point that Indonesians have conducted themselves nonviolently and responsibly during the many national and local elections held since 1998, and that the worst distortions of the system have been at the hands of oligarchs, Syahnakri insisted the blame rests with average citizens. "The problem is not that the people are violent, it is that they are ill-prepared for the choices they are making in elections and end up letting themselves be more influenced by money than anything else."[16]

Even some academics have added their voices to the democratic critique. After reviewing the higher growth rates achieved during the Suharto dictatorship and lamenting Indonesia's weaker economic performance since the transition to democracy, Duncan and McLeod write: "According to Sir Winston Churchill: 'It has been said that democracy is the worst form of government, except all those other forms that have been tried from time to time.' The post-Soeharto decline in Indonesia's economic performance *calls this view into question.*"[17] In fact, it is

---

[14] "In Religion's Name: Abuses against Religious Minorities in Indonesia," Human Rights Watch, February 2013, at http://www.hrw.org/sites/default/files/reports/indonesia0213 _ForUpload_0.pdf, accessed July 31, 2013.

[15] Interview with the author, Jakarta, May 12, 2012.

[16] Ibid.

[17] My emphasis. Duncan and McLeod (2007, 75) press on: "Can we actually say that the institutional changes that constitute Indonesia's recent democratisation are generally for the better? To put it more bluntly: was democratisation the right approach? Or was it a mistake to

misguided to suggest that democracy is to blame for slower growth rates since the inception of *Reformasi*. If anything, Indonesia's democracy works remarkably well considering the political damage inflicted on the body politic for a decade by Sukarno and then for three decades by Suharto. An alternative explanation is that it was Indonesia's other transition in 1998, from a tamed to an untamed oligarchy, that caused risks and costs to rise for those controlling capital, resulting in more uncertainty, higher costs for reliable wealth defense, and lower rates of investment. Indonesia's overarching "problem" is that the country is burdened by a group of powerful oligarchs and elites whose pathological behaviors are barely constrained. And, regrettably, electoral democracy is poorly designed to tame them. Indeed, Indonesia's oligarchs and elites have actually captured and now thoroughly dominate the country's democratic institutions, and yet do not appear capable of using them collectively to achieve a civil oligarchy with a strong legal infrastructure that would defend property rights in exchange for oligarchs themselves submitting to the rule of law.

Oligarchic Scale, Intensity, and Material Power Index

One of the most dramatic transformations in Indonesia's political economy since the end of World War II, but especially after the collapse of Sukarno's Old Order, is the rise of extreme material stratification. As the data presented at the outset showed, this development produced a crop of fabulously wealthy and powerful actors at the apex of the system. Indeed, wealth in Indonesia today is probably more concentrated in the hands of a few oligarchs than it has been for most of the archipelago's recorded history. Table 1 presents comparative data on the forty richest Indonesians. The data focus on oligarchic scale, intensity, and their Material Power Index (MPI). These indicators provide insights into the proportion of the country's total material endowments concentrated in the hands of a tiny segment of the population, as well as the relative material power of oligarchs compared to that of the average Indonesian.

With an average net worth of US$2.13 billion, the oligarchic scale of the forty richest Indonesians is substantially larger than that of their counterparts in Southeast Asia. Indonesia's top billionaires are, on average, over 50 percent richer than those in Singapore, own wealth at roughly double the scale of those in Thailand, and have accumulated fortunes more than 250 percent larger than those of Filipino oligarchs. Robert and Michael Hartono, who own the Djarum empire valued at US$14 billion (an increase of US$3 billion in one year), control the single largest fortune in Southeast Asia. A different pattern is evident for the measure of oligarchic intensity (the weight of the upper oligarchs' wealth-power in the overall economy). The combined fortunes of the top forty oligarchs in Indonesia equal 10 percent of GDP.

impose such a system on Indonesia at this stage of its development, simply because it has been highly successful in the West? Certainly, the changes allow wide participation in politics by citizens and their organisations, but what about the impact on economic performance? As noted at the outset, the record does not look good so far, eight years down the track. Will matters eventually improve of their own accord? Not necessarily." Ron Duncan and Ross H. Mcleod, "The State and the Market in Democratic Indonesia," in *Indonesia: Democracy and the Promise of Good Governance*, ed. Ross H. McLeod and Andrew MacIntyre (Singapore: Institute of Southeast Asian Studies, 2007), pp. 73–92.

This figure is modest, however, compared to 20.4 percent in Singapore and 26 percent in Malaysia.

Table 1. Wealth of Top Forty Oligarchs
Oligarchic Scale, Intensity, and Material Power Index in Selected Countries, 2011

	Material Power Index (MPI)	Oligarchic Scale (bln)	Total of 40 (bln)	Rank 1 (bln)	Rank 40 (bln)	GDP/ capita	Oligarchic Intensity
China	726,504	$3.78	$151	$9.30	$1.86	$5,203	2.2
Indonesia	632,740	$2.13	$85	$14.00	$0.63	$3,361	10.2
Philippines	408,261	$0.85	$34	$7.20	$0.09	$2,082	15.7
USA	347,141	$16.66	$667	$59.00	$7.00	$47,992	4.4
Thailand	221,316	$1.14	$45	$7.40	$0.20	$5,151	13.1
Malaysia	189,881	$1.61	$64	$12.40	$0.16	$8,479	26.0
Hong Kong	112,276	$3.78	$151	$22.00	$0.95	$33,667	62.3
Taiwan	106,207	$2.32	$93	$8.80	$0.93	$21,844	18.4
South Korea	68,896	$1.64	$66	$9.30	$0.53	$23,804	5.7
Singapore	27,557	$1.36	$54	$8.90	$0.21	$49,352	20.4

Notes: Data on forty richest oligarchs is from *Forbes* "40 Richest," 2011, www.forbes.com. Data on GDP and GDP/capita are from the *CIA Factbook*. Oligarchic scale (second column) is the average wealth of the top 40 oligarchs (in US$ billions). Oligarchic intensity (last column) is the total wealth of the top 40 oligarchs (column 3) as a percent of GDP. The Material Power Index (first column) is the average wealth of the top 40 oligarchs (column 2) divided by GDP/capita (column 6). The MPI is a measure also presented in Jeffrey A. Winters and Benjamin I. Page, "Oligarchy in the United States?" *Perspectives on Politics* 7,4 (December 2009): 731–53; and Winters, *Oligarchy*, although in those studies median income was used instead of GDP/capita. Calculations by the author.

The most telling figures are contained in the Material Power Index (column 1), which measures the gap in material resources separating oligarchs from average citizens in their societies. Although there were rich and poor Indonesians at independence in 1945, the distribution of wealth was relatively egalitarian by twenty-first century standards. The MPI separating political leaders from common Indonesians was a multiple in the hundreds, while the MPI separating the richest traders from the median citizen was at most a multiple in the low thousands.[18] In 2010, the MPI of the richest Indonesians was over 630,000 to 1. This extreme stratification in Indonesia is 50 percent higher than in the Philippines, more than twice that seen in Thailand, over three times the gap in Malaysia, and more than *twenty times* the gap between the fortunes of the very rich and the rest in Singapore.

---

[18] Amry Vandenbosch, "A Problem in Java: The Chinese in the Dutch East Indies," *Pacific Affairs* 3,11 (1930): 1001–17. See also M. C. Ricklefs, *A History of Modern Indonesia Since c. 1200* (Stanford, CA: Stanford University Press, 2008).

Although individual wealth is a key power resource across all polities and throughout history, the political potency of that wealth varies significantly. Policy changes, legal regimes, institutional arrangements, and countervailing power resources such as coercion and mass mobilization can amplify or diminish the impact of wealth-power (though rarely neutralize it completely or permanently). Weaknesses in Indonesian civil society, the rapid dispersion of popular forces after Suharto's fall, and the institutional capture of Indonesian politics by oligarchs (especially via political parties and the media) has allowed the power of wealth to expand with each new round of electoral contestation.

This is not to say that Indonesia's democracy is a sham. On the contrary, by the procedural standards of Schumpeter's "free competition for a free vote" and Dahl's criteria of "contestation and inclusiveness,"[19] Indonesia performs reasonably well. It is true that candidates sometimes unleash dirty tricks against each other, that there have been irregularities with voter lists, and the biggest portion of campaign finance is off the books (an important point revisited below). And yet, the country has held three national elections since 1999, on time, every five years. It has also held hundreds of regional elections on a regular basis. Unlike in the Philippines, where election-related fatalities are high and candidates are assassinated, democracy in Indonesia is passionate but generally peaceful. Candidates follow most electoral rules, parties take turns campaigning according to the published schedules, voters cast their ballots in secret, and losing candidates overwhelmingly step down without resistance. There is freedom of assembly, expression, and the press. Although there is little ideology involved, and party platforms are fairly meaningless, various matters get raucously debated as parties and candidates try to shape the discourse. Most importantly, the winners are not known in advance. There have been surprising and sometimes spectacular wins and losses.

All of this political activity unfolds in a context of a poorly organized civil society, which augments the influence of oligarchs. In one sense, civil society in Indonesia is active and robust. Reflecting the country's liberal freedoms, there is a proliferation of organizations, causes, seminars, workshops, and publications. This political engagement can sometimes deliver defeats to oligarchs and elites. But for reasons of history and culture, civil society in Indonesia is also badly fragmented, poorly mobilized, and provides an ineffective counterbalance to the captive grip oligarchs have on how democracy functions. As in other democracies where the power of wealth is deployed with few limitations, oligarchs play a central role in shaping who can contend for office or get appointed to top political posts. The result is that Indonesians get to choose among options that are strongly oligarchically determined.

OLIGARCHS FUND JOKOWI

The election of Jakarta governor Joko Widodo (Jokowi) in 2012 provides a useful illustration of the role oligarchic intervention plays in the democratic choices available to Indonesians. Jokowi challenged and defeated the incumbent Jakarta governor, Fauzi Bowo, a classic oligarchic apparatchik. Part of Jokowi's strategy was

---

[19] See Joseph A. Schumpeter, *Capitalism, Socialism and Democracy*, 3rd edition (New York, NY: Harper Perennial, [1942] 2008), chapter 22; and Robert A. Dahl, *Polyarchy: Participation and Opposition* (New Haven, CT: Yale University Press, 1972).

to pretend he did not have a strategy. Instead, he adopted an "aw shucks" public posture of relaxed simplicity, made a lot of jokes, and spent much of his time visiting ordinary people and the poor across the capital. The intended message was that, as an outsider from the city of Surakarta, he was untainted by the notorious "money politics" game that infuses most Indonesian political contests. As a candidate, he presented very few concrete plans for solving Jakarta's chronic problems and never explained how he would confront the capital's powerful and deeply entrenched interests.

His efforts to distance himself from the fact that his candidacy was possible only because he had major oligarchic backers reached comical proportions during the campaign. The following exchange unfolded on live television in July 2012, soon after Jokowi outpaced Fauzi in the first round of voting:

Karni (*TVOne* host): Bagaimana dengan adanya tuduhan sekarang ini bahwa ternyata timnya Pak Jokowi melakukan *money politics*? [What about accusations lately that it turns out your team has engaged in money politics?]

Jokowi: [Laughs] *Money politics* duitnya dari mana, Pak Karni? Untuk kampanye saja saya harus jualan baju … Lihat spanduk saya paling sedikit. *Money politics* di mana? Duitnya dari mana? [Money politics, money from where, Mr. Karni? Just to campaign I have to sell T-shirts. Notice I've got the fewest banners. Where is the money politics? Money from where?]

Karni: Habiskan berapa kalau kampanye kemarin? [How much did you spend on your recent campaign?]

Jokowi: Kurang-lebih antara … [stuttering] … lima-belasan. [More or less around … fifteenish.]

Karni: [Incredulous] Lima-belasan … milyard!? [Fifteenish … billion [rupiah]!?] [which is about US$1.5 million]

Jokowi: Ya … itupun hampir 90 persen itu dari sumbangan. [Yeah … and even that was almost 90 percent from donations.] [The candidate then mentions a list of ordinary folk, friends, and family who donated.]

Karni: Lima-belas milyard itu hampir tidak masuk akal untuk [kampanye] gubernur Jakarta, Pak, karena bupati saja di Jawa sekarang paling kurang lima-puluh [milyard], Pak.[20] [Fifteen billion makes almost no sense in a campaign for governor of Jakarta, sir, because even running for regent in Java now costs at least fifty, sir.]

Days later, *Tempo* magazine published a revealing article focusing on the oligarchs backing Jokowi's candidacy.[21] The key enablers were tycoon Hashim

---

[20] "Jokowi vs Fauzi Bowo di Indonesian Lawyers Club (ILC) 1…" Video clip, YouTube, July 17, 2012. http://www.youtube.com/watch?v=mzjl1vkWuwo, accessed July 31, 2013.. This forum, hosted by Karni Ilyas, was televised live by *TVOne* from the Indonesia Lawyers' Club in Jakarta. Guests interviewed via satellite included Joko Widodo and Governor Fauzi Bowo.

[21] This section draws on Widiarsi Agustina et. al., "Who Owns Jokowi?" *Tempo*, July 24 2012, http://asiaviews.org/index.php?option=com_content&view=article&id=38312:who-owns-jokowi&catid =1: headlines&Itemid=22, accessed July 31, 2013; and Widiarsi Agustina et. al., "Jokowi Tak Mau Didikte Prabowo dan Mega," *Tempo*, July 23, 2012,

Djojohadikusumo and his brother Gen (ret.) Prabowo Subianto, who will contest the presidency in 2014 as the candidate of the Gerindra party, which Hashim also heavily subsidizes. At the last minute, a supportive role was also played by former president and PDI–P (Partai Demokrasi Indonesia–Perjuangan, Indonesian Democratic Party–Struggle) head Megawati Sukarnoputri (against the designs of her husband, Taufik Kiemas).[22]

Despite Jokowi being a recently elected PDI–P mayor of a medium-size city, it was Gerindra that set his candidacy in motion. Muhammad Taufik, chairman of Gerindra Jakarta, noted that communications with Jokowi intensified toward the end of 2011. Prabowo met him in February of 2012 following an invitation arranged by Hashim, who had known Jokowi for several years. Within weeks the candidate had an audience with Hashim himself. It was at this meeting that Jokowi was asked by Hashim to enter the Jakarta gubernatorial contest. Funding commitments were also made.[23] Meanwhile, Prabowo met with a reluctant Megawati to urge her to back her own party's candidate. If she did not agree, he was ready to cobble together an alliance of smaller parties to back the plan. It was Hashim and Prabowo who selected Jokowi's running mate (Basuki Tjahaja Purnama, nicknamed "Ahok") and announced to the press the duet's intention to run. Prabowo told the reporters he was even willing to serve as chairman of the campaign team.

In early March 2012, the PDI–P had invited Jokowi to Jakarta to subject him to a five-minute "fit and proper" test, and to explore his readiness to seek Jakarta's top office. He informed Megawati that he was willing, but that despite the fact that he was a minor millionaire, the obvious obstacle was money. With a personal net worth of only US$3 to US$5 million,[24] he lacked the funds to mount an effective Jakarta-scale campaign against the well-heeled incumbent. Only oligarchs had the power resources to convert Jokowi's potential as a candidate into a reality. In the event, Prabowo had already signaled to Jokowi via Ahok that the necessary resources would be provided. *Tempo* reports:

> Prabowo first met Ahok around [the] end of February [2012] at the Intercontinental Hotel in Jakarta. Ahok said, "I don't have money," and Prabowo responded, "I'm not asking for your money. We will bear all the expenses." Feeling odd, Ahok asked, "Then how do I return the favor? Do you want [the] MRT [mass rapid transportation] project for Pak Hashim?"[25]

---

http://www.tempo.co/read/news/2012/07/23/078418627/ Jokowi-Tak-Mau-Didikte-Partai-Pengusungnya, accessed July 31, 2013.

[22] According to a leading official in one of the smaller parties close to the action, Megawati was offered between US$2 to US$3 million in "party assistance" to side with the incumbent in the Jakarta race. After she backed Jokowi, the offer was withdrawn. Confidential interview, January 30, 2013.

[23] Confidential sources indicate that Hashim's outlay for the first round exceeded US$5 million. Other oligarchs were also tapped for contributions.

[24] The Corruption Eradication Commission's (KPK, Komisi Pemberantasan Korupsi) June 2012 report on Jokowi estimated his assets to be Rp. 28.9 billion. Some estimates of his wealth reach as high as US$15 million. Most of his holdings are in the form of property, a factory, and deposits.

[25] "Who Owns Jokowi?" *Tempo*, July 24, 2012.

Prabowo, Hashim, and Gerindra were vying for something much larger than Jakarta's stalled transit project. They wanted to strengthen their strategic position in the capital while forging closer bonds with Megawati and PDI–P—vital partners in Prabowo's bid for the presidency and for Hashim's wealth defense goals.

The wildly popular Jokowi's victory over the sitting governor was due to a groundswell of support from scores of groups ranging from students to housewives' associations that helped propel him to victory. This important democratic part of the story was made possible, however, by a prior oligarchic move in which the power of wealth placed Jokowi before the voters in the first place. Even if he did come to enjoy grassroots support, he did not arrive at the gubernatorial contest as a consequence of grassroots initiatives or politics.

MEDIA, OLIGARCHS, AND PARTIES

Politically ambitious oligarchs also pursue a strategic position in Indonesia's mass media market. Following a short burst of new media voices that emerged after 1998, big money moved aggressively to consolidate most sources of information and communication into roughly a dozen hands.[26] Table 2 (on the next page) presents a snapshot of the dominant groups. This process accelerated once big political players realized the media could make or break a candidate. A small number of oligarchs now own the vast majority of Indonesia's print, television, radio, and online media outlets. In 1997, on the eve of Suharto's collapse, there were 289 print media outlets. This exploded during the democratic transition to 1,381 in 1999 and 1,881 in 2001. But by 2006 the number had dropped back to 889.

Major media groups own five out of the six Indonesian newspapers with the highest circulation and all of the four biggest online news media sites. They also own the overwhelming majority of flagship radio networks originating from Jakarta and the largest cities, and a large proportion of local radio stations. The vitally important TV market is dominated by national TV stations that control over 90 percent of viewer hours across the archipelago. Ownership of TV stations is concentrated into five companies that control 96.6 percent of all national stations.[27] Indonesia's media outlets are free in the sense that muscular intimidation from the state is now rare. But they are also thoroughly corporate and dominated by super-powerful oligarchs.

The ideological spectrum for the media ranges from conservative to extreme right-wing. Most conflicts and debates among the media arise because of clashes between the oligarchic personalities or political groups that own them. The only other major variation across publications or broadcasts is whether they are stuffy and up-market (like *Kompas* and MetroTV) or churn out sensationalist, burlesque, or even superstitious fare for the wider market (of which there are too many examples to mention).

---

[26] Data in this section draw on Nugroho, Yanuar, Dinita Andriana Putri, and Shita Laksmi, "Mapping the Landscape of the Media Industry in Contemporary Indonesia," Report Series: "Engaging Media, Empowering Society: Assessing Media Policy and Governance in Indonesia through the Lens of Citizens' Rights," Jakarta: CIPG and HIVOS, March, 2012, https://www.escholar.manchester.ac.uk/api/datastream?publicationPid=uk-ac-man-scw: 168565 &datastreamId =FULL-TEXT.PDF, accessed July 31, 2013.

[27] These are MNC (34.7 percent), TransTV and Trans7 (24.7 percent), Emtek's SCTV and Indosiar (23.9 percent), TVOne and ANTV (10.8 percent), and MetroTV (2.5 percent). The only stations not owned by, or closely linked to, major political figures are SCTV and Indosiar.

Table 2. Oligarchic Dominance of Media in Indonesia, 2011

	Group	TV	Radio	Print Media	Online Media	Other Businesses*	Owner
1	Global Mediacomm (MNC)	20	22	7	1	Content production, Content distribution, Talent management	Hary Tanoesoedibjo
2	Jawa Pos Group	20	NA	171	1	Paper mills, printing plants, Power plant	Dahlan Iskan Azrul Ananda
3	Kelompok Kompas Gramedia	10	12	88	2	Property, Manufacturing, Bookstore chain, Event organizer, University	Jacob Oetama
4	Mahaka Media Group	2	19	5	NA	Event organizer, PR consultant	Abdul Gani, Erick Thoir
5	Elang Mahkopta Teknologi	3	NA	NA	1	Telecommunications and IT solutions	Sariatmaadja Family
6	CT Corp	2	NA	NA	1	Financial services, Lifestyle and Entertainment, Natural resources, Property	Chairul Tanjung
7	Visi Media Asia	2	NA	NA	1	Natural resources, Network provider, Property	Bakrie and Brothers
8	Media Group	1	NA	3	NA	Property (Hotel)	Surya Paloh
9	MRA Media	NA	11	16	NA	Retail, Property, Food and beverage, Automotive	Adiguna Soetowo and Soetikno Soedarjo
10	Femina Group	NA	2	14	NA	Talent agency, Publishing	Pia Alisjahbana
11	Tempo Inti Media	1	NA	3	1	Documentary-making	Yayasan Tempo
12	Beritasatu Media Holding	2	NA	10	1	Property, Health services, Cable TV, Internet service provider, University	Lippo Group

* "Other Businesses" refers to businesses run by the same owner or group owner.

Source: This table is from Nugroho, Yanuar, Dinita Andriana Putri, and Shita Laksmi, "Mapping the Landscape of the Media Industry in Contemporary Indonesia," Table 4.1, p. 39.

Serious presidential contenders for the 2014 elections (and major local elections) must buy media access, which in some cases has meant buying television and radio stations and newspapers outright. Prabowo and his brother Hashim are in the market to buy TV stations.[28] Another major oligarch has invested heavily in television and is planning to launch his own national polling outfit in 2013 with the explicit goal of influencing the 2014 presidential contest.[29]

Oligarchic candidates also buy political parties—or buy their way up the party ranks. This happens in several ways. At the regional and local level, candidates pay large sums to party leaders to gain national party support. But the flow also goes downward. Those seeking to be party leaders compete by making enormous payouts to delegates at national party congresses to outflank opponents for posts like party chairperson or secretary general. And in some cases, oligarchs use their money power (or that of their supporters if they are not yet big fish) to create new parties out of nothing. This is what Hashim and Prabowo did with Gerindra, and Surya Paloh did with NasDem. The idea is to make yourself party chair so that you can be catapulted to the presidency. The strategy worked well for President Susilo Bambang Yudhoyono, who was financed by fewer than a dozen oligarchs until he became one himself.

The last phase of buying a party unfolds during the frenzied process of trying to cobble together enough representation in the DPR (Dewan Perwakilan Rakyat, Indonesia's parliament) to meet the threshold to be a presidential contender. In 2009, candidates for the presidency required the support of parties that held at least 20 percent of DPR seats, or which had won 25 percent of the vote. There is always plenty of political horse trading regarding vice-presidential running mates and promises of cabinet posts. But such deals are never enough to make a successful alliance or coalition in Indonesia. A presidential hopeful must also be ready to pay many millions of dollars in cash to his or her party allies. A portion of the payoff flows to the other parties' coffers, and some goes directly into the pockets of party

---

[28] Nugroho et. al. sum up the concentration and consolidation of Indonesia's media this way: "Today, twelve large media groups control nearly all of Indonesia's media channels, including broadcasting, print media, and online media. They are MNC Group, Kompas Gramedia Group, Elang Mahkota Teknologi, Visi Media Asia, Jawa Pos Group, Mahaka Media, CT Group, Beritasatu Media Holdings, Media Group, MRA Media, Femina Group, and Tempo Inti Media. MNC Group has three free-to-air television channels—the highest number owned by any media group—with twenty local television networks and twenty-two radio networks under its subsidiary, Sindo Radio. Jawa Pos Group has 171 print media companies, including its Radar Group. *Kompas,* Indonesia's most influential newspaper, has expanded its network to include a content provider by establishing KompasTV, besides the existing twelve radio broadcasters under its subsidiary Sonora Radio Network, and eighty-nine other print media companies. Visi Media Asia has grown into a powerful media group with two terrestrial television channels (ANTV and tvOne) and its quickly growing online media channel *vivanews.com*. A new media company under Lippo Group, i.e., Berita Satu Media Holding, has already established an Internet-Protocol Television (IPTV) BeritasatuTV, online media channel *beritasatu.com*, and additionally owns a number of newspapers and magazines. […] Some important M&As have taken place recently: *Indosiar* was acquired by Elang Mahkota Teknologi, a holding company of SCTV; *detik.com* was bought out by CT Group, the owner of Trans TV and Trans 7; a number of local television channels were taken over by large groups such as MNC Group with its Sindo TV network and *Jawa Pos,* which has its own TV network. Laws and regulations seem to be toothless in controlling the concentration of the industry as such." See Nugroho, et. al., "Mapping the Landscape," pp. 4–5.

[29] Confidential interview, Jakarta, July 18, 2012.

leaders as a political closing fee for being the direct negotiators of the deals. Oligarchic and elite forms of power tend to be mutually supporting within Indonesia's electoral ruling oligarchy. Table 3 summarizes the oligarchic moorings of major political figures within Indonesia's democracy.

Table 3. Indonesia's Oligarchic Democracy

Politician	Oligarch	Oligarch Backers	Media	Owns/Bought Party
Aburizal Bakrie (11% of TV)	Yes	Self (also SBY links)	TVOne, ANTV, Visi Media Asia, Vivanews.com (Anindya) Dahlan Iksan Jawa Pos Group (Radar, TV network)	Yes (Golkar)
Susilo Bambang Yudhoyono (27% of TV)	Hidden (Yes)	Budi Sampoerna, Sunaryo Sampoerna, Ramadhan Pohan Chairul Tanjung James Riady (Peter Gontha) [2004 Aburizal Bakrie, Jusuf Kalla] Squeezed Chinese	Media Nusa Pradana (*Jurnal Nasional*) Trans Corp (TransTV, Trans 7), Detik.com Lippo Media, Berita Satu Media Holdings (*Suara Pembaruan, Jakarta Globe, Investor Daily,* BeritaSatu.com)	Yes (Democrat Party)
Surya Paloh (36% of TV)	Yes	Self	MetroTV, Media Indonesia	Yes (NasDem)
Prabowo	Yes	Self Hashim (brother)	Trying to buy TV stations	Yes (Gerindra)
Wiranto	Yes	Self (Cendana?) Hary Tanoesoedibjo (had SBY links, then Surya Paloh links)	— MNC Group, RCTI, Global TV, MNC TV, Sindo Radio, Seputar Indonesia, Okezone.com	Yes (Hanura)
Megawati	Hidden	Taufik Kiemas Arifin Panigoro	—	Genetic (PDIP)
Jusuf Kalla	Yes	Self	—	Yes (Golkar 2004, 2014?)

If one wants to win at this money-driven game—and not already an oligarch who commands a large personal fortune—one must get the financial backing of big Indonesian oligarchs who can supply the political cash. The risk parameters are sufficiently understood and anticipated by most oligarchs so that they supply funds strategically and "voluntarily." But sometimes persuasion is needed, often involving a strong element of extortion. Candidates and their backers threaten—implicitly or explicitly—to harass or punish oligarchs who refuse to provide financial support. Past or dormant legal cases can always be revived (for instance, to target Prabowo, President SBY suddenly backed an initiative to form an *ad hoc* body to investigate alleged human rights abuses perpetrated in 1998), and key business permits can suddenly be revoked or mysteriously require review. One of the most important political calculations an oligarch can make—and this is especially true for vulnerable ethnic Chinese oligarchs who have severely limited opportunities to augment their material power via the wealth-defense levers of office—is deciding which candidates to support and how much cash to supply.[30]

There is no shortage of illegality behind the major fortunes in Indonesia. This leaves oligarchs permanently vulnerable to being squeezed. Even if these oligarchs wanted to play strictly by institutionalized legal rules (and many of them probably do), this presumes that there are clear legal codes and procedures to follow in the first place. Such is not the case in Indonesia. This is partly because of outdated and contradictory laws dating back to Dutch colonial times, and partly a reflection of greater regional autonomy after 1998, which has resulted in conflicting laws across multiple jurisdictions (nowhere is this problem more prevalent than in the regulations and mappings covering land status, boundaries, ownership, and use).

But an equally important reason why there is so much legal disarray is that legal uncertainty plays a vital role in the constant game of extortion and forced-sharing that redistributes wealth among Indonesia's oligarchs and elites. The biggest game in town is not energetic wealth creation via industry and services, but aggressive wealth redistribution among the powerful after it has been extracted from the country's declining natural resource endowments. Oligarchs and politicians must master this game of money, elections, office, law, and extortion if they are to win (or just survive) in the country's challenging political economy. This is not a transient aspect of Indonesian politics that is likely to fade as the "quality of democracy" improves in the electoral cycles that lie ahead. Rather, it is a defining characteristic of how oligarchy and democracy are blended in contemporary Indonesia. And however much those playing the game at the top may complain about the distortions all of this causes for the nation's politics, or how disgusted they feel personally taking part in it, these relationships between the power of money and politics are deep and self-regenerating.

BEYOND OLIGARCHY?

Recent work on oligarchs and oligarchy has generated welcomed debate, some of which is represented in this volume. One criticism, raised by Aspinall and by

---

[30] Another motivation mentioned by the oligarch seeking to launch a polling firm was to gain access to more reliable data about who was doing well to ensure funds were more effectively channeled to politicians who could be helpful or damaging to him. Confidential interview, Jakarta, July 14, 2012.

Caraway and Ford, is that oligarchic theory does not sufficiently emphasize politics from below and says very little about potentially important actors like activists, workers, and unions.[31] These authors do not seriously dispute the claim that the current distribution of power in Indonesia favors oligarchs and elites over much weaker, fragmented social forces. But they do advance the fairly uncontroversial observation that a comprehensive perspective on politics (of which oligarchic theory is a part) must incorporate all serious contenders for power. It is certainly true that dominance by a relatively small group of oligarchs and elites in one period hardly means these power positions are fixed.

It is noteworthy that neither my study of oligarchy (2011) nor that by Robison and Hadiz (2004) argues that other social forces are irrelevant, even if these other groups and actors are not the focus of these works. My own approach to oligarchy is explicitly grounded in power resource theory, which emphasizes power capacities ranging from the material resources of oligarchs to the mobilizational, coercive, and organizational–positional power of other players. The distributions of these power resources are understood to vary both within and across cases. For instance, non-material power resources (including the mobilizational power of unions and parties) were vastly more important in Indonesia prior to the decline of Sukarno in the late 1960s. It was only after Suharto took over that oligarchic power arose and mobilizational power was systematically attacked and subverted. In my treatment of the United States case, I emphasize how the populist movement of the 1890s and early 1900s delivered major setbacks to oligarchs when a federal income tax exclusively targeting the ultra-rich was imposed twice—the second time by an enormous popular victory in the form of a constitutional amendment oligarchs resisted vigorously. Reading Aspinall and Caraway and Ford, one could get the mistaken impression that theorists of oligarchy believe oligarchs dominate everything everywhere, crowd out all other politics, and always win. Oligarchs not only lose many wealth-defense battles, but throughout history they have repeatedly been extinguished as a group. In the division of labor that is academia, it is fortunate that researchers analyze different elements of very complex political economies involving oligarchs, elites, states, warlords, students, activists, workers, and farmers. That said, scholars are not really engaging the work of their colleagues if their main criticism amounts to: You do not pay enough attention to the part I study.

The point of *Oligarchy* is to offer a re-theorization of oligarchs and oligarchy by excavating, refining, and partly redefining the concepts involved. Important facets of oligarchy—especially its many intersections and fusions with various forms of politics and rule—are developed in the book through multiple cases that overlap with Indonesia as often as they diverge from it. The justification of a book-length exploration focused on oligarchs is not the proposition that oligarchs are the only actors worthy of sustained attention. Rather, it is that the power of oligarchs is wildly disproportionate to their numbers (including in democracies), that there are specific political challenges oligarchs face inherent in the conflicts generated by extreme wealth stratification (and their position at the top rather than the bottom), and that concentrated material power manifests unique qualities that deserve careful and separate theorization. It is for these reasons, among others, that an understanding of

---

[31] Edward Aspinall, "Popular Agency and Interests in Indonesia's Democratic Transition and Consolidation," this volume, pp. 117–37; and Teri L. Caraway and Michele Ford, "Labor and Politics under Oligarchy," this volume, pp. 139–55.

oligarchs and oligarchy is not amenable to being folded into a generic "pluralist" optic of the sort Pepinsky advocates in this issue.[32]

Aspinall presents a second and rather different critique centered on how to interpret the collapse of the Suharto regime, the democratic transition, and the politics that followed. Going beyond the general call for keeping the analytical lens wide, he advances a much more specific claim that Indonesia's democratic transition in 1998 was driven from below. His argument is not merely that mass actions played a vital conclusive role in toppling a regime that was already damaged. It is that Suharto stepped down because of a political process he says was "society-initiated." The position Aspinall is critiquing acknowledges that societal forces played a role in the collapse of the New Order, but contends that activists and demonstrators followed and finished rather than led and initiated. This view posits that students in particular arose as a relatively inchoate "mobilization of the last minute" that took advantage of an already weakened regime reeling from the worst economic shock it had endured since the hyper-inflation of the 1960s, a regime that was badly fragmented from within and was less enthusiastically supported by foreign allies than at any time since Suharto came to power (with US Treasury Secretary Robert Rubin taking the lead in tightening the noose around the aging dictator's neck).

This interpretation argues that the financial crisis that erupted in 1997 was more destabilizing than past ruptures because the regime was less solidly backed by oligarchs and elites at home (including in the military) and strategic partners abroad.[33] Students and other actors in civil society read the signals that Suharto was exposed and vulnerable—some communicated directly through players within the New Order regime. Pouring into the fissures opened by the financial crisis and the disarray at the top, emboldened students formed the backbone of a people-power moment that convinced Suharto to step aside. The popular moment was so weak and unthreatening, however, that after one of the twentieth century's most murderous and corrupt dictators concluded his impromptu resignation, he calmly went home, watched TV for several years in his living room, and eventually died in a hospital bed surrounded by family and cronies.

Aspinall's counter-argument is that powerful movements from below, which had been gaining strength and momentum since the early 1990s, split open the regime. This is not an easy interpretation to sustain.[34] Although Aspinall grants that

---

[32] Across the decades, pluralism has come under sustained and effective criticism for its explanatory weaknesses when applied to cases like the United States. Pluralism lacks a sophisticated theory of the state and, by design, ignores material power rooted in social class. It is thus surprising to see calls for its transfer to Indonesia, where it promises to explain even less. The refashioned version of pluralism that Pepinsky wants to apply in Indonesia has its most important "interest group liberalism" component removed to better fit the Indonesian context. But the obvious question is: without this crucial element, what's left to apply? Compounding the problem is Pepinsky's effort to reduce the study of all politics and power to the analysis of policy outcomes.

[33] The financial crisis hit Indonesia particularly hard because the country was more exposed to the risks of highly mobile capital flows than in earlier decades and relative to other countries in the region. See Jeffrey A. Winters, "The Determinants of Financial Crisis in Asia," in *The Politics of the Asian Economic Crisis*, ed. T. J. Pempel (Ithaca, NY and London: Cornell University Press, 1999): 79–97.

[34] Pepinsky's argument that Suharto's regime collapsed because of conflicting "coalitions" of investors who disagreed over currency and other policy options as the regime was reeling from a financial crisis is equally difficult to sustain. First, if such coalitions existed, there is no evidence the members ever met, strategized, or were even aware they were in a coalition.

societal forces in Indonesia are chronically fragmented, he wants to credit them with constituting a mobilized movement that *caused* the cracks in the regime rather than took advantage of them. Curiously, he admits that the democratic transition immediately following Suharto's departure was dominated by elites and oligarchs rather than by societal forces. This suggests that the power position of civil society experiences unexplained oscillations. Thus, despite fragmentation, social forces were strong during the period leading up to 1997, and yet suddenly became weak during the transition years (which arguably should have been a period of triumph since the citizenry had just toppled a dictator). For reasons Aspinall does not explain, the disempowering effects of fragmentation were only temporary. Empowerment (despite chronic fragmentation) suddenly reappears in his approach to explain why Indonesia's oligarchs and elites do not win every political battle in the decade that follows.[35]

No one in this debate is arguing that forces from below were or are irrelevant. The fundamental question is whether it was a people-power movement or moment that pressured Suharto to abandon the presidency. For it to be a movement proper, we would have to see evidence of organization, networking, leadership, and some minimum of ideological coherence. These elements were scarcely present at the height of the mass actions, much less in the years leading up to 1998. A mobilization of the last minute—a people-power moment that is not the source of the regime's rupture, but which is cobbled together quickly to challenge an already weakened regime facing a crisis—is attainable even by fragmented social forces presented with an opening.

The various people assembled in protest in those months agreed on only one thing—that Suharto must go. Beyond that, there was very little consensus and a minimum of organization. Deep divisions were apparent almost immediately when one major student faction accepted the succession of Vice-President Habibie (because of his Islamic credentials), while another rejected him as a New Order leftover. It was

---

Second, if there existed a faction or coalition of oligarchs still committed to maintaining Suharto's rule, it was at most a very tiny set of actors comprising his children, Bob Hasan, and perhaps a couple others like Liem Sioe Liong, who regularly met Suharto face-to-face (suggesting loyalty of a decidedly personal nature). There was far more unity than disagreement among oligarchs of all stripes that Suharto had to go. Even oligarchs who are nostalgic today for the "pre-kids era" under Suharto freely admit that they stood aside and did not come to his aid, financially or otherwise, as the New Order fragmented and crashed. The determining differences that resulted in the collapse of Suharto's regime in Indonesia and stability of Mahathir's regime in Malaysia, respectively, were not coalitional conflict or unity among investors, but rather the significant differences in oligarchic posture across the two cases, the scale of mass mobilization, and the decisive refusal of the military to defend Suharto in the Indonesian case. See Thomas Pepinsky, *Economic Crises and the Breakdown of Authoritarian Regimes: Indonesia and Malaysia in Comparative Perspective* (Cambridge: Cambridge University Press, 2009). For an illuminating treatment of military defection and the durability of authoritarian regimes, see Eva Bellin, "Reconsidering the Robustness of Authoritarianism in the Middle East: Lessons from the Arab Spring," *Comparative Politics* 44,2 (2012): 127–49.

[35] In the political struggles between oligarchs and mass groups, effective organization is vitally important for the latter to sustain its victories. When activists, workers, or peasants are unable to mobilize themselves, material power is dominant by default. As Huber and Stephens observe, "power resource theory assumes that property and organization are political power resources and that, in the absence of organization, political power resources will be highly asymmetrically distributed and political decisions will reflect the interests of property holders." Huber and Stephens, *Democracy and the Left*, p. 35.

into this crumbling people-power moment that the formidably empowered oligarchs and elites came forward to supplant *revolusi* with *Reformasi* and redirect the democratic transition toward an electoral politics they could embrace and dominate.[36]

CONCLUSIONS

Wealth-power always matters in politics, democratic or otherwise. In many respects, the interplay of oligarchs, wealth, media, parties, and democracy in Indonesia displays increasing similarities with the expression of oligarchic power in democracies such as the United States (including extreme concentration in media ownership). The main differences—and they are important—are that civil society and the rule of law are vastly stronger in the latter. Strong legal regimes do a double service of constraining individual oligarchs while providing the primary firmament for property and wealth defense. The two functions are intimately related in the politics of oligarchy, and the absence of these conjoined elements accounts for why Indonesia is best described as an electoral ruling oligarchy (in which being an oligarch is closely intertwined with governing) rather than the civil type as in the United States or Singapore.

The trend is clear. As Indonesian democracy consolidates, oligarchs are increasingly positioned as key arbiters of the country's political life. Their grip is particularly evident in the structure and operation of political parties—including oligarchic control over who can rise as contenders for party leadership, who can run for major offices, and how the political apparatus is used for purposes of wealth defense. Insofar as the media are heavily dominated by the same actors and political forces, it is unlikely that a critical free press or parties will provide the venues or vehicles for challenging this particular form of oligarchic domination. As for the potential of law to constrain oligarchs in the near or medium term, the prospects are equally grim. There is an expectation in the scholarly literature that as democratic consolidation progresses, gains will be made in the rule of law (typically portrayed as a "quality of democracy" matter). But there is no inherent reason for this to be so. A democracy thoroughly captured by oligarchs has no strong inherent incentives to impose independent and punishing legal constraints on itself. Nor is democracy necessarily unstable or vulnerable to crippling illegitimacy just because the legal regime is feeble at the top. Evidence from a broad sample of transitions to democracy globally suggest that "democracy without law" can persist for decades. It is a scenario Indonesia has been playing out since 1998.

---

[36] In his critique of "leaderless" revolutions, Berkeley sociologist Cihan Tugal warns against the "fallacy that the people can take power without an agenda, an alternative platform, an ideology, and leaders." He continues: "Those who cannot represent themselves will be represented. This old statement regarding the French peasantry warns us against the beautification of non-organized masses, a romanticization now in high fashion. Multiple anti-representation theses from rival ideological corners (anarchist, liberal, autonomist, postmodernist, etc.) all boil down to the following assumption: when there is no meta-discourse and no leadership, plurality will win." If this assumption is true at all, Tugal suggests, it holds only in the short run. See Cihan Tugal, "The End of the 'Leaderless' Revolution," *Counterpunch*, July 10, 2013, at http://www.counterpunch.org/2013/07/10/the-end-of-the-leaderless-revolution/, accessed on July 31, 2013.

THE POLITICAL ECONOMY OF OLIGARCHY AND THE REORGANIZATION OF POWER IN INDONESIA

Vedi R. Hadiz and Richard Robison

When three decades of authoritarian rule unravelled in Indonesia following the fall of President Suharto in 1998, it was widely expected that this would also open the doors for a dramatically different sort of politics in which individuals and social organizations could demand accountable governance and rule of law. It was indeed true that the old centralized authoritarian regime gave way to a remarkably open system of electoral democracy and to the devolution of state administrative authority. A vibrant and often chaotic media emerged to debate ideas previously proscribed, and new figures flooded onto the political landscape. And in the volatile period that followed the Asian financial crisis just a few years previously, successive Indonesian governments had been forced to agree to the demands of the IMF (International Monetary Fund) and other global organizations for widespread reforms in finance and banking, in public and corporate governance, and in the judiciary, especially in the commercial courts.

However, such institutional changes were not reflected in the way social and economic power was concentrated or imposed in Indonesia. Well over a decade after the fall of the Suharto regime, access to and control of public office and state authority continues to be the key determinant of how private wealth and social power is accumulated and distributed. Many of the old faces continue to dominate politics and business, while new ones are drawn into the same predatory practices that had defined politics in Indonesia for decades. Even political parties that presented themselves as the new champions of good governance, such as the Islamic party, PKS (Partai Keadilan Sejahtera, Prosperous Justice Party), became enmeshed in corrupt practices and dubious alliances. Rather than opening the door for political parties to emerge on the basis of claims to ideological or policy agendas, the same Suharto-era political parties continue to operate as escalators for careers and wealth, even if this function is now shared with some new political vehicles. And far from providing a new dimension of accountability and representation, the decentralization of administrative authority and parliamentary politics has extended the old ways of politics from the political center of Jakarta down to a bewildering range of individuals and organizations in the regions and towns of Indonesia.

In this paper we argue that these seemingly counter-intuitive developments are best analyzed within a structural political economy approach and understood in the context of the vast political conflicts that precede and follow democratic and market transitions and that preserve or reshape the social order that defined the old regime.[1] In other words, the disintegration of authoritarian rule and the introduction of democratic and market institutions do not in themselves give rise to a broader liberal transformation of society and politics. The forces and interests that had established their preeminence within the previous regime do not necessarily disappear along with the institutions of centralized authoritarian rule. As Nigel Harris has observed, "... when the state establishes a system for forced accumulation, this is not simply a set of arrangements that can be changed at will. It constitutes a social order, with a weight of inertia constituted by vested interests, the immediate beneficiaries, that inhibits the creation of any new order."[2]

The influence of previous authoritarian regimes on new democracies and market economies is also expressed in other ways. As Sheri Berman has reminded us in her analysis of the Arab Spring and of the rise of Fascism in Germany and Italy in the 1920s and 1930s, the prospects for a coherent liberal politics are diminished where the previous order has disorganized civil society and destroyed liberal forces as part of its formula for rule.[3] These circumstances can open the door for political chaos or money politics and for the entry of extremist, resentful, and violent political interests that appeal to the basest of xenophobic sentiments. At the very least, such cases show that so-called "transitions" to liberal forms of democracy are likely to be severely impeded where the social interests that support such a transition are weak or politically disorganized.

The central task of this study is to explain how those interests that had established political ascendancy within the previous Indonesian regime have been able to reorganize their power and preserve salient features of the old social and political order within the shell of the new democratic and market society. Specifically, we propose, it has been the rise of a highly cohesive and complex oligarchy that has led to these conditions, an oligarchy that embraces both a particular form of dominance over state power and a distinct social and economic character that is the key to the puzzle in Indonesia.[4] The paper begins with an explanation of what this specific form of oligarchy is and is not, on the basis of a

---

[1] This thesis is most comprehensively set out in Richard Robison and Vedi R. Hadiz, *Reorganising Power in Indonesia: The Politics of Oligarchy in an Age of Markets* (London: RoutledgeCurzon, 2004). Given that this paper is a development of that thesis, and its defense in the current debate, the arguments in the book are necessarily referred to and repeated.

[2] Nigel Harris, "New Bourgeoisies," *The Journal of Development Studies* 24,2 (1988): 47.

[3] Sheri Berman, "The Promise of the Arab Spring: In Political Development, No Gain without Pain," *Foreign Affairs* 92,1 (January/February 2013): 64–74.

[4] See Richard Robison and Andrew Rosser, "Surviving the Meltdown: Liberal Reform and Political Oligarchy in Indonesia," in *Politics and Markets in the Wake of the Asian Crisis,* ed. Richard Robison, Mark Beeson, Kanishka Jayasuriya, and Hyuk Rae Kim (London: Routledge, 2000), pp. 171–91; and Vedi R. Hadiz, *Localising Power in Post-Authoritarian Indonesia: A Southeast Asia Perspective* (Stanford, CA: Stanford University Press, 2010). The same broad proposition is made by Jeffrey Winters in his wider historical and comparative analysis of different forms of oligarchy. See Jeffrey Winters, *Oligarchy* (Cambridge: Cambridge University Press, 2011).

political economy theoretical framework. The aim is to clarify factors that have been often lost in translation between the parallel universes of pluralist liberal political science, rational choice neoliberalism, and critical political economy, and to set a firm basis for debate.

This explanation is followed by an examination of how our thesis is located in the larger terrain of political and political economy analysis of Indonesia in the post-Suharto era. In this evaluation, the theoretical focus is more firmly placed on the agency of rational individuals and the transformative capacity of institutions. In the final and largest part of the paper, we provide a detailed analysis of how oligarchy has shaped state authority and social power in contemporary Indonesia and how this system of power has survived and colonized the political and economic upheavals of 1997 and 1998 and remains the defining force in contemporary Indonesia.

THE OLIGARCHY THESIS: WHAT IT IS AND IS NOT

It is fair to say that the broader debate about the evolution of political power in Indonesia since the fall of Suharto has been largely focused on the critique (or defense) of the oligarchy thesis developed by Richard Robison and Vedi Hadiz and by Jeffrey Winters. Such critiques have included arguments that the oligarchy thesis neglects the possibilities of agency and presents a pessimistic picture of a country caught in a structural straitjacket; that it denies the importance of institutions as mechanisms of change; that it denies the significance of non-material factors in politics; and that it denies the real inroads made by local and grassroots political and social movements in questions of policy, accountability, and representation.[5] A discussion of these critiques requires some brief clarification of the oligarchy thesis, what it argues and what it does not.

The Oligarchy Thesis: What It Is

Oligarchy is treated here as a system of power relations that enables the concentration of wealth and authority and its collective defense. It is a concept of oligarchy that is set in a larger theoretical framework of structural political economy. Thus, the construction of oligarchy is understood in the context of capitalist development, especially as manifested in late developing capitalist countries. The rise of oligarchy in Indonesia at a time of growth and expansion of market capitalism during the New Order is seen as the product of struggles over the accumulation of private and corporate wealth and the way control of public institutions and state authority became essential to this process. This particular fusion of political authority and economic power has been a common characteristic of countries in the earliest stages of capitalist development, as evidenced by cases ranging from the South Sea Bubble and the joint stock scandals of early English capitalism to the "robber barons" of late-nineteenth-century America. This phenomenon has been variously described as "primitive accumulation" or "political capitalism."

Importantly, oligarchy is not conceived as a type of economic or political regime in itself nor tied to any specific form of regime in this analysis. In fact, we propose that oligarchy can survive and flourish in a range of regime types, including

---

[5] In fact, the rationale for the workshop in Sydney that is the basis of the papers in this collection was to bring such critiques into a direct conversation with the proponents of the idea of oligarchy as an explanatory concept. Critiques, including those above, are found in other contributions to this volume.

democracy, as we currently see in post-Suharto Indonesia. Nevertheless, oligarchies are historically defined. Significantly, for example, a plutocracy cannot rule from outside the apparatus of the state in Indonesia in the same way it does in the United States. This is partly because its biggest players in Indonesia are and have been ethnically Chinese and are therefore constrained in their public political role. It is also because Indonesian capitalism was incubated within the state itself, establishing a distinct relationship between state capitalism and private interest that did not exist in America.

The focus of the analysis is, therefore, on the structural factors that gave rise to a particular form of politico–business oligarchy in Indonesia, specifically on how state authority and bourgeois interest historically evolved, interacted, and became fused during the New Order. It is important that the relationships between state authority and the bourgeoisie in Indonesia changed from a Bonapartist form in the early Suharto era to one that took an oligarchic form in the later New Order period. This was a state that had become the possession of its own officials and that acted to preserve its own institutional underpinnings and on behalf of major capitalist interests. Such a state was transformed to one that was defined by an increasing fusion of wealth and politico–bureaucratic power, articulated in the relationships and interminglings between the leading families of business and those of politics and the bureaucracy as they became enmeshed directly in the ownership and control of capital.

Perhaps the most controversial aspect of this treatment of oligarchy is the suggestion that democracy has not undermined the oligarchy that emerged under the New Order, although the theory does acknowledge that Indonesia's dominant elite has been forced to sustain its ascendancy in different ways. For example, oligarchic power in Indonesia now more distinctly accommodates members of the growing apparatus of administration and politics at the local level. Many of these local members have successfully reinvented themselves as parliamentarians and political party leaders and forged new kinds of alliances with local business interests, leaders of mass organizations old and new, and, sometimes, even with military or police commands. Many former political, business, and criminal elements have used the diffusion and decentralization of government to establish quite new political identities.

The Oligarchy Thesis: What It Is Not and What It Rejects
a) The Primacy of Institutional Change
The oligarchy thesis does not dismiss the significance of institutions in influencing political behavior, although it does place primacy on the coalitions of power that underpin them. In other words, we place emphasis on where institutions come from and how they are constructed or expropriated by powerful forces to serve their own needs.[6] Nevertheless, the thesis does not argue that "nothing has changed in Indonesia." There is little doubt that the "shock therapy" of change in both economic and political institutions after 1998 has meant that entrenched oligarchies and others have to find new ways of surviving and operating within an increasingly globalized market and a democracy that is both decentralized and based on electoral

---

[6] S. N. Sangmpam, "Politics Rules: The False Primacy of Institutions in Developing Countries," *Political Studies* 55,1 (2007): 201–24.

politics.[7] Moreover, it is no longer possible for those holding power to ignore the demands and resentments of social coalitions of interests that may emerge at the local level of politics.

b) Ideas about Indonesian Uniqueness

The critical political economy approach that infuses the oligarchy thesis refutes exceptionalist or relativist explanations of politics or ideas, including those based on cultural or behavioral factors. One of the key advantages of utilizing the concept of oligarchy within a critical political economy framework is to better enable historically informed comparisons of the Indonesian case with those of others, including countries outside the developing world.[8] Even the case of the United States, where oligarchic power has been a traditional feature of US politics in big cities as well as in the form of rural populism, provides important comparative insights that can illuminate the Indonesian case.[9] These comparative cases highlight the way oligarchic and plutocratic politics can be constrained by entrenched and organized social forces in quite different ways. The relative feebleness of such influences in Indonesia, in spite of the developments observed by Edward Aspinall and by Teri Caraway and Michele Ford, provides a particularly telling insight.[10]

c) The "Matter of Time" Argument

This theory does not assume that there will be linear progression from authoritarianism to a predatory form of democracy and then to a liberal form. In other words, we propose that there are clear limits to the utility of arguments regarding the "growing pains of democracy." Indeed, the factors that historically made possible the transformation to liberal forms of democracy elsewhere are not easily transposed to Indonesia. These may be the result of a conjuncture of historical circumstances that will not be repeated. Given these distinctions, the question is not about whether Indonesia has "transitioned to democracy," or whether its democracy has now "consolidated," but instead asks what are the configurations of social and political power that are shaping the evolution of Indonesian democracy. The product may be a form of democracy that is anomalous to the idealized liberal democratic template but which may thrive nevertheless. As Patrick Chabal and Jean-Pascal Daloz have argued in the case of Africa, what appear to be highly dysfunctional and chaotic political systems may, indeed, be highly efficient in terms of guaranteeing the interests of specific groups.[11] And the cases of Russia, China, and even Singapore, for

---

[7] Hadiz, *Localising Power in Post-Authoritarian Indonesia*.

[8] In our various studies, we have brought in such cases as post-Soviet Russia, Egypt, and the broader Middle East. See Robison and Hadiz, *Reorganising Power in Indonesia*; Vedi Hadiz and Richard Robison, "Neo-Liberal Reforms and Illiberal Consolidations: The Indonesian Paradox," *Journal of Development Studies* 41,2 (February 2005): 220–41; and Vedi R. Hadiz and Richard Robison, "Political Economy and Islamic Politics: Insights from the Indonesian Case," *New Political Economy* 17,2 (2012): 137–55.

[9] Winters, *Oligarchy*.

[10] Edward Aspinall, "Popular Agency and Interests in Indonesia's Democratic Transition and Consolidation," this volume, pp. 117–37; and Teri L. Caraway and Michele Ford, "Labor and Politics under Oligarchy," this volume, pp. 139–55.

[11] Patrick Chabal and Jean-Pascal Daloz, *Africa Works: Disorder as Political Instrument* (Oxford and Bloomington, IN: The International African Institute with James Currey, and Indiana University Press, 1999).

example, suggest a range of models in which illiberal politics and capitalism can survive and flourish together over time.

d) Exclusion of Non-Material Factors

There is no suggestion in structural political economy that non-material factors are unimportant in shaping conflicts over power and the way state authority is exercised. As we shall see, the influences of ideas of nationalism, populism, and corporatism, for example, are integral to our understanding of the rise of oligarchy throughout the Sukarno and Suharto periods and of the ways in which oligarchy defended itself against liberal and social democratic critics. We do not, however, see material and non-material factors as separate and independent—a matter of choice for participants or scholars—but rather as always being bound in complex relationships.

e) Agency Trumps Structure

It is not generally suggested in political economy approaches that individuals are powerless to resist structural imperatives. Individuals and organizations have room to move within the circumstances they inherit. The demise of the New Order and the advent of electoral democracy have clearly made possible the emergence of new players and widened alliances that influence politics in substantive ways. Nevertheless, the oligarchy thesis rejects the liberal pluralist idea that individuals may simply accumulate resources such as wealth, authority, status, media control, and so on by virtue of the voluntary exercise of individual skills, including that of leadership.[12] Instead, it is argued that, in the Indonesian case, individuals invariably find themselves required to accommodate the logic of the existing power structure. The difficulties of operating outside this logic are illustrated by the fall from grace of such former reformers within the Democratic Party as Anas Urbaningrum and Andi Mallarangeng as well as in the case of the PKS previously mentioned. Even the swashbuckling reformer from Solo, Joko Widodo (Jokowi), has had to enter dubious alliances in his time as mayor of Solo and as a Jakarta gubernatorial candidate; the gubernatorial campaign involved no less than accommodation with Gerindra, the political vehicle of former Suharto son-in-law, Prabowo Subianto.

f) A Theory of Pessimism

These disagreements over agency and structure have led to claims that the Robison–Hadiz thesis is inherently pessimistic about the prospects for progressive change in Indonesia. We will deal with this critique more thoroughly in the final part of this paper. Such claims of pessimism conflate the rejection of institutional or agency based explanations of change and transition in Indonesia with a larger rejection of the possibility of change itself.

CRITICAL POLITICAL ECONOMY AND CONTENDING THEORETICAL EXPLANATIONS

The central claim of a critical political economy approach is not merely that economics and politics are interrelated but that conflicts over wealth and power are

---

[12] See R. William Liddle, "Improving the Quality of Democracy in Indonesia: Toward a Theory of Action," this volume, pp. 57–77.

part of the same broad process of social change.[13] The rise of new forms of production and property give rise to new forces and interests and to new conflicts over the rules that will govern markets on such issues as property rights, working conditions, the provision of public welfare and public goods. Such rules and the institutions of economic life are, if judged from the political economy perspective, not simply based on questions of efficiency but is also about power and how it is distributed. It is due to the way in which the distribution of economic power and the nature of the state itself is formed that different levels of political resources and economic leverage are constructed.

Thus, the central task of political economy analysis is to explain the forces and interests that are historically thrown up in the evolution of capitalism and how conflicts between these shape economic and political life and the institutions in which they operate. It is important in explaining the evolution of this configuration of power that capitalism in Indonesia has moved from a colonial agrarian export economy to a nationalist import-substitution industrialism and, finally, to an export-oriented resources and industrial system more closely integrated within the global market economy. Concern with these issues distinguishes structural political economy from the main contending theoretical explanations of social and political change in contemporary Indonesia.

Modernization theory has been perhaps the most pervasive influence in the study of Indonesia over several decades. In its classical version, it has conceived of a process of political development synonymous with progress toward democratic pluralism and regarded as the natural accompaniment of economic development.[14] As R. William Liddle argues, economic growth is positive for democracy in that it gives rise to a progressive middle class that demands personal autonomy, freedom, rule of law, and participation.[15] That such a flowering of middle class/civil society failed to eventuate in Indonesia, even where economic growth took place, was explained in the 1960s and 1970s as a result of traditional culture's resistance to such a change, manifest in the consolidation of successive forms of despotic rule. Not surprisingly, a common point of reference was the feudal and hierarchical nature of Javanese court culture, the resilience of which was thought to lead to irrational political behavior that was not in conformity with the ideal type of Western liberal democracy.[16]

---

[13] Some examples of this general approach to explaining social and political change include: Colin Leys, *The Rise and Fall of Development Theory* (Oxford: James Currey, 1996); and Kiren Aziz Chaudhry, *The Price of Wealth: Economies and Institutions in the Middle East* (Ithaca, NY, and London: Cornell University Press, 1997). Such approaches are not confined to developing economies. See Andrew Gamble, *The Free Economy and the Strong State: The Politics of Thatcherism* (London: Macmillan, 1994).

[14] See Gabriel Almond and Sidney Verba, *The Civic Culture: Political Attitudes and Democracy in Five Nations* (Princeton, NJ: Princeton University Press, 1963).

[15] Liddle, "Improving the Quality of Democracy in Indonesia."

[16] A recent expression of this approach is found in Webber, who maintains that the greatest obstacle to Indonesia's successful transition to democracy is cultural in nature. He suggests, however, that the values and norms associated with Javanese feudal culture—which obfuscate corruption and abuse of power—may be on the verge of breaking down because Indonesia's electoral democracy forces leaders and parties to behave more accountably and rationally. See Douglas Webber, "Consolidated Patrimonial Democracy? Democratization in Post-Suharto Indonesia," *Democratization* 13,3 (2006): 396–420.

The apparent absence of democratizing agents was resolved in a different way in the work of Samuel Huntington, where the main marker of modernity shifted from pluralist politics and democratic culture to the institutionalization of state power and political order.[17] The product of heightened Cold War anxieties, revisionist modernization theory placed great emphasis on political stability because disorder could open up opportunities exploitable by the Left. Reflecting such concerns, Emmerson[18] and Liddle[19] thus pondered whether the alternative to New Order authoritarianism was descent into chaos. For Liddle, especially, the authoritarianism of Suharto appeared to underpin economic development, for he believed that the president's personal interest was to support policies that promoted growth via the macroeconomic reforms advanced by international development organizations, especially after the fall of international oil prices in the early 1980s.[20]

The appeal of this version of modernization theory was severely eroded, however, as Indonesia's economy almost collapsed as a result of the Asian Economic Crisis of 1997–98. The idea of authoritarianism as the spearhead of modernization rather than the expression of specific economic and social interests was undermined when Suharto initially attempted to resist the macroeconomic reforms insisted upon by the International Monetary Fund rather than rise above the interests of the powerful oligarchic alliance that had underpinned the regime, including not least those of the Suharto family itself.[21]

Interestingly, some facets of this version of modernization theory have reappeared in different guises within neoliberal political economy and economic neo-institutional approaches. Theorists within these camps had long argued that it is the very power of the state to intervene in markets that provides the conditions for the rise of the rent-seeking economy, preventing good policy made in the public interest, diverting scarce resources from productive investment, and strangling economic growth.[22] However, neoliberals in the World Bank and elsewhere began to question the idea that simply dismantling the state would produce efficient markets and to embrace the idea that the successful transplanting of markets required a strong framework of regulatory institutions that could only be supplied by the state.[23] Reminiscent of Huntingtonian concerns for political institutionalization, some

[17] Samuel Huntington, *Political Order in Changing Societies* (New Haven, CT: Yale University Press, 1968).

[18] Donald K. Emmerson, "The Bureaucracy in Political Context: Weakness in Strength," in *Political Power and Communications in Indonesia,* ed. Karl Jackson and Lucian W. Pye (Berkeley, CA, and London: University of California Press, 1980), pp. 104–5.

[19] R. William Liddle, "Development or Democracy," *Far Eastern Economic Review* 9 (November 1989), p. 23.

[20] R. William Liddle, "The Relative Autonomy of the Third World Politician: Soeharto and Indonesian Economic Development in Comparative Perspective," *International Studies Quarterly* 35 (1991): 403–27.

[21] Robison and Rosser, "Surviving the Meltdown."

[22] Deepak Lal, *The Poverty of Development Economics* (London: Institute of Economic Affairs, 1983); James M. Buchanan and Gordon Tullock, *The Calculus of Consent* (Ann Arbor, MI: University of Michigan Press, 1962); Robert Bates, *Markets and States in Tropical Africa* (Berkeley, CA: University of California Press, 1981); and Mancur Olson, *The Rise and Decline of Nation: Economic Growth, Stagflation, and Structural Rigidities* (New Haven, CT: Yale University Press, 1982).

[23] World Bank, *Indonesia: Developing Private Enterprise* (Washington, DC: World Bank, 1991); World Bank, *Managing Development: The Governance Dimension,* discussion paper (Washington,

neoliberals began to argue that benign authoritarian leadership could enforce free markets in the face of predatory officials and rent-seeking robber barons.[24] Prominent neo-classical economist Deepak Lal proposed that "a courageous, ruthless, and perhaps undemocratic government is required to run roughshod over these newly created special interest groups."[25] Such sentiments became the basis for the World Bank's growing attraction to the notion of rule by a corps of enlightened technocrats or persons who are somehow liberated from the pursuit of self-interest and thus able to see beyond short-term goals to the public interest."[26]

The residual influences of modernization theory, whether in its liberal pluralist or institutional, technocratic managerial versions, shape the way post-Suharto Indonesia is understood outside the political economy approach. While pluralists search among the middle classes and in the institutions of elections for signs of liberal transformation, neoliberals place the blame for growing disorganization and chaos on democracy itself and the opportunities it offers to self-seeking interests and predatory raiders.[27]

Other influences can also be seen in the application of the democratic transitions literature in Indonesia.[28] With its origins in the analysis of political change in the Iberian Peninsula and Latin America in the 1970s and 1980s, democratic transitions theory was distinguished by its reassertion of the primacy of social agency in political analysis and the crafting of benign pacts following the demise of authoritarian regimes—pacts through which democratic institutions replete with new rules for politics can be forged. This theory also reasserts the proposition that institutions can shape social and political behavior, dismissing the necessity of social revolution or transformation as a precondition for democratic change.[29]

These themes became attractive to many Indonesian analysts who hoped that the post-Suharto era would ultimately produce benign and liberal outcomes even if

DC: World Bank, 1991); World Bank, World Development Report, *Building Institutions for Markets* (Washington, DC: World Bank 2002); World Bank, *Indonesia: Accelerating Recovery in Uncertain Times,* report from the East Asia Poverty Reduction and Economics Management Unit, October 13, 2000.

[24] T. N. Srinivasan, *Neo-classical Political Economy: The State and Economic Development* (New Haven, CT: Economic Growth Center, Yale University, 1985).

[25] Lal, *The Poverty of Development Economics,* p. 33.

[26] Merle S. Grindle, "The New Political Economy: Positive Economics and Negative Politics," in *Politics and Policy Making in Developing Countries,* ed. Gerald M. Meier (San Francisco, CA: International Center for Economic Growth, 1991), pp. 41–67.

[27] See, for example, Ron Duncan and Ross McLeod, "The State and the Market in Democratic Indonesia," in *Indonesia: Democracy and the Promise of Good Governance,* ed. Ross McLeod and Andrew MacIntyre (Singapore: Institute of Southeast Asian Studies, 2007), pp. 73–92.

[28] R. William Liddle, *Crafting Indonesian Democracy: International Conference toward Structural Reforms for Democratization in Indonesia: Problems and Prospects* (Bandung: Penerbit Mizan, 2001); R. William Liddle, "Indonesia's Democratic Transition: Playing by the Rules," in *The Architecture of Democracy: Constitutional Design, Conflict Management, and Democracy,* ed. Andrew Reynolds (Oxford: Oxford University Press, 2002); Edward Aspinall, *Opposing Suharto: Compromise, Resistance, and Regime Change in Indonesia* (Stanford, CA: Stanford University Press, 2005); and Paul J. Carnegie, *The Road from Authoritarianism to Democratization in Indonesia* (Basingstoke: Palgrave Macmillan, 2010).

[29] Guillermo O'Donnell, Philippe C. Schitter, and Laurence Whitehead, *Transitions from Authoritarian Rule: Comparative Perspectives* (Baltimore, MD, and London: Johns Hopkins University Press, 1986).

those outcomes developed after an initial period of confusion. What they offered was the possibility that good decisions made by the right kind of individuals, able to rise above patrimonial politics, could somehow bypass the structural constraints to democratization and empower those who had been marginalized under the authoritarian New Order.[30]

It soon became clear, however, that Indonesian democratization had provided a lifeline to the oligarchs incubated and nurtured within the previous centralized system of authority and patronage. This was a democracy driven by money politics and in which competition between an array of predatory interests over the spoils of state power, institutions, and resources would take more chaotic forms than under the New Order. Political parties and parliaments were largely unencumbered by programs or ideologies, and certainly free of liberal policies, and only occasionally subject to the demands of broader social interests that remain largely disorganized.

As the democratic transitions problematic began to lose its luster,[31] a new literature has begun to emerge that appears self-consciously to place emphasis on civil society movements and new developments in such arenas as organized labor. Initiated by labor, new waves of strike action have taken place in some localities, making use of opportunities provided by democratization, and to which the Indonesian press has devoted considerable attention. The point of such works is, again, to explore the possibly of social agency trumping structural constraints, although these studies are focused on local and grassroots organizations rather than on technocrats and political leaders. Some but not all of this discourse is influenced by the broad literature on social movements and contentious politics as put forward by Doug McAdams, Charles Tilly, and Sidney Tarrow.[32] Writing on the Indonesian labor movement, Benny Hari Juliawan, for example, ponders whether Indonesia is becoming a "movement society"[33]—a concept borrowed from David Meyer and Tarrow's analysis of public protest in advanced industrial societies.[34]

Social movement theory has its parallels with political economy theory in that it places an emphasis on change as a process driven by conflicts among politically organized social interests. A central point of divergence separating these two perspectives, however, lies in the different ways of understanding the relationship between the state and social power. In the political economy view, the rise of a vigorous civil society historically requires not the shrinking of state power, but its consolidation in a form that provides the guarantees of civil rights and rule of law.[35] In other words, incremental sniping at the margins by social movements and NGOs has limited effectiveness. Real change in Indonesia requires that state power itself be

---

[30] See, for example, Gerry Van Klinken, "How a Democratic Deal Might be Struck," in *Reformasi: Crisis and Change in Indonesia*, ed. Arief Budiman, Barbara Hatley, and Damien Kingsbury (Melbourne: Monash Asia Institute, 1999), pp. 59–68.

[31] For the reasons, see Thomas Carothers, "The End of the Transition Paradigm," *Journal of Democracy* 13,1 (2002): 15–21.

[32] See, e.g., Doug McAdams, Charles Tilly, and Sidney Tarrow, *Dynamics of Contention* (Cambridge: Cambridge University Press, 2001).

[33] Benny Hari Juliawan, "Street-level Politics: Labour Protests in Post-authoritarian Indonesia," *Journal of Contemporary Asia* 41,3 (2011): 349–70.

[34] David Meyer and Sidney Tarrow, eds., *The Social Movement Society: Contentious Politics for a New Century* (Oxford: Rowman and Littlefield, 1998).

[35] See E. M. Wood, "The Uses and Abuses of Civil Society," *The Socialist Register* 26 (1990): 60–84.

wrested from the hands of a reconstituted oligarchy whose authority is embedded in the enforcement of institutional and legal practices that are antithetical to liberal notions of society and markets.

THE IDEA OF OLIGARCHY AND THE EXPLANATION OF POWER IN POST-AUTHORITARIAN INDONESIA

How, then, does a political economy analysis and a thesis that is focused upon oligarchy explain the way power and authority are reconstructed in the wake of authoritarian regimes? A pluralist might look for individuals able to construct their own power resources as a result of a capacity for leadership. Institutional theorists will assess the design and capacity of institutions and the levels of efficient governance able to insulate technocratic authority from vested interests. Other social theorists may investigate the extent of social capital, identifying this resource as the basis for a vibrant civil society. Structural political economists, on the other hand, will look at the way social power and interest are forged and configured and how this configuration is organized politically.

The questions to be asked are to some degree suggested by the strikingly different ways that authoritarian regimes around the world have collapsed and been transformed into various forms of democracy over the past several decades.[36] The fall of the Mubarak regime in Egypt, for example, raises the question of why Indonesia has not descended into the political chaos, or at least the gridlock, that has defined the Egyptian situation and why the threat of retreat into some variant of illiberal politics, whether Islamic or military, has not been a real possibility in the Indonesian case. Or why have there been no prolonged power struggles within the ruling political and social forces and their military allies and emerging business interests as occurred in Thailand? There, the political struggles that followed the economic crisis of 1997–98 culminated in the victory of elected business politicians within a new form of nationalist and populist political alliance.[37]

What is required in the political economy approach is an investigation of the genesis of Indonesia's oligarchy and how its political relations with other social forces and interests evolved. Several propositions emerge. Most important is that we understand oligarchy and the political regimes it spawned not simply as political phenomena but recognize their social character. Thus, the Suharto regime can be seen as resting upon a broad system of oligarchic relations that had, in themselves, become the central glue for a social order and determined the way power and wealth were accumulated and allocated from Jakarta down to the regions and towns of Indonesia. Oligarchy's growing political coherence and social pervasiveness meant it was no longer dependent specifically upon the institutions of centralized authoritarian rule but could embrace and colonize both market capitalism and political democracy. It was able progressively to shed its reliance on the coercive power of military or security forces, at least compared to the extent that defined Mubarak's oligarchy, for example.[38]

---

[36] Clearly we do not intend to enter into any extended comparative analysis in the context of this paper.

[37] Kevin Hewison, "Neo-liberalism and Domestic Capital: The Political Outcomes of the Economic Crisis in Thailand," *The Journal of Development Studies* 41,2 (2005): 310–30.

[38] Samer Soliman, *The Autumn of Dictatorship: Fiscal Crisis and Political Change in Egypt under Mubarak* (Stanford, CA: Stanford University Press, 2011), pp. 63–65.

A second factor that has shaped Indonesia's political economy since the fall of Suharto is the way the emerging oligarchy organized its political relations with other forces. It is important that the previous Sukarno and Suharto regimes had thoroughly disorganized and fragmented social and political organizations and ideologies that threatened their absolute ascendancy, whether these were based within the liberal middle class, a radical and working class, or even a reactionary Islamic petty bourgeoisie. This effective disruption of civil society was achieved not simply through repression by the security apparatus but also within a more complex corporatist co-option of the civil society organizations. So long as prosperity was increased, Indonesia's middle class embraced Suharto and failed to grasp liberal ideas with any enthusiasm. As a consequence, when the old regime fell, despite the initial enthusiasm and energy of reformist movements, those with the most potential to strengthen civil society have never been able to recover any substantial ideological or organizational cohesion or build a substantial social base.

At the same time, the answer to the Indonesian "puzzle" also lies in the fact that attempts by the IMF and other international financial institutions to enforce constraints on the politics of oligarchy by means of institutional reform following the financial and economic crises of 1997–98 have been limited. This is not because of a successful resistance to democracy or markets on the part of the oligarchs but because these now suited their needs and provided a framework within which they could consolidate their authority and economic power. Liberals and neoliberals were to search vainly for progressive forces to support technocratic rule or the broader scope of liberal democracy or to dismantle the tentacles of oligarchy throughout the public bureaucracy or in the new parliaments.

Oligarchy and the Neoliberal Challenge

How, then, did oligarchy embrace the market and the rules that defined it? Neoliberalism and oligarchy have had a long and complex relationship in Indonesia. The rise of Suharto in 1965 had been welcomed by Western governments, especially when the new regime appointed a team of Western-trained economists to key economic ministries and began to wind back the system of nationalist state capitalism established by former President Sukarno.[39]

Nevertheless, the relationship between the neoliberal reformers and the oligarchs was to become tense and sometimes hostile. Despite the moves to dismantle the "guided economy" of the Sukarno period, important aspects of state capitalism were retained. Many state corporations continued to control access to key sectors of the economy, including in transport and communication, banking, trade, electricity generation, mineral resources, and agriculture. In part, such state-owned behemoths as Bulog and Pertamina served the old agendas of economic nationalism and protected industrial development, stabilizing commodity prices and subsidizing strategic industries, notably in steel, petrochemicals, shipping, engineering, fabrication, and in the communications sector.[40]

In reality, the authority exercised by the state over state bank credit, import licenses, forestry and mining concessions, and government contracts and procurement increasingly became the basis of a vast system of patronage and favor.

---

[39] J. Panglaykim and K. D. Thomas, "The New Order and the Economy," *Indonesia* 3 (April 1967): 73–120.

[40] Richard Robison, *Indonesia: The Rise of Capital* (Sydney: Allen and Unwin, 1986).

At one level, rents raised by such activities became important sources of funding for the military and other state bodies and for individual officials and their families. At the same time, they were to be the underpinnings of a substantial domestic class of capitalists and associated swarms of *rentiers* and "fixers." The most important of these capitalists were drawn from the ethnic Chinese community and included the leaders of business empires like those of Liem Sioe Liong and William Soerjadjaja. To a much lesser extent, indigenous Indonesian business groups also launched their business ventures as recipients of contracts and monopolies allocated by powerful patrons within the state.[41]

By the 1980s, those interests controlling the terminals of this system began to take a more oligarchic form as the families of powerful officials and military officers, no longer satisfied with simply collecting tolls, now directly entered the world of business in their own right as owners of capital and as shareholders. This metamorphosis of officials and politicians into a putative bourgeoisie has been a common feature in developing capitalist economies, especially in places where they emerged from engagement in various forms of state capitalism.[42] In the case of Indonesia, the way was led by the president's family, which constructed a vast business empire that extended from banking, forestry, and agriculture to automobiles and petro-chemicals. Other families from the ranks of political leaders, state officials, and military officers followed, not only at the national level but in a pattern to be repeated down to the provinces and towns and involving the families of governors, *bupatis,* and local military commanders.[43]

At the same time, policies also became more directly the instruments by which oligarchic interest was enhanced. Legislation to reserve government contracts and procurement for domestic business, under regulations Keppres 10 and 14 in 1979 and 1980, channelled vast amounts of state funds into the hands of the State Secretariat and its Team 10 and through the president's special fund, Banpres, for the same purposes.[44] Among its beneficiaries were a growing and politically important group of indigenous (*pribumi*) business figures, many of whom, notably Aburizal Bakrie, have continued to be key business and political players to the present time. In other words, the system of oligarchy had increasingly become the defining framework within which political power and wealth in Indonesia were drawn together and in which a divergence of families and groups were encompassed.[45]

It is important that oligarchy sought to consolidate itself not by simply negating the rules of the market but by selectively exploiting and expropriating them. In some cases, the state sector and its lucrative monopolies, including in banking, power generation, and telecommunications, were dismantled and transferred into private

---

[41] Ibid.

[42] Events in the Middle East have provided an insight into the rise of family business dynasties from political origins in that region. Much of the vitriol of reformers was directed at the venality of the sons and relatives of various dictators, including Gaddafi, Ben Ali, Hosni Mubarak, and Saddam Hussein.

[43] Robison, *Indonesia: The Rise of Capital.*

[44] See Robison and Hadiz, *Reorganising Power,* pp. 58, 60. The amounts of state funds involved: US$20 billion between 1980 and 1986. See Jeffrey Winters, *Power in Motion: Capital Mobility and the Indonesian State* (Ithaca, NY: Cornell University Press, 1996), pp. 151–64; and Robinson Pangaribuan, *The Indonesian State Secretariat 1945–1993* (Perth: Asia Research Centre, 1995), pp. 35–41.

[45] See Robison and Hadiz, *Reorganising Power,* pp. 57, 60.

hands. In particular, the deregulation of the finance sector enabled a dramatic inflow of global capital for domestic investors. The rapid establishment of private banks, with little regulatory control, enabled private conglomerates to mobilize vast new sources of private funding for their own enterprises.[46]

Organizations like the World Bank and their Indonesian technocratic allies had only limited influence over this runaway system of oligarchy, especially with Indonesia's economic growth surging ahead in the 1980s and 1990s. There were other constraints on neoliberal agendas from unlikely quarters. Western governments were unwilling to upset governments and forces that opened the doors to their investors and served their larger geostrategic interests, and which kept radical and reactionary threats at bay. And large Western corporate investors competed with each other to get a place at the table where huge infrastructure and resource projects figured as important prizes; these investors proved willing to enter into the murky politics of oligarchy in the process. When the edifice of highly leveraged growth came apart in 1997 and 1998, Western banks, contractors, and resource companies were deeply implicated in the practices and relationships at the heart of the crisis.

Surviving the Crisis: How Economic Power Was Reorganized

The long coalescence of authoritarian politics, market capitalism, and oligarchy appeared to come to a dramatic end with the Asian Financial Crisis of 1997–98, as Indonesia was plunged into a destructive economic collapse that exposed the real and fragile political underpinnings of its economic miracle. An economy that had enjoyed decades of growth was forced to submit to the humiliating demands for policy and institutional reform by the IMF as Indonesia confronted a crisis of public and private debt that paralyzed its financial and banking institutions and engulfed its major corporate conglomerates.[47] While some neoliberal economists placed the blame for the crisis upon dysfunction in the global financial architecture,[48] it was more widely accepted that Asian economies fell under the weight of their own inefficiency and the widespread cronyism that permeated the governments of the region. IMF managing director, Michel Camdessus, argued that the crisis resulted from Asian governments' and corporations' refusal to adhere to the disciplines of global markets and was a lesson for Asia's policy-makers and a "blessing in disguise" that would pave the way for better policy choices.[49]

The huge catalogue of demands set by the IMF as conditions for its US$30 billion rescue package included stringent requirements for reforms in governance and rule of law, as well as transparency and disclosure of information that enabled prices and risks to be set at their true value. [50] More immediately, the IMF set out plans for an

---

[46] Ibid., pp. 82–84.

[47] Ibid., pp. 6–10.

[48] Ross McLeod, "Indonesia," in *East Asia in Crisis: From Being a Miracle to Needing One,* ed. Ross McLeod and Ross Garnaut (London: Routledge, 1998), pp. 31–48; Ross Garnaut, "The Financial Crisis: A Watershed in Economic Thought about East Asia," *Asian Pacific Economic Literature* 12,1 (May 1998): 1–11; and Hal Hill, *The Indonesian Economy in Crisis: Causes, Consequences, and Crises* (Singapore: Institute of Southeast Asia Studies, 1999).

[49] "Socialist International," editorial, *Asian Wall Street Journal,* December 18, 1997; "An $18 Billion Inoculation," *Asian Wall Street Journal,* February 5, 1998.

[50] See Gary Hamilton, "Asian Business Networks in Transition: Or, What Alan Greenspan Does Not Know about the Asian Business Crisis," in *The Politics of the Asian Economic Crisis,* ed. T. J. Pempel (Ithaca, NY: Cornell University Press, 1999), p. 47.

extensive recapitalization of banks and debt repayment by Indonesia's struggling corporate moguls.[51] Yet, the expectation that the bitter lessons of the crisis would be, in themselves, sufficient to change things failed to take into account the real factors that defined any social or economic order. As Pranab Bardhan has argued, the significance of crisis in bringing about real change lies not so much in the lessons it offers to improve efficiency but in the way crisis undermines existing political forces and enhances new and reformist ones.[52] Because reforms are not simply about the efficiency of markets, but have real implications for the way power is distributed and how existing elites are sustained, such interests will resist reforms even where the economic costs are severe.

In the Indonesian case, attempts to close insolvent banks and to force insolvent groups to part with assets and repay debt have met with fierce resistance. This was not only true in the dying days of the Suharto regime.[53] Despite the starkness of the "lessons" of the financial crisis and the huge leverage of the IMF and other agencies in pressing for specific reforms in policy and governance, oligarchy and its major players were ultimately able to survive. The key to this "success" was the resilience of the networks of political authority and economic interest that underpinned and defined oligarchy and permeated the institutions of the state itself. Neoliberal reformers and their allies were never able politically to dismantle these.

One critical illustration of this failure to reform and uproot Indonesia's oligarchy can be found in the way the IMF program of bank recapitalization was carried out. Despite the fact that most of Indonesia's beleaguered and insolvent banks were revealed to have contravened capital adequacy provisions and the IMF's laws on intra-group lending, these institutions were provided with large injections of funds by Bank Indonesia in the form of so-called liquidity funds (BLBI, Bantuan Likuiditas Bank Indonesia) intended to enable the banks to remain liquid, but which, in reality, were often sent offshore immediately to prop up other parts of the corporate groups. While the establishment of IBRA (the Indonesian Bank Recapitalization Agency) was intended to secure the assets of the disabled banks to fund a government bailout, in reality it enabled many of the conglomerates to warehouse their assets, write down debts at inflated values assigned to assets, and, in some cases, to repurchase assets at much reduced prices.[54]

One of the reasons for this great escape was the continuing grip of oligarchy on the critical parts of the bureaucracy, including in many key financial ministries and in the judiciary and commercial courts, where the will to pursue corruptors and debtors was undermined as the central elements in the judiciary proved reluctant to convict corrupt political and business figures.[55]

Two of Indonesia's presidents, Abdurahman Wahid and now Susilo Bambang Yudhoyono, made the fight against corruption a central plank in their political programs. This struck a responsive chord with the public. The Corruption

---

[51] Robison and Hadiz, *Reorganising Power*, pp. 6–10.

[52] Pranab Bardhan, "The New Institutional Economics and Development Theory: A Brief Critical Assessment," *World Development* 17,9 (1989): 1389–95.

[53] Robison and Rosser, "Surviving the Meltdown."

[54] Discussed in detail in Robison and Hadiz, *Reorganising Power*, pp. 187–222.

[55] Timothy Lindsey, "Black Letter, Black Market, and Bad Faith: Corruption and the Failure of Law Reform," in *Indonesia in Transition: Social Aspects of Reformasi and Crisis*, ed. Chris Manning and Pierre van Dierman (Singapore: Institute of Southeast Asian Studies, 2000), pp. 278–92.

Eradication Commission (KPK, Komisi Pemberantasan Korupsi) was thus established and has been successful in bringing charges against a range of politicians and business figures that were not possible under the previous regime, although its reach remains limited.[56] The investigations of non-government organizations, the KPK, and the media continue to provide detailed insights into the way politics and business continue to be inextricably entangled, as was shown in the spectacle that was the Bank Century case, which reached into the very heart of the Democratic Party, led by the president. This is a pattern that reaches from the heights of national politics and the most powerful corporate figures down into the arenas of provincial and subprovincial politics.[57]

It is significant that, despite the new leverage of reformers and regulatory institutions, oligarchy and its beneficiaries still operate openly. KPK continues to be pressured by powerful interests seeking to discredit its officials, and in some cases influential figures still appear to possess immunity from legal redress, as demonstrated in the case of Aburizal Bakrie.[58]

Oligarchy and the Challenge of Liberal Politics

Middle-class liberalism, with its emphasis on individual rights and rule of law, has been a slender but consistent thread in the political history of Indonesia. Through the political prominence of middle-class intellectuals and professionals, those advocating liberalism exercised an influence beyond its numbers in the brief period of parliamentary democracy in the 1950s. Student movements, sometimes involving street demonstrations, arrests, and imprisonment, continued to punctuate even the deepest periods of authoritarian rule under Suharto. Yet, middle-class liberalism was never translated into an effective or coherent force in Indonesia during authoritarian rule.

It is natural that authoritarian regimes are hostile to liberal political movements and ideas. In Indonesia, the particular corporatist and functionalist influences in authoritarian politics provided especially effective weapons in keeping civil society and liberal politics at bay. The notion of a single national interest embodied in the corporatist and populist ideals of both "guided democracy" and Suharto's development state denied the legitimacy of claims by liberals for political participation and representation outside the prescribed functionalist frameworks.[59] In this Orwellian circumstance, there was no room for the incubation of the sort of progressive civil society and its independent institutions expected by liberal pluralists.

The disorganization of liberal politics was not reliant on repression. Rather, the co-option of the middle classes, including critics and more moderate opponents, was to be the primary means of defusing and domesticating potential opposition. For the middle class, access to patronage, jobs, and careers, and to the benefits of economic

---

[56] Simon Butt, *Corruption and Law in Indonesia* (London: Routledge, 2012).

[57] Hadiz, *Localising Power in Post-Authoritarian Indonesia*.

[58] For example, one of his companies, Lapindo Brantas, is widely considered responsible for massive mudflows that have destroyed the ecology of a significant swath of East Java, as well as the homes and livelihoods of tens of thousands of ordinary people.

[59] David Bourchier, "Lineages of Organicist Political Thought in Indonesia" (PhD dissertation, Monash University, Melbourne, 1996); and David Reeve, *Golkar of Indonesia: An Alternative to the Party System* (Singapore: Oxford University Press, 1985).

growth, came at the cost of accepting that the arena of politics was bounded by a single state ideology (Pancasila) and confined within a form of state-managed electoralism dominated by a state political party (Golkar) and smaller, approved political parties (PDI, Partai Demokrasi Indonesia, Indonesian Democratic Party; and PPP, Partai Persatuan Pembangunan, United Development Party).

At another level, it is critical that political liberalism was never able to become the ideological basis for wider alliances between the middle class and the bourgeoisie, while an emerging working class was largely separated from social democratic political traditions.[60] Importantly, Indonesia's bourgeoisie had been formed in circumstances where the state controlled the gateways through which private interests might enter the economy—the vast networks of licenses, monopolies, concessions, and contracts that provided access to resources, trades, and bank credit. It was an accommodation that suited Indonesia's bourgeoisie, providing a broad shelter for a bourgeoisie that was predominantly ethnic Chinese and therefore vulnerable to the threats of both social radicalism and reactionary populism so important in the 1950s and 1960s. The political agenda of the Chinese bourgeoisie has always been to protect these arrangements and to develop close alliances and relationships with powerful officials and political power-holders rather than replacing them with open markets and transparent and general rules.[61]

It is important, too, that the social and political basis of the regime was changing. These changes were manifest, not least, in deepening struggles for control of the military, often depicted as conflicts between secular and "green" (Islamic) political factions, but, in reality, a conflict in which oligarchy had begun to assert its authority over the old institutions and interests of state capitalism and over the officials of Benedict Anderson's "*state qua state.*"[62] Oligarchy had, in fact, become constrained by state capitalism and economic nationalist policy as the public monopolies of state capitalism were progressively and selectively expropriated and transformed into private monopolies. However, it is significant that, in this drift towards a kind of market politics where money and oligarchic power were increasingly ascendant, the old authoritarian structures became less necessary.

When the Suharto regime collapsed, political liberals believed they were going to play a central role in deciding the way politics was to be reconstructed in Indonesia. The *reformasi* movement made strident demands for a new political era to be based on the classical liberal principles of individual rights and popular democracy. The World Bank, the IMF, and other international development organizations played a pivotal role in driving the new laws on politics and decentralization that were to define democratic politics and administrative authority after Suharto. However, the movement ultimately faded into a relatively uncoordinated series of mainly student actions sporadically connected with the activities of a small liberal intelligentsia. Compared with the middle-class liberals and their leftist allies subsequently involved in the Arab Spring, for example, the would-be Indonesian reformers were even more disorganized and bereft of a real political or social narrative.

---

[60] Vedi Hadiz, *Workers and the State in New Order Indonesia* (London: Routledge, 1997).

[61] Robison, *Indonesia: The Rise of Capital*; Robison and Hadiz, *Reorganising Power in Indonesia*.

[62] Benedict Anderson, "Old State, New Society: Indonesia's New Order in Comparative Historical Perspective," *Journal of Asian Studies* 42,3 (1983): 477–96; Robison and Hadiz, *Reorganising Power in Indonesia*.

In fact, those who might be considered the representatives of progressive liberal-minded civil society have been pitched into a political arena defined by proliferating corruption and money politics and the rise of extra-legal forms of social and political violence and coercion. They were quickly marginalized in an ongoing struggle where a resurgent oligarchy was able to build new and more pervasive social and political alliances and settle comfortably into the new democratic ambience.

Despite their early efforts to impose institutional changes and subsequent attempts to prop up the reforms through various programs of capacity building, "good governance," and democracy promotion, the international development organizations had limited influence over the course of change in Indonesia. In any case, neoliberals have always harbored suspicion of democracy as a form of government that could open the door to distributional coalitions and predatory raiders and frustrate the efficient workings of markets.[63] Some neoliberal commentators have even looked back with some degree of nostalgia to the certainties that authoritarian rule provided to technocratic planners and investors alike.[64]

As a proliferation of political parties emerged to contest the elections, it was significant that no new parties emerged on the basis of liberal or social democratic ideas to seize the moment. The long-awaited presidency of Megawati failed to deliver on its claims to the populist legacy of Sukarnoism. Megawati's tenure was to be defined instead by policy failure and murky alliances with the military and business. Not surprisingly, parliaments and the political parties became widely regarded as major realms for corruption. The former state political party, Golkar, quickly became the home of many former leading figures of the Suharto era, even if some have migrated to other parties, including the Democratic Party. If there are any signs of something different, they come from the populist and xenophobic Right and from parties like Gerindra, led by Prabowo Subianto. In this context, the parallels with Thailand's Thaksin Shinawata and his fusion of populism and business interests are clear.

Surviving Decentralization: How Local Power Was Reorganized

Decentralization of government and administration has been long regarded by neoliberal policy makers, not least in the World Bank and the IMF, to be ideally suited to ensure government accountability and the liberation of individuals and businesses from stifling centralized control to enable them to be innovative and enterprising. At another level, populist NGOs have regarded decentralization as a path to the empowerment of local citizens and grassroots social organizations.[65] There is no doubt that the decentralization of government and administration in Indonesia under Laws 22 and 25 of 1999 has been far-reaching. This so-called "big bang" of decentralization saw real administrative and financial authority shifted into the hands of regents (*bupatis*) and mayors and to local parliaments.[66]

---

[63] See James Dorn, "Economic Liberty and Democracy in East Asia," *Orbis* 37,4 (1993): 599–619; and F. A. Hayek, *The Road to Serfdom* (London: Routledge, 2001).

[64] Ron Duncan and Ross McLeod, "The State and the Market in Democratic Indonesia," in *Indonesia: Democracy and the Promise of Good Governance*, ed. Ross McLeod and Andrew MacIntyre (Singapore: Institute of Southeast Asian Studies, 2007), pp. 73–92.

[65] Hadiz, *Localising Power in Post-Authoritarian Indonesia*.

[66] Nankyung Choi, *Local Politics in Indonesia: Pathways to Power* (London: Routledge, 2011).

These new institutional arrangements have enabled a vigorous electoral politics to emerge at these lower, regional levels and have allowed the expression of local opposition and demands in a way not possible before. Voters have proven willing to throw incumbents out of office if they displease them, and, in some cases, reformist mayors and *bupatis* have been elected even when they ran against the heavyweights of established parties and cliques. Some of these successful candidates have even made progress in cleaning up moribund bureaucracies and cleaning out corrupt cliques and individuals.[67] However, these accomplishments are not necessarily indicative of the early stages of a more general rise of progressive interests at the local level.

Moreover, Hadiz has argued that the decentralization of political and administrative institutions has more generally provided opportunities for the same kinds of social interests previously at the heart of Suharto's New Order to assert their power at the local level.[68] Thus, the vast majority of local parliamentary candidates, as well as individuals vying for positions as *bupatis* and mayors, have been drawn from a pool of former officials, party apparatchik, as well as business figures and gangsters, many of whom had helped to exercise authority at the local level on behalf of the old authoritarian regime.[69] Even where reformist and progressive figures have emerged, they necessarily have had to make accommodation with entrenched political and economic forces and to operate within circumstances already in place. The point is that while the new institutions may have made some things newly possible, what really matters, at the local level as well as the national level, are the kinds of interests that are able to organize politically to influence and profit from the institutions.

CONCLUSIONS: WHERE TO NOW?

As we noted earlier, the oligarchy thesis has been criticized for an underlying pessimism about the prospects for social and political reform in Indonesia and for dismissing the significance of democratic transformation and of the efforts to reform public institutions. One source for these criticisms is to be found among pluralist scholars, including R. William Liddle and Thomas Pepinsky.[70] For Liddle, the oligarchy thesis denies not only the possibility of progressive liberal transformation but also the possibility of individual agency in politics and of political action by individuals on behalf of democratic consolidation. In Liddle's view, politics operates in Machiavellian terms, so that the accumulation of power resources by individuals, such as wealth, position, and status, is achieved by astute strategic decisions, including decisions made when building political and economic alliances or capturing votes in elections.

Thomas Pepinsky argues that the oligarchy thesis cannot provide an account of the complexity of power struggles or the importance of non-material power resources, nor can it acknowledge and explain the sheer number or fluidity of

---

[67] Luky Djani, "Reform Movements and Local Politics in Indonesia" (PhD dissertation, Murdoch University, 2013).

[68] Hadiz, *Localising Power in Post-Authoritarian Indonesia.*

[69] Ibid., especially Chapter 4.

[70] See Liddle, "Improving the Quality of Democracy in Indonesia"; and Thomas B. Pepinsky, "Pluralism and Political Conflict in Indonesia," this volume, pp. 79–98.

elements that constitute the oligarchic system, which is often intent on survival rather than any enduring ideas or policy agendas. The theoretical key to the analysis of Indonesian politics lies, therefore, according to Pepinsky, in a form of critical pluralism that recognizes the fluid and shifting processes wherein coalitions are formed and dissolved according to changing circumstances and based on interacting material and non-material resources, including that of identity.

A further criticism is that the oligarchy thesis underplays the importance of political conflicts taking place at the margins and within the lower orders of society, not least at the local level. Edward Aspinall, for example, points to the widespread rise of reformist movements and cites their—sometimes successful—demands for reforms in labor and in the provision of social safety nets and services in health and education, protection for the environment, the elimination of corruption, and so on.[71] This evidence can be interpreted either as proof of a fundamental theoretical failure of the oligarchy thesis or, more simply, proof of the theory's adherents' failure to recognize and give proper weight to the importance of politics from below within the basic theoretical framework of the oligarchy thesis.

What is disputable from the structural political economy perspective is the larger transformative significance of these forms of oppositional politics. Such a concern can be illustrated if we imagine a circumstance—that the current oligarchy in Indonesia has disintegrated, due to internal fractures or perhaps in combination with another deep global economic crisis. In such a case, there would be no guarantee that an alternative form of rule could take its place, sustained by a set of coherently organized social interests. In other words, there could be a repeat of the situation that came about at the end of the Suharto era, when there was no reformist coalition ready to step into the temporary void before old interests reorganized, thus ensuring that the New Order legacy continues to this day. What set of circumstances, then, can break this cycle?

Our basic propositions are that real change cannot be achieved so long as the social order of the previous regime and its ascendant political forces remain intact and in charge of the state. Attempts to induce change by institutional fixes and programs of "good governance" cannot bypass the bitter and sometimes violent conflicts over power that historically accompany social and political transformation. Incremental demands for reform by individuals or groups can only be piecemeal if they do not achieve a broader political ascendancy and control over the state. This means that a transformation of substance, rather than a descent into chaos or simply more of the same, requires both the disintegration of the old order and its social underpinnings and the forging of a new social order with its political forces.

All this does not mean that Indonesia is necessarily caught in a state of permanent atrophy or that oligarchy is unassailable. Where, then, should we look for the potential sources of change? We propose that, rather than looking outside the broader system of oligarchy itself, to those attempting to bring it down, we should look within the framework of oligarchy, for that is where the dynamics of change are most likely to be forged. From the perspective of structural political economy theory, one potential source is generated as capitalism outgrows its predatory roots and where capital begins to see its interests in more predictable and transparent

---

[71] See Aspinall, "Popular Agency and Interests" and *Opposing Suharto: Compromise, Resistance, and Regime Change in Indonesia.*

regulation and in rule of law.[72] In Indonesia, these tensions are shown in disputes over mining regulation, investments laws, and corporate governance (as revealed in the conflict over Bumi Plc, involving the Bakries and the Rothchilds). They are also crystallized in battles over the authority and reach of the KPK and other regulatory institutions, battles that take place with government and within the oligarchy itself.

However, there are difficulties here. One is that capital has historically been politically opportunist rather than reformist, reluctant to accept the risks of attaching itself to reformist politics. Indonesia's middle classes, too, have been incubated within the framework of the state and have shown little appetite for engaging in reformist opposition or for establishing political relationships with, for example, organized labor, as was sometimes the case in Europe. Invariably, the reform of capitalism has required the intervention of the state itself throughout history. And numerous systems of authoritarian rule and/or oligarchy have shown a remarkable resilience in the face of neoliberal policy and institutional reforms.[73] Nor is there necessarily any fundamental disjuncture between illiberal politics and market capitalism.[74] Waiting for the logic of the machine to drive reform may be a forlorn prospect. Singapore and China are only two examples of countries where successful capitalist economies can flourish within highly illiberal political systems.

It is also true that the growing reach of global governance over the rules of trade, investment, and public management is offset by the extensive relations that exist among various governments and oligarchies in the developing world with international investors and Western governments, relations that are important in sustaining those less developed states and their economies.[75] International capitalists are often enthusiastic about the way authoritarianism can sweep away environmental, labor, and welfare coalitions and remove regulatory constraints on their commercial ambitions. For Western governments and international organizations, activities that involve them in the fortunes of oligarchies are often intermingled with strategies to preserve these special advantages for investors.

A second potential source of contradiction within an oligarchy can be found in the highly diffuse, decentralized, and corruption-ridden system of money politics that has emerged in Indonesia. Significantly, it is a system that may prove to be increasingly exclusionary as the cost of gaining access to the spoils of state power generally grows beyond the reach of all but a few. Maybe it is in this way that decentralization will ultimately reveal its true significance: by opening new sites of localized conflict caused by the failure of an oligarchic power structure to absorb properly the ambitions of the growing armies of apparatchiks, local fixers, entrepreneurs, and enforcers that it has assembled across the archipelago.

---

[72] See, for example, Paul D. Hutchcroft, *Booty Capitalism: The Politics of Banking in The Philippines* (Ithaca, NY: Cornell University Press, 1998). In this study, Hutchcroft provides an extensive overview of Weberian and other theories about the progression of capitalism and its implications for politics and administration.

[73] See, for example, Joshua Stacher, *Adaptable Autocrats: Regime Power in Egypt and Syria* (Stanford, CA: Stanford University Press, 2012).

[74] Garry Rodan, *Transparency and Authoritarian Rule in Southeast Asia: Singapore and Malaysia* (London: RoutledgeCurzon, 2004).

[75] Mick Moore, "Political Underdevelopment: What Causes Bad Governance?," *Public Management Review* 3,3 (2000): 385–418.

Our analysis concludes that for the cycle to be broken and a new social order put in place nothing less is required than a deeper social and political revolution, whether in liberal or other directions.

Improving the Quality of Democracy in Indonesia: Toward a Theory of Action

R. William Liddle

In mainstream political science, most discussions of the quality of democracy, particularly in new democracies like Indonesia, highlight the performance of key institutions and procedures. Larry Diamond and Leonardo Morlino identify four of these: "(1) universal, adult suffrage; (2) recurring, free, competitive, and fair elections; (3) more than one serious political party; and (4) alternative sources of information." They continue: "Once a country meets these basic standards, further empirical analysis can ask how well it achieves the three main goals of an ideal democracy—political and civil freedom, popular sovereignty (control over public policies and the officials who make them), and political equality (in these rights and powers)—as well as broader standards of good governance (such as transparency, legality, and responsible rule)."[1]

Within this frame, this essay attempts to develop the rudiments of a theory of action that can empower scholars and activists to improve the quality of democracy in Indonesia and elsewhere. Following Robert Dahl, it argues that the basic obstacle to achieving the goal of political equality highlighted by Diamond and Morlino is market capitalism, an economic system that everywhere creates inequalities. To be sure, this is an old critique. Perhaps the most vigorous and long-lasting attack on capitalism was launched by Karl Marx in the nineteenth century. Nonetheless, contemporary Marxist analysts do not help us much to understand how to improve democracy.[2] Mostly they tell us to throw out the baby, democracy, together with the bath water, capitalism. In reality, both need to be saved.

In this effort, the ideas of sixteenth-century political philosopher Niccolo Machiavelli are more useful than those of Marx. Machiavelli focused on the individual as an independent actor who creates, possesses, and deploys political

---

[1] Larry Diamond and Leonardo Morlino, "The Quality of Democracy: An Overview," *Journal of Democracy* 15,2 (2004): 21.

[2] There are, to be sure, many variants of Marxism today, although the common thread is perhaps a materialist interpretation of history. This essay, as elaborated below, focuses on analysts who call themselves "critical theorists."

resources. In the twentieth and twenty-first centuries, his framework has been brilliantly developed by several American political scientists. Each has contributed to the formulation of a theory of action that will help us better understand politics and improve the quality of democracy. Their contributions, with Indonesian applications, will be discussed below.

ROBERT DAHL: RESOURCE INEQUALITY AND DEMOCRACY

In *On Democracy*, Robert Dahl summarized five key arguments about the relationship between market capitalism and democracy.[3] First, throughout modern history, democracy has only endured in countries with capitalist market economies, never in countries with non-market economies. According to Dahl, this empirical finding is astonishing; in the social sciences there is almost never so strong an association between two factors.

Second, this relationship has an empirical foundation. In market economies, the main participants are individuals and private companies acting on their own, motivated by profit and loss incentives, without direction from a center. Following Adam Smith, Dahl argues that this incentive-regulated pattern of behavior produces highly efficient economies. Efficient economies in turn tend to grow quickly, reduce the percentage of the absolute poor, and produce economic resources that can be distributed to resolve conflicts among interest groups.

Economic growth also produces more economic resources available to create a literate and educated population, factors proven positive for democracy. Most importantly, economic growth tends to produce a property-owning middle class, which typically demands education, personal autonomy, individual freedom, rule of law, and participation in government. "The middle classes, as Aristotle was the first to point out, are the natural allies of democratic ideas and institutions."[4]

Conversely, a non-market economy is not only inefficient but tends to place most economic resources in a single set of hands, the hands of the government of the state. That monopoly is used by government officials to construct or defend authoritarian rule. The twentieth century's most prominent examples were the communist and fascist governments. Dahl reminds us that those governments were responsible for the murder of millions of their own people, something that has not occurred in democratic countries. Third, democracy and market capitalism are in continuous conflict while simultaneously shaping and reshaping each other profoundly. In Great Britain, toward the middle of the nineteenth century, capitalism as *laissez-faire* ideology succeeded in overcoming its competitors. But capitalism as an economic force had also created new economic interests, including labor unions demanding state intervention and regulation. At the beginning of the twentieth century, British workers created the Labour Party. With the building of modern economies, similar developments occurred in almost all European and overseas British states.

Dahl's argument: *laissez-faire* ideology is impossible to maintain in a democratic country. Logically, key market institutions need to be regulated by a body external to the market, the most effective of which is the state. Market competition, ownership of economic units, the implementation of contracts, the prevention of monopoly, and the protection of property rights all need the involvement of the state to work

---

[3] Robert Dahl, *On Democracy* (New Haven, CT: Yale University Press, 1998).

[4] Ibid., p. 168.

properly. Empirically, we observe that *laissez-faire* ideology has never been implemented in a democratic country.

Moreover, markets simultaneously provide benefits and create losses. In a democracy, individuals and groups who feel disadvantaged will demand reform of that characteristic or element of the market thought responsible for their losses. The result everywhere is economic policies and rules that regulate the economy and reduce market freedom. As evidence, Dahl lists several categories of economic behavior that are regulated in the United States, the state ostensibly "famous for its commitment to market capitalism."[5]

Dahl's fourth argument contends that market capitalism limits the potential for high quality democracy by creating important inequalities in the distribution of political resources. Political resources "include everything to which a person or a group has access that they can use to influence, directly or indirectly, the conduct of other persons."[6] As potential resources, Dahl lists "physical force, weapons, money, wealth, goods and services, productive resources, income, status, honor, respect, affection, charisma, prestige, information, knowledge, education, communication, communications media, organizations, position, legal standing, control over doctrine and beliefs, votes, and many others." Among these possibilities, in a modern democracy, the most important and, at the same time, the most vulnerable to the depredations of market capitalism are wealth, income, status, prestige, information, organization, education, and knowledge.[7]

Dahl's fifth and final argument describes an ineluctable present-and-future tension that constitutes a powerful irony. On the one hand, the creation of democratic institutions was made possible and is undergirded by market capitalism. Everywhere and for centuries, authoritarian governments have collapsed when land-owning classes (who control almost all the political resources in pre-modern societies) and ordinary farmers (who have few political resources) are replaced by a more complex class structure. Rural politics, which puts two main classes in opposition to each other, is replaced by urban politics, which empowers many groups. The politics of the illiterate is replaced by the politics of the educated. Knowledge and organization become important political resources.

On the other hand, capitalism as the creator of many inequalities becomes the main obstacle to the further development or deepening of democracy. Here is the great irony. It is precisely those political resources that are most valuable in citizens' struggles for their rights and interests that are distributed unequally by market capitalism. This reality only becomes visible, however, after the basic electoral and governmental institutions and interest and party organizations of modern democracy have been established.

THREE IMPLICATIONS FOR SCHOLARS OF INDONESIA

Dahl's conclusions have three key implications for scholars of contemporary Indonesia. First, the political resources in the hands of those who would like to improve the quality of Indonesian democracy are extremely limited. Other players, though small in number, are vastly superior in amount and weight of resources.

---

[5] Ibid., p. 175.

[6] Ibid., p. 177.

[7] Ibid.

Even so, democracy as the best political system and the capitalist market as the best economic system are both highly valued by most Indonesians (as reflected, for example, in opinion surveys).[8] At the same time, citing Isaiah Berlin's value pluralist terms, we note that economic and political freedom may be incommensurable.[9] If the two systems, capitalism and democracy, sometimes clash, democratic theorists and those who would like to improve the quality of Indonesian democracy must live with that reality.

Second, recognition of this resource imbalance requires us to reassess our understanding of the bases of political action. Analysis of resources cannot be separated from conceptualization of the political system as a whole, including demand-making, governmental formulation of policy responses, decision-making, and policy implementation. In other words, a theory of action is needed that can conceptualize the role of the actor in the political system while placing that role in the context of the constraints that limit action and the opportunities that facilitate it. The concepts of constraints and opportunities will be elaborated below.

Third, scholars of contemporary Indonesia are urged by Dahl, again implicitly, to study the ways in which the key political resources he has identified can be developed and distributed as widely and democratically as possible. This third task is more comprehensive and long term.[10] This essay focuses on the first and second, the recognition of a resource imbalance and the formulation of a theory of action to reduce the level of imbalance.

In my view, the conclusions to be drawn from Dahl's analysis are clear. Scholars need to develop a theory of action that recognizes but does not exaggerate the influence of material resources in achieving political equality in modern democracies. Such a theory should specify the factors constraining and facilitating action by individuals and groups that want to reduce political inequality and thereby improve the quality of democracy. And it should further specify and elaborate how to develop and distribute those resources most critical to increasing equality.

Unfortunately, in Indonesia and elsewhere, there are influential analysts who have drawn other conclusions. The analysts I have in mind call themselves "critical theorists," connoting hostility to the capitalist organization of domestic and international economies. In their view, the institutions of democracy constitute a mere mask obscuring the power of the wealthy. According to such theorists, those institutions reflect not rule by the people, but instead by a small wealthy elite, upper class, or oligarchy. Even in the strongest democracies, these elites will prevail.

The argument posed by critical theorists assumes that material wealth is virtually the only potent resource in politics. In this respect, they differ with Dahl, who regards wealth as important but only one of many resources mobilizable in politics. The original source of the critical theorists' position is the mid-nineteenth-century theory of Karl Marx, developed to explain the social and political impact of early industrialization.

---

[8] R. William Liddle and Saiful Mujani, "Indonesian Democracy: From Transition to Consolidation," in *Democracy and Islam in Indonesia,* ed. Mirjam Kunkler and Alfred Stepan (New York, NY: Columbia University Press, 20013), pp. 24–50.

[9] Isaiah Berlin, *The Crooked Timber of Humanity* (London: Fontana Press, 1991).

[10] The most promising research in this area is being conducted by Amartya Sen and associates under the label of the "capabilities approach." See Amartya Sen, *Development as Freedom* (New York, NY: Anchor 1999); see also R. William Liddle et al., *Memperbaiki Mutu Demokrasi di Indonesia: Sebuah Perdebatan* (Jakarta: Yayasan Wakaf Paramadina, 2012), pp. 37–40.

For Marx, the principal actor in history is not the individual, but social classes based on control of property. Social change is shaped and moved by class conflict. Not all Marxists today focus primarily on classes or class conflict, though that theme remains prominent. Perhaps the defining feature of twenty-first-century Marxism is an unmitigated and implacable hostility to capitalism and all its works. A contemporary example, which also retains the class focus, is the critique mounted by widely cited anthropologist David Harvey of "neoliberalism," which he claims "provide[s] a benevolent mask full of wonderful-sounding words like freedom, liberty, choice, and rights, to hide the grim realities of the restoration or reconstitution of naked class power, locally as well as transnationally, but most particularly in the main financial centers of global capitalism."[11]

In Indonesia, critical theory has been developed most fully and persuasively by Richard Robison and Vedi Hadiz.[12] Their book describes not a classical Marxist confrontation of bourgeoisie and proletariat but rather the way in which certain Indonesian business and governmental elites responded *à la* Harvey to the opportunities and constraints of the global capitalist order. According to Robison and Hadiz, a "complex oligarchy" was formed during Suharto's New Order. A complex oligarchy is defined as "a system of government in which virtually all political power is held by a very small number of wealthy ... people who shape public policy primarily to benefit themselves financially ... while displaying little or no concern for the broader interests of the rest of the citizenry."[13] When formed, this Indonesian oligarchy consisted of three elements: state officials, "politico-business families," and business conglomerates.

According to Robison and Hadiz, the complex oligarchy is still in power today, even though the authoritarian New Order regime fell in 1998 and was replaced with formally democratic institutions. The authors also deny that decentralization has had any impact on the quality of Indonesian democracy. Those in power now, both in the center and the regions, more than a decade after *reformasi* (reform, the Indonesian term for the democratic transition begun in 1998), are still individuals or their representatives from the three elite groups listed above.

Robison and Hadiz's prediction is pessimistic: "[T]he possibility that cohesive reformist parties might emerge from the wreckage, driven by a coherent agenda of market liberalism rather than being swallowed in a system of power relations embedded in the pursuit of rents appears even more remote than ever ... [This

---

[11] David Harvey, *A Brief History of Neoliberalism* (Oxford: Oxford University Press, 2005), p. 119. "Neoliberalism" is defined by Harvey as "a theory of political economic practices that proposes that human well-being can best be advanced by liberating individual entrepreneurial freedoms and skills within an institutional framework characterized by strong private property rights, free markets, and free trade" (p. 2). In fact, the concept, "neoliberalism," is a polemical term of abuse employed by Marxist scholars like Harvey. As far as I can determine, no scholars use it to label their own approach. Substantively, the Marxist claim is that the current small government approach of classical liberals inspired by Friedrich von Hayek, *The Road to Serfdom* (Chicago, IL: University of Chicago Press, 1994), is being used to justify world domination by capitalist elites. In truth, Hayekian liberalism is only one of many contemporary economic theories in play, and has been increasingly challenged since the 2007–08 global financial crisis by more interventionist theories.

[12] Richard Robison and Vedi Hadiz, *Reorganising Power in Indonesia: The Politics of Oligarchy in an Age of Markets* (London and New York, NY: RoutledgeCurzon, 2004).

[13] Ibid., p. 16, note 6.

means] a system of democratic rule where the state apparatus will provide some form of order in which oligarchies rather than markets will prevail."[14]

Long-time observers of Indonesian politics can readily understand the appeal of Robison and Hadiz's argument, both as empirical observation and as moral complaint. During the New Order, it was reasonable to believe that many high officials violated their oath of office in return for material reward. It also seemed apparent that officials' family members and private businesspeople were part of a patron–client system that profited them at the expense of the nation and the state. Even so, the argument of critical theorists is incorrect, either as moral complaint or empirical analysis. As moral complaint, it is incomplete. Of course, it is undeniable that many officials, members of the families of officials, and businesspeople with government connections profited corruptly during the New Order. Nonetheless, the nearly 8 percent growth rate maintained for more than a quarter century benefited the majority of the population. This history has been well told by several economists, including Anne Booth,[15] Hal Hill,[16] and Peter Timmer.[17]

Empirically, the ruler of the New Order was not an oligarchy but a single dictator, Suharto. All important decisions were taken by Suharto himself to realize many different objectives, probably first and foremost the perpetuation of his own rule. The so-called oligarchic elements of the New Order acted at once as a support base for Suharto and an instrument or political resource deployed by him. Without an appreciation of Suharto's role as self-conscious ruler, it is impossible to understand the ebbs and flows in the fortunes of particular economic groups during the New Order and the ways in which those shifts affected the larger economy and polity.[18] Also important were a number of other resources not emphasized by Robison and Hadiz, most critically the armed forces, the coercive resource that enabled Suharto to keep his grip on his office for thirty-three years.

At the very least, it is incumbent upon scholars who employ abstract constructions—such as complex oligarchy, but also mainstream political science variables like interest groups, social movements, and religious beliefs—rather than the actions of concrete individuals as their independent or dependent variables to specify the nature of the evidence that persuades them and might persuade others of the validity of their claims. In the case of Suharto's New Order, for example, it is epistemologically much easier in at least three senses to provide broadly acceptable evidence for the proposition that Suharto or the relevant minister in each case promulgated a particular economic policy rather than to show that an oligarchy did it. If one focuses on the policies of Suharto and his state officials, then, first, the act will have been publicly reported. Second, the impact on others of the act is readily traceable. Third, questions of collusion, division of responsibility, and so on do not

---

[14] Ibid., p. 265.

[15] Anne Booth, ed., *The Oil Boom and After: Indonesian Economic Policy and Performance in the Soeharto Era* (Singapore: Oxford University Press, 1992).

[16] Hal Hill, *The Indonesian Economy since 1966* (Cambridge: Cambridge University Press, 1996).

[17] Peter Timmer, "The Road to Pro-Poor Growth: The Indonesian Experience in Regional Perspective," *Bulletin of Indonesian Economic Studies* 40,2 (2004): 177–207.

[18] See, for example, Thomas Pepinsky's analysis of the political economic causes of the fall of the New Order. Thomas Pepinsky, *Economic Crises and the Breakdown of Authoritarian Regimes: Indonesia and Malaysia in Comparative Perspective* (Cambridge: Cambridge University Press, 2009).

arise if claims are made only about individual human actors. These concerns are not raised in the critical literature on Indonesia.

Of course, as individuals, state officials (including armed forces officers), the families of officials, and private businesspeople had their own objectives, including objectives that could be realized through favorable government action. Throughout the New Order, most of these individuals seem to have been relatively satisfied that their demands were receiving a sufficient response. The evidence: there were few individuals, not to mention significant interest groups, who rebelled or broke their relationship with Suharto.

That fact does not, however, imply that those groups ruled the country. They supported the New Order because Suharto served their interests. Their political resources—including wealth, status, prestige, information, organization, knowledge, and positions—were mobilized by Suharto to establish and defend his rule. No more than that.

That system of rule changed dramatically after May 1998. Since *reformasi*, there have been thousands of rulers, that is, the presidents, governors, district heads, and mayors in the executive branch, plus the legislators in the center and the regions. In Weberian terms, the basis of authority of the New Order, personal rule (in that respect not different from Sukarno's Guided Democracy), is now legal-constitutional rule. Elective governmental office has become an autonomous and powerful political resource. It is difficult to imagine a more fundamental political transformation.

Through the amendment process, the 1945 Constitution, previously manipulated to maintain two authoritarian rulers in power, has become the solid foundation of a modern presidential democracy. No less important, Laws 22/1999 and 25/1999 concerning regional government have laid the legal foundation for the decentralization of authority, including its all-important financing, channeling that authority to the provinces, districts, and municipalities. Presidents, governors, district heads, and mayors are now directly elected by the people.

Of course, that transformation does not mean that political demand-making by diverse interest groups has disappeared or even decreased after *reformasi*. What has happened in Indonesia was described clearly by Dahl when he wrote the following about European industrialization in the eighteenth century and later. "Democracy and market-capitalism are locked in a persistent conflict in which each modifies and limits the other."[19]

On the one hand, support for economic liberalization, which found its initial adherents and application during the New Order in the technocrats led by Professor Widjojo Nitisastro, has strengthened and even become dominant in state policy-making since the fall of Suharto. President B. J. Habibie (during the New Order a notorious state protectionist on behalf of his aircraft industry) and his successors, including the current President Susilo Bambang Yudhoyono (SBY), have all maintained the macroeconomic policies pioneered by Suharto. Nonetheless, economic groups that have not benefited from these policies have lobbied hard against them. Sometimes they use the newly opened democratic channels, but they also continue to rely on their old connections and resources, engaging in bribery and other illicit means.

For Robison and Hadiz, this mixing of politics and markets proves that the New Order oligarchy has come back to life. For the future, "a coherent agenda of market

[19] Dahl, *On Democracy*, p. 173.

liberalism" will likely be "swallowed in a system of power relations embedded in the pursuit of rents."[20] For Dahl, and me, this mixing is normal and unavoidable. There has never been a coherent agenda of market liberalism pursued by a democratic government because that agenda is always disrupted by the demands of those who have been disadvantaged by market capitalism and therefore sought rents (defined by neoclassical economists as payments for goods and services that are determined by non-market forces). The evidence for this is hard to miss in Indonesia in the form of legal subsidies distributed to many different groups of producers and consumers, most notably and controversially fuel oil consumers. According to economists, rents make markets less efficient. Without denying the economists' conclusions, which are accurate depictions of outcomes in the world constructed by their models, Dahl emphasizes that in the actually existing world, rents are the natural and ineluctable result of the marriage of democracy and market capitalism.

In sum, what has occurred post-*reformasi* in Indonesia is not the continuation of a complex oligarchy but instead a process of governmental fragmentation on the political side and market-capitalist continuity in the economy. Beginning in 1999 and continuing since that time, the rulers of the country have been chosen democratically. From Dahl we know that market capitalism has multiple effects on democracy. The economic, social, and political policies of the New Order created or augmented several political resources held by members of society, as individuals and as groups. Those individuals and groups now act in the democratic system that they themselves have built. At the same time, throughout and after the New Order, the distribution of political resources has never been equal. Today, this inequality represents what is probably the biggest challenge to the quality of democracy in Indonesia.

More recent writings by Hadiz,[21] Hadiz and Robison,[22] and Jeffrey Winters[23] do not add complexity to this picture. Hadiz's *Localising Power in Post-Authoritarian Indonesia* is an unrelievedly negative portrayal of post-decentralization politics in North Sumatra and East Java. Moreover, his evidence is entirely illustrative and by example. No attempt is made to define systematically leadership characteristics that would enable him or his readers to weigh which leaders are more and which less representative and accountable to local voters.[24] Hadiz's conclusion repeats the themes of his and Robison's earlier work: "This book has shown that the main contenders in the contest in Indonesia are essentially shifting locally-based coalitions of predatory power rooted in the now demised [sic] New Order."[25] Moreover, there is no way out, according to Hadiz, certainly not via the "good governance" programs

---

[20] Robison and Hadiz, *Reorganising Power in Indonesia,* p. 265.

[21] Vedi Hadiz, *Localising Power in Post-Authoritarian Indonesia* (Stanford, CA: Stanford University Press, 2010).

[22] Vedi Hadiz and Richard Robison, "The Political Economy of Oligarchy and the Reorganization of Power in Indonesia," this volume, pp. 35–56.

[23] Jeffrey A. Winters, *Oligarchy* (Cambridge: Cambridge University Press, 2011); Jeffrey A. Winters, "Oligarchy and Democracy in Indonesia," this volume, pp. 11–33.

[24] Two systematic studies that do enable the reader to identify more and less successful cases of leadership at the local level are Ryan Tans, *Mobilizing Resources, Building Coalitions: Local Power in Indonesia* (Honolulu, HI: East–West Center, 2012); and Christian von Luebke, "The Political Economy of Local Governance: Findings from an Indonesian Field Study," *Bulletin of Indonesian Economic Studies* 45,2 (2009): 201–30.

[25] Hadiz, *Localising Power in Post-Authoritarian Indonesia,* p. 172.

supported by international donors or the actions of local reformist politicians. The former are dismissed as technocratic know-nothings and tools of "neoliberal" capital, while the latter are characterized as "goons and thugs."[26]

Jeffrey Winters's understanding of oligarchy is more narrowly conceptualized and ultimately even less persuasive than Robison and Hadiz's arguments. The focus is not on classes or the components of a complex oligarchy but rather on extremely wealthy individuals and the defense of their wealth. Other power resources beyond great material wealth—"formal political rights, official positions, coercive power, mobilizational power"—are in principle taken into account.[27] The extent to which lesser amounts of wealth count as a political resource in a democracy is, however, totally left out. This, as we have seen, is a key variable for Dahl, who argues convincingly that economic development creates not just great wealth but a complex pattern of economic concentration and dispersion that both supports and challenges democracy.[28]

In Winters's view, Indonesian politics is dominated by the extremely wealthy. "The central argument is that from a power resource perspective, oligarchs are disproportionately influential actors within Indonesia's political economy, that they arose and gained power during Suharto's New Order, and that the transition to democracy does not constitute a significant disruption or even diminution of their power."[29]

Winters makes no systematic effort to link causally his main independent variable, material power resources held by a small number of extremely rich people, with policy outputs or outcomes. "The politics of wealth defense by materially-endowed actors"[30] is a near-tautological definition of oligarchy. Most of *Oligarchy*'s long discussion of wealth accumulation and its defense in Indonesia retells a well-known story.[31] No one denies that Suharto accumulated great wealth, for both personal and political purposes, and allowed others to do so as well, under his tight control. Nor would anyone deny that wealth accumulation and defense by wealthy individuals continues to this day, as it does in all capitalist market economies, where the whole point of being a capitalist is to build one's business.

What is missing from Winters's interpretation is serious consideration of other variables and what effect they might have had on New Order politics or might be having on today's democracy, which he characterizes both as criminal[32] and untamed.[33] Potentially positive trends in the development of civil society or of the

---

[26] Ibid., p. 14.

[27] Winters, "Oligarchy and Democracy in Indonesia," p. 23; Winters, *Oligarchy*, pp. 11–20.

[28] "Democracy refers to *dispersed formal political power* based on rights, procedures, and levels of popular participation. By contrast, oligarchy is defined by *concentrated material power* based on enforced claims or rights to property or wealth." Winters, *Oligarchy*, p. 11, emphases in the original. Moreover, "ending oligarchy is impossible unless the power resource that defines oligarchs—concentrated wealth—is dispersed. This has happened many times in history ... However, it has never been successfully attempted as a democratic decision." Ibid., p. 285.

[29] Winters, "Oligarchy and Democracy in Indonesia," p. 16.

[30] Winters, *Oligarchy*, p. 7.

[31] Ibid., pp. 139–93.

[32] Ibid., p. 142.

[33] Ibid., pp. 181ff. To his credit, Winters does recognize that "a campaign to tame oligarchs ... is an achievement that can improve the absolute welfare of average citizens," though he still

Anti-Corruption ✳   *Popular mobilization on behalf of KPK*

· mapping corruption ?

KPK

rule of law that might provide counterweights to material power get particularly short shrift in *Oligarchy*. One of the most important political developments in recent years, in my view, is the repeated and indeed growing intervention by civil society in defense of the Komisi Pemberantasan Korupsi (KPK, Corruption Eradication Commission). In 2012 alone there were two instances of successful popular mobilization on behalf of the KPK, the "coins for the KPK" movement in June and the support for the KPK against attempts by the National Police to undermine its autonomy in October.[34]

Finally, a favorite rhetorical device of both Winters and Hadiz is to assert that supposedly reformist politicians have feet of clay. The 2012 gubernatorial election success in Jakarta of Joko Widodo, the reformist mayor of Solo, "was possible only because he had major oligarchic backers."[35] For Hadiz, the performance of the district head of Jembrana, Bali—praised by other observers—is diminished if not negated by the fact that this official was "widely believed to have won power by bribing members of the local parliamentary body that voted him into office ..."[36] These arguments are not the product of a systematic analysis of the range of variables potentially constraining and enabling the behavior of political actors. They are polemical point-scoring.

DEVELOPING A THEORY OF ACTION

How should scholars of Indonesian democracy respond to Dahl's challenges while avoiding the conceptual and empirical errors made by the oligarchy theorists? To repeat, we need a theory of action that is capable of explicating the role of the actor in context while appreciating that the distribution of political resources is highly unequal. In particular, we need to specify and elaborate the factors constraining and facilitating political action to reduce this inequality. For this purpose, we can learn much from the clearing first cut nearly five hundred years ago by the political philosopher Niccolo Machiavelli and later expanded by four American political scientists: Richard E. Neustadt, James MacGregor Burns, John W. Kingdon, and Richard J. Samuels.

From its day of publication, Machiavelli's *The Prince*[37] has been notorious as a handbook of evil for unscrupulous politicians. But *The Prince* could not have endured, indeed, become a classic, for nearly half a millennium if its advice was only that. Three positive contributions of *The Prince* resonate today. First, Machiavelli inspired future thinkers to separate the actual from the ideal. Mid-twentieth-century empirical political scientists praised Machiavelli because he affirmed their intent to develop a genuinely scientific political science. Second, rereading Machiavelli reminds us, against Machiavelli's purpose, that the tension between private and

concludes pessimistically to the effect that "even if the relative gap between them and oligarchs widens rather than narrows" (p. 285).

[34] "Masyarakat Menyumbang," *Kompas*, June 27, 2012; *Tempo*, October 8–14, 2012; *Tempo*, October 15–21, 2012; and *Tempo*, October 22–28, 2012.

[35] Winters, "Oligarchy and Democracy in Indonesia," p. 23.

[36] Hadiz, *Localising Power in Post-Authoritarian Indonesia*," p. 29.

[37] Niccolo Machiavelli, *The Prince*, trans. Peter Constantine (New York, NY: Random House Modern Library, 2008 [first published in 1527]).

public morality is ineluctable. Morality for a politician, including in modern democracies, differs from individual private morality.

Third, and most important, Machiavelli offered an elegant new framework, consisting of the concepts *virtu* and *fortuna,* for empirical political analysis. *Virtu* means skill or masculinity, from the word *vir*, male, in Latin. Its meaning is different from "virtue" in English, which denotes high moral purpose. In the language of this essay, *virtu* is considered a collection of resources held by a person or that can be created, mobilized, and deployed to achieve his or her goals as a political actor. Examples of political resources mentioned by Machiavelli are diverse. Among other things he noted: intelligence, strategic and tactical courage, conscientiousness, firmness, a reputation for a willingness to forgive, support from one's own people, support by the leader of a neighboring state, and ability to choose aides and to read the signs of the times. Also, of course: cunning and readiness to lie and to use force in a calculated and cold-blooded fashion.

Fortuna means chance or luck, but in the sense of natural and social conditions and events to which actors respond, without the implication that necessity or fate are involved. Two well-known explications from Machiavelli himself: (1) "*Fortuna* seems to be the arbiter of half our actions, but she does leave us the other half, or almost the other half, in order that our free will may prevail;"[38] and (2) "It is better to be impetuous than cautious, because *Fortuna* is a woman, and if you wish to dominate her you must beat and batter her."[39]

In our time, Machiavelli's approach to the study of political leadership has been applied by the political scientists Richard E. Neustadt and James MacGregor Burns (of course, after rejecting his views on violence and women). The first edition of *Presidential Power*,[40] Neustadt's most influential book, was published several months before John F. Kennedy's presidential inauguration. After Kennedy's death, Neustadt founded the Harvard Kennedy School (HKS), today the most celebrated public policy graduate school in the United States.

In *Presidential Power*, Neustadt extends Machiavelli's approach to the analysis of American presidents in the modern era (the "modern era" is Neustadt's term, which he uses to emphasize the importance of time and place in political analysis). For Neustadt, the power to persuade is the chief political resource a president can deploy. The success of his programs and policies is highly dependent on his willingness and capacity to persuade three types of people: members of his own government; Washington society (especially Congress and the Supreme Court); and the voting public (including the press and public opinion survey institutions). In Neustadt's words: "The essence of a president's persuasive task is to convince such men that what the White House wants of them is what they ought to do for their sake and on their authority."[41]

Based on his research on three presidents—Franklin Roosevelt, Harry Truman, and Dwight Eisenhower—Neustadt argues that there are five factors that determine the success or failure of a president's policy or program. The president himself must be fully involved in the process of decision-making on any specific issue. His words

---

[38] Ibid., p. 115.

[39] Ibid., p. 118.

[40] Richard E. Neustadt, *Presidential Power and the Modern Presidents: The Politics of Leadership from Roosevelt to Reagan* (New York, NY: The Free Press, 1990 [first published in 1960]).

[41] Ibid., p. 30.

must be unambiguous. His view must be publicized widely. The instruments and resources that are available for implementation must be up to the task. And the recipients of his instructions must accept his authority and legitimacy in terms of that particular policy or program.

This is a simple and seemingly obvious list of factors. Nonetheless, in the hands of the expert and experienced analyst Neustadt, employing them as a conceptual framework deepens our understanding of the meaning and causes of presidential achievement in America. In Indonesia, there has so far been no comparable study of any of Indonesia's democratic presidents. Abdurrahman Wahid and Megawati Sukarnoputri's relatively short presidencies, under the quasi-parliamentary institutional rules prevailing during their tenures, are probably less suitable for a Neustadt-style analysis than that of the two-term, directly elected SBY.

What such a study might show is that, in comparison to the records of all three of his non-democratic predecessors—Sukarno, Suharto, and Habibie—there have been few policy areas in which SBY has been fully involved, let alone unambiguous in his policy position, and he has not publicized his views widely or paid attention to implementation or to whether his constituents accepted his legitimacy in that particular policy area.[42] In the economy, SBY has been criticized for failing to deal with burgeoning fuel subsidies that have several times threatened to overwhelm the state budget. He has arguably failed to formulate, let alone implement, a broad plan for infrastructure development, according to most economists a prerequisite for future growth. In social affairs, he is criticized for failing to protect a range of religious minorities, including Christians, Shi'ites, and Ahmadis. In foreign relations, he has carried out few significant initiatives.

How to explain this lackluster performance, especially when we recall that this is a president who was directly elected twice by large majorities—in 2009, by 61 percent in the single-round presidential election? In a democracy, popular support is typically the single most important resource that can be deployed by an elected official to achieve his or her goals. In the hands of political parties and civil society groups, it is also a key resource for reducing the political inequality created by capitalism in Dahl's account. In SBY's case, the puzzle appears to be why he has not made better use of that resource. One possible answer, which calls for systematic research to test it, is the relative organizational weakness of parties and interest groups. With regard to fuel subsidies, for example, the mass constituency that can be mobilized to support pro-market reform has arguably been much weaker than the defenders of the status quo.

Neustadt specifies three target audiences for presidential persuasive power, one of which is the voting public. In Indonesia, systematic studies of voting behavior have been pioneered by Saiful Mujani, who wrote the first scientific study of Indonesian voting behavior after *reformasi*.[43] For the first time in Indonesian history, several large national random-sample surveys using up-to-date methodology have been conducted since 1999.

Analysis of this data shows that the factors that have most influenced the voter's choice in parliamentary and presidential elections since 1999 have been

[42] But see the discussion later in this article about Djayadi Hanan's analysis of SBY's leadership.

[43] Saiful Mujani, R. William Liddle, and Kuskridho Ambardi, *Kuasa Rakyat* (Jakarta: Mizan, 2012).

psychological and political economy factors, including voters' perceptions of the national economic condition. If his or her perception is positive, the voter tends to choose the incumbent president or governing party; if negative, the voter tends to choose the opposition candidate or party. This finding directly contradicts the conventional wisdom of the 1950s (based in part on anthropological data) that most voters in Indonesia are influenced by religious, regional or ethnic, and social class solidarities.

In consequence, analysts and players today have an understanding of Indonesian electoral politics that is much more accurate, sophisticated, and reliable than before modern surveys were conducted. President SBY, for example, is known to place a high degree of trust in the findings of pollsters and to have used them to help define his election campaign themes and even his choice of a running mate in 2009.[44] Excessive sensitivity to poll-based evaluations of his actions may also help to explain his lackluster performance, as noted above. We may hypothesize that he has often failed to act in a particular policy area because of a calculation that public opposition to his preferred policy in that area is too great. Again, this points to the value of future systematic research examining the effect on elected officials of pressure from mobilized groups in society.

James MacGregor Burns's most influential book, *Leadership,* was published almost two decades after Neustadt's.[45] By the late 1970s, the times had changed dramatically in America, where political activists had mobilized to oppose discrimination against African-Americans and the war in Vietnam. *Leadership* was Burns's response. His world view was more to the left than that of Neustadt, placing greater emphasis on the necessity of conflict to bring about social change. Moreover, Burns's approach was more psychological and moralistic than political scientific in the empirical sense that I have characterized as the mainstream of the discipline.

Burns introduced two new analytical elements: the concept of followership as inseparable from leadership; and the division of leadership into two prominent types, transactional and transforming. Transactional leadership, the much more common form, he defined as the exchange of political resources in the form of goods and services, including votes in elections, between leaders and followers. Both sides obtain something valuable from the transaction, and the society may also benefit. But in transactional leadership there is no higher objective that binds together leaders and followers in the pursuit of a higher moral purpose. This second type of leadership Burns called transforming.

Burns's contribution to the development of a theory of action is impressive and promising. The understanding of followership as a concept that highlights the voters' continuing interaction with leadership can help us to understand the rise and fall of social movements that potentially reduce political inequality. In Indonesia, Burns's followership concept can be used to investigate all forms of social and political movement, from the early nationalist period to the present. The relatively successful defense today of the KPK by civil society groups, discussed above in my critique of the oligarchical perspective, is an obvious topic for further research. Another example is the interaction between leaders and followers within Islamic movements, with their generally high level of ideological commitment. What

---

[44] Ibid., Chapter 3.

[45] James MacGregor Burns, *Leadership* (New York, NY: Harper Perennial Political Classics, 2010 [first published in 1978]).

difference do leaders make in such a context? A valuable study might be conducted of former Masjumi leader Mohammad Natsir's leadership during the New Order in laying the foundation of today's Islamist resurgence. The Islamist organizations PKS (Partai Keadilan Sejahtera, Prosperous Justice Party), HTI (Hizbut Tahrir Indonesia), and FPI (Front Pembela Islam, Islamic Defenders Front) may also be usefully compared in these terms. Have individual leaders played a relatively small role in PKS and HTI but a dominant one in FPI, and, if so, what have been the consequences for these movements?

Indonesia has by now had enough presidents (though of course not all democratic) to enable scholars to compare their levels of achievement in terms of Burns's framework. Sukarno was arguably a transforming leader until 1949, after which he failed both as a transforming and transactional leader. Far more than any other leader, as he engaged with millions of followers, he shaped his fellow Indonesians' pan-ethnic, pan-religious identity and their stance toward the outside world. His subsequent efforts to pump Third World populism into that identity and to maintain himself in power transactionally through balancing PKI and army support led, perhaps inevitably, to economic decline and political instability, if not to the cataclysm of 1965. During Guided Democracy, Sukarno's unique deployment of the combined political resources of charisma and coercion arguably left most Indonesians less politically equal to the established elites than they had been in the 1950s.

During the New Order, Suharto succeeded in transforming the Indonesian economy, but his successes came at a high price, as they increased political repression and inequality. Measured in Burns's frame, Suharto was not a genuine leader, that is, he did not build and learn from a genuinely engaged followership from below but instead relied on heavily managed elections and "floating masses." Under the leadership of B. J. Habibie, Indonesian politics was transformed from dictatorship to democracy. The result was a huge increase in political equality, but the actions of Habibie himself were more transactional than transforming, which perhaps helps explain why he was not elected president in his own right in 1999.[46] Abdurrahman Wahid, Megawati Sukarnoputri, and Susilo Bambang Yudhoyono have been at best transactional presidents. Their successes and failures must be measured by the extent to which, given the constraints and opportunities of their time, they adopted strategies and tactics that improved the quality of the democratic institutions they inherited and thus increased political equality.

Two substantial objections may be raised to Burns's approach. First, his moral compass is distorted. Like many Left intellectuals of his time, Burns is too quick to forgive brutal behavior in the name of higher purpose.[47] Second, and analytically more relevant, Burns demands too much from us as ordinary citizens of large modern states. His approach evokes normative theories of participatory democracy, in which citizens participate directly in policy making, and deliberative democracy,

---

[46] R. William Liddle, "Indonesia's Democratic Transition: Playing by the Rules," in *The Architecture of Democracy*, ed. Andrew Reynolds (Oxford: Oxford University Press, 2002), pp. 373–99.

[47] Of course, it is not only observers from the anti-capitalist Left who have a one-sided view of their times. I, myself, conducting research from the center–left, have not yet written in a balanced way about the leadership of Suharto, who was arguably responsible both for the mass murders of 1965–66 and the subsequent economic development that has so benefited the Indonesian people.

in which citizens are urged to deliberate until a consensus is achieved. Initially inspired by Athenian democracy, these ideas probably are most applicable today to small social groups or communities. In Indonesia, they might give new life to discussions about village democracy, which many Indonesians value positively but believe has been undermined by modernization. Providing more resources to village government and social institutions might be one way to reduce political inequality.

The approach of John W. Kingdon differs considerably from that of Neustadt and Burns, who focus exclusively on the most important national-level actors like presidents and their most critical decisions. Neustadt and Burns are also often dismissed as unscientific by mainstream political scientists. Their concepts are ostensibly too high level, grand, vague, and opaque; difficult to turn into operational variables that can be tested in the form of empirical hypotheses. From the title alone, *Agendas, Alternatives, and Public Policies*, it is clear that Kingdon's focus is on practical problem solving.[48] The actor only appears as a potential cause of a policy outcome in his systematic comparison of twenty-three cases of decision-making in the health and transportation sectors, most of them during the US presidency of Jimmy Carter (1977–81).

The potential value of *Agendas, Alternatives, and Public Policies* for developing a democracy-relevant theory of action is enormous, greater perhaps than the work of any other modern scholar discussed in this essay. Kingdon's principal findings are as follows:

- The actors with the greatest influence on outcomes are the elected politicians and others visible to the researcher, not hidden actors behind the screen.

- Policy entrepreneurs often play an important role in policy reform. They can come from anywhere, but most are policy insiders who have long played a role in the policy-making process.

- Policy entrepreneurs swim in a sea (Kingdon's metaphor) of three separate and independent streams: problem recognition, generation of policy proposals, and political events. In short, problems, policies, and politics.

- These three streams meet in decision windows that open and close continuously and constitute unique opportunities for problem-solving. The chief role of the policy entrepreneur is to know when a window has opened and to act based on that knowledge.

- Because they take place within the flow of three autonomous streams, most policy processes are highly uncertain and unpredictable.

The characterization of three streams that flow freely in a sea of policy brilliantly specifies Machiavelli's *fortuna*. *Virtu* is interpreted by Kingdon as the substantive knowledge, willingness to act, and strategic and tactical skill of the policy entrepreneur. His theory of action is completed with the addition of the concept of a decision window that connects the *virtu*-possessing actor with *fortuna* in the form of the three streams.

---

[48] John W. Kingdon, *Agendas, Alternatives, and Public Policies* (New York, NY: Longman, 1995 [first published in 1984]).

For Indonesia, the governance scholar Sofie Schuette has written an excellent analysis of the important law creating the KPK, passed in December 2002.[49] The KPK is generally regarded, both inside and outside Indonesia, as an example of a relatively successful anti-corruption commission. It reduces political inequality in at least two ways: by shrinking the amount of money available as a political resource to the small number of actors who are caught; and by dissuading many others from engaging in corrupt acts for fear of being punished. The first consequence is, of course, the most easily demonstrable by analysts. The second is less obvious and requires further research, perhaps through surveys and interviews of officials and business people.

Schuette does not refer directly to Kingdon's book, but we can describe her argument in his frame. Schuette's actors, including donors and foreign consultants, were all visible. *Reformasi* opened a decision window, but the process was still slow. Before the 1999 election, several members of the New Order-era DPR (Dewan Perwakilan Rakyat, People's Representative Council) promoted the establishment of the KPK for electoral purposes but failed to enact it. From then until 2002, the most important role was played by the DPR, especially members of the steering committee. Donor influence was limited. "Rather than being a foreign legal transplant, the KPK was the result of a commonly perceived solution among Indonesian and international reformers to Indonesia's problem of enforcing its anti-corruption legislation."[50]

From Kingdon's point of view, the passing of the KPK law is a clear example of the resolution of a significant problem. His three streams—problem, policy, and politics—flowed separately and only came together in December 2002. The process was uncertain and unpredictable. Several policy entrepreneurs in the DPR played important roles in determining the final outcome. The decision window that was only opened prior to the 1999 election after being closed for decades was also crucial.

Djayadi Hanan's analysis of Indonesian legislative–executive relations during the SBY presidency is also very much in the Kingdon spirit.[51] Hanan's frame is based on the most recent comparative-politics literature on presidential governments with multiparty systems, a combination that has been considered prone to instability and gridlock, especially in Latin America. His Indonesian cases are organized in three categories: annual state budget decisions; six cases of specific legislation (the election law, the freedom of information law, the law on governmental ministries, the law on national and local legislatures, the election implementation law, and the law establishing social security implementing institutions); and three cases of legislative oversight (the Bank Century scandal, fuel oil subsidies, and corruption in tax collection).

Hanan's first finding is that the president and the DPR are about equal in their formal constitutional powers. This assessment challenges Jakarta public discourse, in which the conventional wisdom since the 2002–04 constitutional amendments has been that the DPR is more powerful than the president. Hanan's second finding is that, measured in terms of the results of the deliberative process, there are no signs of

---

[49] S. A. Schuette, "Against the Odds: Anti-corruption Reform in Indonesia," *Public Administration and Development* 32,1 (2012): 38–48.

[50] Schuette, "Against the Odds," p. 43.

[51] Djayadi Hanan, *Making Presidentialism Work: Legislative and Executive Interaction in Indonesian Democracy* (PhD dissertation, Department of Political Science, Ohio State University, 2012).

gridlock. After SBY became president, a budget has been passed every year. The same is true for the six substantive bills. The oversight cases of Bank Century, the fuel oil subsidy, and tax corruption all ended with compromises accepted by the president and the DPR. In short, according to Hanan, the Indonesian case represents an example of executive–legislative relations in a multiparty system that has "apparently performed reasonably well."[52] It has also arguably reduced political inequality by making the political process more transparent, increasing the role of legislators, and raising the ability of the executive to formulate and implement policies that promote the public welfare.

What factors explain this success? Hanan highlights several institutions, formal and informal, that pressured the two sides to compromise in order to achieve their separate goals. Some examples: constitutionally mandated deliberation and agreement requirements from beginning to end of each legislative process; long-standing personal relationships, predating the Yudhoyono government, between presidential and DPR staff; and collective internal organization and decision-making structures in the DPR (in the form of caucuses, commissions, and committees). Hanan proposes that gridlock occurs more often in the US Congress because it is a much more individualistically structured institution than the collectivist DPR.

Hanan also mentions culture as a causal factor, citing a general Indonesian tendency to be accommodative and look for *mufakat*, consensus. No less important, he praises the conscious choices of President Yudhoyono and leaders of other parties to form coalitions. "Finally, the problem of a minority president with minority legislative support (low partisan power) is overcome by the existence of a coalition. This study finds that the coalition has been working in mitigating immobilism and deadlock in legislative–executive relations in multiparty presidentialism comparable to most multiparty presidentialism systems in Latin America in the last two decades."[53]

The fourth and final action theorist is Richard Samuels, a leading Japan specialist at the Massachusetts Institute of Technology and author of *Machiavelli's Children: Leaders and their Legacies in Italy and Japan*.[54] Like Kingdon, Samuels attempts to explain the causes and consequences of important policies. Where Kingdon limited himself to the United States and one presidential administration, however, Samuels's wide canvas covers the history of Italy and Japan as late modernizers. For Samuels, the success of modernization and its special qualities in Italy and Japan were caused by policy choices made by twenty-four leaders, eleven in Italy and thirteen in Japan. Those choices were intentional and consequential, though constrained by social forces. The leaders he studies were involved in nine important cases of decision-making that Samuels presents in parallel analyses to highlight his comparative argument.

The first case is nineteenth-century state-building, liberal in Italy and authoritarian-nationalist in Japan. The key decision-makers were Count Camillo Benso di Cavour in Italy and Ito Hirobumi and Yamagata Aritomo in Japan. These three individuals, according to Samuels, shaped the substantive content of modern institutions in Italy and Japan. The other eight cases, presented chronologically, focus

---

[52] Ibid., p. ii.

[53] Ibid., pp. 406–7.

[54] Richard Samuels, *Machiavelli's Children: Leaders and their Legacies in Italy and Japan* (Ithaca, NY: Cornell University Press, 2003).

on economic development, the death of liberalism, the birth of corporatism, foreign alliances after World War II, controlling corruption, the impact of the death of communism in the Soviet Union and Eastern Europe, and the balance of authority between regions and the center. Samuels concludes that his actors possessed considerable freedom of action. He argues persuasively that, in each case, the leaders formulated goals, strategies, and tactics while weighing various alternatives. Morally and in the eyes of history, they were responsible for their choices.

Samuels's social forces derive from anthropology (culture), sociology (social structure), psychology (perception and cognition), and political science (governmental and political institutions). They are treated analytically as both constraints that obstruct and resources that facilitate political action. Quoting Samuels: "leadership is that constrained place where imagination, resources, and opportunity converge."[55]

Beyond the soaring rhetoric, Samuels offers three practical contributions to a theory of action. First, he describes three mechanisms of mobilization used by political actors to achieve their goals: buying, bullying, and inspiring. Citing a key term of Machiavelli's, the author explains that these mechanisms specify dimensions of *virtu*. Each mechanism is connected by Samuels to several commonly encountered political resources: in buying, actors seek money, goods, services, and positions; in bullying, coercion and violence are employed by state institutions like the police and the armed forces and by social groups outside the state; for inspiring, actors rely on ideology, symbolic policies, and other resources that have to do with affect, legitimacy, or culture.

Samuels's three-element model can be used to analyze leadership successes and failures. In Indonesia, the perdurance of the New Order can be explained as a result of the mobilization of all three mechanisms in shifting combinations, depending on the situation and needs of Suharto, the primary actor.[56] At the beginning, the primary mechanism was bullying. The army was used to destroy the communist party and control other political forces. Golkar's victorious 1971 election campaign was also guaranteed by armed force. After that, buying became more important, in the narrow (and democratically illegitimate) sense of corruption, but also the broader (and democratically legitimate) sense of economic development that created the foundations of broad prosperity. As Dahl predicted, this prosperity ultimately reduced political inequality by distributing more widely resources of wealth, knowledge, social status, and organizational skills. Post-*reformasi*, these resources are available to political actors throughout the system. Returning to the New Order, from beginning to end inspiring mechanisms were also deployed, for example, in the form of anti-communism, anti-Islamism, and, of course, the promotion of the state doctrine of Pancasila, an all-purpose, all-period ideology.

Samuels's emphasis on the role of legacy as the chief constraint for the next generation of leaders is also useful. In the case of Indonesia, scholars who write about the *reformasi* period must weigh carefully the impact of important decisions made by previous governments, perhaps extending back to precolonial times, while realizing that legacies represent only constraints, not determinants or causes.

---

[55] Ibid., p. 6.

[56] R. William Liddle, "Indonesia: A Muslim-Majority Democracy," in *Comparative Governance*, ed. W. Phillips Shively (New York, NY: McGraw-Hill PRIMIS, 2007), paging various.

An obvious example of a legacy, with great promise for reducing political inequality, is today's governmental decentralization, which has channeled authority primarily to districts and municipalities rather than to provinces. This reform was powerfully influenced by Indonesian nationalist aversion to Dutch-imposed federalism in the 1940s and to separatist and perceived separatist movements in the 1950s. Another example is the preference for presidentialism over parliamentarism. This inclination is traceable to the instability of the 1950s multiparty parliamentary system as perceived by national politicians during the democratic transition in the late 1990s and early 2000s. A third legacy, perhaps less obvious and more controversial, is the debt owed by democrats to Suharto's electoral institutions, designed to legitimize a dictatorship. These turned out to be readily usable with only minor adjustments for the first genuinely democratic elections in 1999, enabling the country to postpone more contentious constitutional reform until the first democratic government had been created.

Finally, the concept of constraint-stretching may be Samuels's most useful contribution to measure the *virtu* or achievements of today's leaders. In Japan and Italy, success is almost always connected by Samuels to the capability of a leader to stretch the major constraints of his time. The highest accolades are awarded by Samuels only to the leaders who act in a way that is original, courageous, and unexpected by friends, enemies, and the outside world. Mere success is not enough.

Can the concept of constraint-stretching be applied to Indonesia? At the end of the 1980s, modernist Muslims were embraced by President Suharto after being ostracized for decades. The new policy startled many people, including the modernists and those who feared them, because Suharto had a well-deserved reputation for hostility to modernists only exceeded by his hostility to communists. After Suharto stepped down, we could see that his embrace had had a significant legacy impact, because all important religious groups now had a place at the national table as Indonesia democratized. Given the results of this highly significant and politicized case involving Muslims, there is now much more equality in the country than had been true during most of the Suharto period.

In 1998–99, new President Habibie made his own bold moves by initiating a promised democratic election, decentralizing authority to the regions, and offering independence to East Timor. All of those policies were his choices. If retired army General Try Sutrisno (vice president until March 1998) had become president instead, his choices would almost certainly have been different. After the 1999 election, Habibie failed to become Indonesia's first democratically elected president, but a genuine democratic transition and increase in political resources for most Indonesians had taken place during his term. Like Samuels's leaders in Italy and Japan, Habibie stretched his constraints and changed the history of his nation. After that, there has not been a president who tried, much less succeeded, in stretching constraints either to achieve personal goals or to enhance political equality significantly.

A final formulation of action theory that summarizes concisely the discussion so far is the following from the leftist sociologist Steven Lukes. In a seminal essay entitled "Power and Structure," Lukes discusses types of structural constraints confronted by political actors, including internal and external, positive and negative, and ends- versus means-oriented constraints. He concludes that "Social life can only properly be understood as a dialectic of power and structure, a web of possibilities for agents, whose nature is both active and structured, to make choices and pursue strategies within given limits, which in consequence expand and contract over time."[57]

CONCLUSIONS

Distributing political resources more equally is the greatest challenge facing modern democracies, if democracy is defined as political equality among all citizens, the definition of democratic theorist Robert Dahl. Unfortunately, this goal is difficult to achieve in capitalist market economies, which, ironically, constitute both a necessary condition for and a constant threat to modern democracy. In this, contemporary Indonesia is no different than any other democracy, past or present.

Karl Marx, who privileged class conflict as the dynamic force in history, launched a vigorous attack on capitalism in the nineteenth century. But Marx's followers in the twenty-first century do not help us much to understand how to improve democracy. The most prominent examples in Indonesian studies have been Richard Robison, Vedi Hadiz, and Jeffrey Winters. There are two fatal weaknesses in their approach. First, they denigrate or dismiss all resources other than great material wealth that might be mobilized to reduce political inequality. In their landscape, there are no more- and less-fertile uplands and lowlands but only one massive and desolate mountain range. Second—remarkably in the works of authors who represent the inheritors of a great revolutionary tradition—there is in their analyses no theory of political change, no specification of factors or processes that might reduce or replace the oppressive weight of material wealth. For well-wishers of democracy, theirs is truly a counsel of despair.

To construct a theory of political change, the sixteenth-century political thinker Niccolo Machiavelli is a better twenty-first-century guide than today's Marxists. To Machiavelli, the individual is an autonomous actor who self-consciously creates, possesses, and deploys political resources. In a modern democracy, this self-consciousness is a necessary (though, of course, not sufficient) condition for holding elected leaders accountable. Most importantly, Machiavelli's concepts of *virtu* and *fortuna* offer a foundation for a new theory of action. Machiavelli's embryonic theory has, in turn, been brilliantly adapted to the needs of the twenty-first century by four prominent American political scientists: Richard Neustadt, James MacGregor Burns, John Kingdon, and Richard Samuels. Each of their frameworks can be applied productively to the analysis of contemporary democratic Indonesian politics.

Neustadt's focus on the presidential power to persuade as a political resource helps to explain the apparent gap between promise and performance in the presidency of Susilo Bambang Yudhoyono. It also enables us to understand better, for SBY as well as his successors, the role played by mass opinion surveys in holding presidents accountable to their electorates, an important dimension of political equality. Burns's distinction between transforming and transactional leaders gives us a tool to evaluate how successful previous presidents and other elected officials have been. It also sets a standard by which voters can judge future candidates for office. Less conventionally, Burns's concepts of followership and mutual engagement between leaders and followers can help explicate the growth and appeal of civil

---

[57] Steven Lukes, "Power and Structure," *Essays in Social Theory* (New York, NY: Columbia University Press, 1977), Chapter 1, p. 28.

society organizations across a broad spectrum of issue areas, guiding research on organizations ranging from the KPK to Hizbut Tahrir Indonesia.

Kingdon-style systematic empirical analysis of the causes of policy outcomes has already yielded valuable studies of the formation of the corruption-fighting KPK and of the relative success of executive–legislative relations during the SBY presidency, both of which have had a positive impact on political equality during the *reformasi* period. Samuels's three mechanisms of political mobilization (buying, bullying, and inspiring) have already been employed to explain the perdurance of Suharto's New Order. His concept of legacy gives us a deeper understanding of today's governmental decentralization, the choice of presidentialism over parliamentarism, and the positive role for political equality played by Suharto's electoral institutions in the democratic transition. Finally, President Habibie truly stretched constraints by conducting a genuinely democratic election, decentralizing governmental authority, and offering independence to East Timor. Each of these actions undeniably enhanced and distributed more equally the quantity and quality of political resources in the hands of Indonesian citizens.

To conclude at a more foundational level, we need to remember Dahl's warning that increasing and distributing political resources to improve the quality of democracy is a Herculean task. A vast, probably growing, abyss separates the resourceful haves from the have-nots in Indonesia as elsewhere. But we can take heart in the knowledge that tools are available to attack this problem. If Indonesians do increase and distribute resources more equally in the twenty-first century, it may well be because they have developed a modern Machiavellian theory of action enabling them to do so.

PLURALISM AND POLITICAL CONFLICT IN INDONESIA[1]

Thomas B. Pepinsky

INTRODUCTION

Contemporary Indonesian politics is characterized by inequality. Scholars of oligarchy have provided the most cogent analysis of Indonesia's extraordinarily unequal distribution of material wealth as a central feature of Indonesian politics. They have also pushed forward the comparative analysis of national political systems by using the Indonesian case to conceptualize oligarchy as a category of political analysis.[2] These analyses draw attention to the manifest weaknesses of Indonesian democracy, and highlight the differences between the formal rules and procedures that constitute democracy, and the exercise of power under democratic rule.

Pluralism is an alternative framework through which to analyze Indonesian politics. Pluralism shares with Marxist and other materialist analyses of politics a "socially determinist"[3] conception of politics. It rejects the position that material interests are fundamentally different from other interests, with fundamentally different consequences for political action. The weaknesses of early pluralist analyses are well-known: they offered a theoretical framework, not a theory of anything; pluralism as a concept is most fruitfully applied to the static analysis of existing cleavages rather than to the dynamic analysis of where cleavages come from and why they persist or change; and most seriously, the conception of power (and of interest itself) typically affirmed by a pluralist analysis is one dimensional and reductive.[4] For these reasons, many recent analyses of contemporary Indonesian politics working outside of the oligarchic tradition have ignored or downplayed their pluralist heritage.

[1] Special thanks to Michele Ford and Matt Winters for comments on an early draft.

[2] Richard Robison and Vedi R. Hadiz, *Reorganising Power in Indonesia: The Politics of Oligarchy in an Age of Markets* (London: RoutledgeCurzon, 2004); and Jeffrey A. Winters, *Oligarchy* (New York, NY: Cambridge University Press, 2011).

[3] Theda Skocpol and Kenneth Finegold, "State Capacity and Economic Intervention in the Early New Deal," *Political Science Quarterly* 97,2 (1982): 259.

[4] Steven Lukes, *Power: A Radical View*, 2nd ed. (New York, NY: Palgrave Macmillan, 2005).

This essay explores the complementarities and the tensions between pluralism and recent analyses of oligarchy in Indonesia. Its goal is to argue that a "critical" pluralism offers a toolkit through which to understand Indonesian politics, as well as a progressive research program that can push the analysis of material wealth and political power further than existing research on oligarchy. This open dialogue between pluralist and oligarchic analyses contributes to the study of material wealth and political power (in Indonesia and elsewhere) in three ways. Conceptually, it helps analysts distinguish between descriptive and causal claims about material wealth, political power, and political outcomes. Theoretically, it challenges oligarchic analyses by offering competing and complementary causal arguments about the effects of the unequal distribution of material resources. Methodologically, it outlines a practice of knowledge production for scholars of Indonesia interested in effects of material wealth on contemporary Indonesian politics, one that invites structured comparison with other national contexts or historical periods and clarifies the role of evidence in adjudicating among contending approaches.

My use of the qualifying term "critical" here is deliberately nonstandard.[5] Rather than serving as a dogwhistle for structural or materialist theories of politics, it is meant as an internal challenge to theories of pluralism themselves, one that follows from the weaknesses outlined above and seeks to address them by questioning why cleavages exist and why interests are or are not articulated; this enables scholars to move beyond one- and two-dimensional analyses of power and interest, and to take history and social structures seriously.[6] None of these pluralist auto-critiques is original to this essay, yet they have not been articulated in sustained conversation with the empirics of contemporary Indonesia for two decades.[7] In my usage, "critical" also rejects the search for a single master narrative in Indonesian politics, and recommends a practice of Indonesian political studies that is concerned first and foremost with middle range theory in the service of social explanation.[8] Pluralism, like any other approach to social analysis, is strongest when it recognizes the limits of its explanatory power.

[5] I borrow the term "critical pluralism" from Gregor McLennan, *Marxism, Pluralism, and Beyond: Classic Debates and New Departures* (Cambridge: Polity Press, 1989), pp. 43–56. Here, McLennan makes passing reference to Robert Dahl and Charles Lindblom's critique of conventional pluralist analyses of the United States political economy. McLennan is also the source of the term "conventional pluralism," as discussed below.

[6] Gabriel Almond has argued that the early pluralist literature was far more conceptually advanced than its later critics have allowed, implying that most of these critiques were actually well understood as early as the 1950s. For a review, see the chapter by Gabriel A. Almond, "Corporatism, Pluralism, and Professional Memory," in *A Discipline Divided: Schools and Sects in Political Science*, ed. Gabriel A. Almond (Newbury Park, CA: Sage Publications, 1990), pp. 173–88.

[7] Stefan Eklöf has observed a general decline of theoretical debate among models of Indonesian politics by the late New Order period: Stefan Elköf, *Power and Political Culture in Suharto's Indonesia: The Indonesian Democratic Party (PDI) and the Decline of the New Order (1986–98)* (Copenhagen: NIAS Press, 2003), p. 11. This may reflect the exhaustion of these debates, or a general shift from a focus on typological theory to quantitative measurement in comparative politics; see David Collier, Jody LaPorte, and Jason Seawright, "Putting Typologies to Work: Concept Formation, Measurement, and Analytic Rigor," *Political Research Quarterly* 65,1 (2012): 217–32.

[8] Daniel Ziblatt, "Of Course Generalize, But How? Returning to Middle Range Theory in Comparative Politics," *American Political Science Association–Comparative Politics Newsletter* 17,2 (2006): 8–11.

Because pluralism is not a theory that predicts any particular outcome, it cannot be falsified or tested. However, a critical pluralism *produces* hypotheses in the study of material wealth in Indonesian politics that can be falsified through empirical analysis. Political conflict during Indonesia's financial crisis and local economic governance in decentralized Indonesia offer two topical studies through which to contrast pluralism and oligarchy as explanatory frameworks for key issues in contemporary Indonesian politics in which massive inequalities in wealth feature prominently.

The essay proceeds as follows. It first traces a brief history of pluralist theory in comparative political analysis, and then highlights applications of pluralism to the analysis of Indonesia's political economy in the New Order period. From this review, it will become clear that, much as scholars of United States politics concluded in the 1960s, pluralist analyses of anything approaching "interest-group liberalism" in Indonesia are inappropriate.[9] From there, I move to a direct engagement with the concept of oligarchy as presented by Vedi Hadiz and Richard Robison and Jeffrey Winters, outlining the points of tension between oligarchic and pluralist analyses. Building on that discussion, I next present the two topical case studies. In each, I begin with what I interpret to be the useful strengths of an oligarchy-based approach to contemporary problems in Indonesian politics, before then introducing the problems that a pluralist critique inevitably raises and the solutions that it provides. The essay concludes by discussing how Indonesianists should build a progressive, cumulative research program[10] to study Indonesian politics without ignoring the extraordinarily unequal distribution of wealth or its corrosive effects on the functioning of Indonesian democracy.

PLURALISM IN INDONESIAN POLITICS

The essence of pluralism is a conception of politics as competition among pressure groups that represent various interests in society.[11] Pluralism has changed

---

[9] The classic statement of this critique in the United States context is Theodore M. Lowi, *The End of Liberalism*, revised ed. (New York, NY: Norton, 1979).

[10] Here, I mean "progressive" in the standard Lakatosian sense; see Imre Lakatos, "Falsification and the Methodology of Scientific Research Programs," in *Criticism and the Growth of Knowledge*, ed. Imre Lakatos and Alan Musgrave (New York, NY: Cambridge University Press, 1970): 91–196.

[11] Even though pluralism was a dominant current in the political science mainstream for most of the twentieth century, it was never definitively articulated as a theory of politics by any of the major scholars associated with it. Before the conceptual debate on pluralism and its alternatives declined in the 1990s, in fact, critics commonly observed that pluralism had no core principles upon which its adherents commonly agreed; see Grant Jordan, "The Pluralism of Pluralism: An Anti-theory?," *Political Studies* 38,2 (1990): 286–301; and McLennan, *Marxism, Pluralism, and Beyond*, p. 35. Commenting on Arend Lijphart's analysis of consociationalism, Gary King, Robert Keohane, and Sidney Verba observe that "it was widely recognized that the concept of pluralism was often used in conflicting ways, none clear or concrete enough to be called a theory. Ronald Rogowski's description of pluralism as a 'powerful, deductive, internally consistent theory' … is surely the first time it has received such accolades." See Gary King, Robert O. Keohane, and Sidney Verba, "The Importance of Research Design in Political Science," *American Political Science Review* 89,2 (1995): 480, note 3.

significantly over the past six decades; here, I outline its evolution only briefly.[12] As originally developed, pluralism had both descriptive and normative ambitions, and was used not only to characterize the nature of political conflict but also to legitimize the practice of democratic life.[13] Later analyses, led by Robert Dahl (himself a key figure in early pluralist debates), began to separate the descriptive from the normative components of a pluralist analysis of politics. While these scholars remained deeply committed to a normative analysis of democratic politics in capitalist states,[14] their critical analysis of pluralism as a descriptive framework became more tightly focused on characterizing the essential axes of political conflict within different polities.[15]

While a useful corrective to the most idealistic and unreflective pluralist analyses, Dahl's most critical approach to pluralism did not save this tradition from losing intellectual currency as political scientists transitioned away from paradigmatic debates in comparative politics. Theodore Lowi's critique of "interest-group liberalism" in the United States also helped to bury conventional pluralism.[16] However, the pluralist impulse to characterize politics and the policymaking process as competition among groups defined by their interests in policy outcomes has survived. This is most apparent in the lineage of Mancur Olson's *The Rise and Decline of Nations*, which used Olson's earlier writings on collective action and group behavior to explore how distributional coalitions shaped politics and policy.[17] Here, the break from the normative aspirations of early pluralism is complete, for Olson's analysis was skeptical that "pressure groups" were representative of anything resembling the public interest, and that their competition would have salutary effects on national politics or on economic performance.[18] Important comparative works following (more or less conspicuously) in this theoretical tradition concerned with

---

[12] A recent, textbook-style overview of the pluralist tradition and its contemporary successors can be found in John S. Dryzek and Patrick Dunleavy, *Theories of the Democratic State* (New York, NY: Palgrave Macmillan, 2009), pp. 35–56 and 131–203.

[13] The standard reference is David B. Truman, *The Governmental Process* (New York, NY: Alfred A. Knopf, 1951).

[14] Most notably, see Robert A. Dahl, *A Preface to Economic Democracy* (Berkeley, CA: University of California Press, 1985).

[15] See, e.g., Robert A. Dahl, "Pluralism Revisited," *Comparative Politics* 10,2 (1978): 191–203.

[16] Lowi, *The End of Liberalism*. Andrew McFarlane labels Lowi's alternative as "plural-elitist theory." Distributive and redistributive politics remain essential to this conception of politics and policymaking; see Andrew S. McFarland, "Interest Groups and Theories of Power in America," *British Journal of Political Science* 17,2 (1987): 129–47.

[17] Mancur Olson, *The Rise and Decline of Nations: Economic Growth, Stagflation, and Social Rigidities* (New Haven, CT: Yale University Press, 1984).

[18] Harmon Zeigler, "Interest Groups," in *Encyclopedia of Government and Politics*, ed. Mary Hawkesworth and Maurice Kogan (New York, NY: Routledge, 1992), pp. 377–92. Public choice theory draws on similar insights, but has grown to encompass a general critique of interventionist government as hopelessly captured by special interests; the standard reference is James M. Buchanan and Gordon Tullock, *The Calculus of Consent: Logical Foundations of Constitutional Democracy* (Ann Arbor, MI: University of Michigan Press, 1962). This "Virginia school" public choice critique of regulation or activist government does not follow logically from a pluralist ontology of political conflict. Olson himself "complained that 'the value of the scientific contributions of Gordon Tullock and his colleagues in the Virginia School is obscured when it is treated as a part of or a justification for any right-wing ideology.'" See Iain McLean, "The Divided Legacy of Mancur Olson," *British Journal of Political Science* 30,4 (2000): 657.

distributional politics, in which sectoral and class interests shape politics and policy, include Peter Gourevitch on politics after economic crises, Ronald Rogowski on trade and political alignments, and Jeffry Frieden on Latin American political economy.[19] Distributional politics figures also prominently in later analyses of economic development, economic reform, and public policy, even if business, sector, or factor interests are only partially determinant of these outcomes.[20]

The important conclusion is that the pluralism of mid-century North Atlantic political science has been discarded almost entirely, rendered obsolete by both internal critiques (Dahl) and external critiques, both moderate (Lowi) and radical (Lukes). Pluralism's intellectual heritage survives, however, in the analysis of distributional politics. My understanding of pluralism as applied to contemporary Indonesian politics begins from the perspective that political actors engage in politics to produce policies that they favor. Political conflict results from differences in the interests of various actors, both individuals and groups. Political outcomes are shaped by the resources available to conflicting groups and the institutions that aggregate or channel individual or collective preferences. These institutions are themselves subject to manipulation by the actors and groups whom or which they are meant to constrain, such that conflict about political institutions reflects more basic conflicts over distribution, redistribution, and recognition. There is no reason to believe that such conflict will always produce balanced or socially optimal policy outcomes, that "interest groups" as conventionally understood always exist, or that the recognizable interest groups that do exist are representative of the interests that they may claim to represent.

MODIFIED PLURALISMS AND THE NEW ORDER POLITICAL ECONOMY

Conventional pluralism was never a serious analytical framework for Indonesian politics. However, pluralism did shape the research agenda on the New Order. The problem was how to square the observation that Suharto's regime faced no significant threat from any organized opposition group with the observation that it was possible to uncover clear evidence of distributional politics with effects on policy outcomes; in areas ranging from financial deregulation to rice and sugar policy, relatively weak groups and interests were able to shape policy outcomes in their favor, and executive preferences rarely determined policy outcomes alone.[21] The search for pluralism in New Order politics was reinforced by parallel currents in the

---

[19] Jeffry A. Frieden, *Debt, Development, and Democracy: Modern Political Economy and Latin America, 1965–1985* (Princeton, NJ: Princeton University Press, 1991); Peter Gourevitch, *Politics in Hard Times: Comparative Responses to International Economic Crises* (Ithaca, NY: Cornell University Press, 1986); and Ronald Rogowski, *Commerce and Coalitions* (Princeton, NJ: Princeton University Press, 1989).

[20] See, for example, Richard F. Doner, "Limits of State Strength: Toward an Institutionalist View of Economic Development," *World Politics* 44,3 (1992): 398–431; Stephan Haggard, Sylvia Maxfield, and Ben Ross Schneider, "Theories of Business and Business-State Relations," in *Business and the State in Developing Countries*, ed. Sylvia Maxfield and Ben Ross Schneider (Ithaca, NY: Cornell University Press, 1997): 36–60; and Hector E. Schamis, "Distributional Coalitions and the Politics of Economic Reform in Latin America," *World Politics* 51,2 (1999): 236–68.

[21] See R. William Liddle, "The Politics of Shared Growth: Some Indonesian Cases," *Comparative Politics* 19,2 (1987): 127–46; and M. Hadi Soesastro, "The Political Economy of Deregulation in Indonesia," *Asian Survey* 29,9 (1989): 853–69.

study of communist Europe, which sought to demonstrate the utility of a pluralist conceptual framework for sharpening the analysis of politics under communism.[22] Thus emerged what might be termed the "modified pluralisms" in the study of the New Order political economy.

Modified pluralisms bring together the concept of group competition with some other feature of the New Order political system—traditionally, either its extensive bureaucracy or its top-down political system—to describe a hybrid political system. Examples include "bureaucratic pluralism" as used by Dwight King and Donald Emmerson,[23] John Bresnan's "managed pluralism,"[24] and Hadi Soesastro and Peter Drysdale's "constrained pluralism."[25] Bureaucratic pluralism is perhaps the most theoretically developed of these modified pluralisms, drawing on a long theoretical lineage that Emmerson traces to early writings by Juan Linz.[26] In this way, the modified pluralisms drew from theoretical models that had been first elaborated to understand the postwar authoritarian regimes of southern Europe and Latin America.

These analyses also reveal a fundamental concern with policy as central to political conflict. The analytical focus on policy outcomes was certainly dominated by economic concerns, but material resources and economic interests occupy no special position in the modified pluralist analyses of Indonesia or in the pluralist literature that was evolving at the same time.[27] That said, the relationship between the modified pluralisms and the broader concept of pluralism (or of, say, bureaucratic-authoritarianism[28]) has never been outlined with much precision.[29] It is not clear if the modified pluralisms are diminished subtypes of pluralism (such as pluralism minus electoral democracy) or proper subtypes of authoritarianism (authoritarian rule plus identifiable group conflict).[30] In general, the problem hindering the comparative analysis of the New Order regime in pluralist terms has been the difficulty of describing the conceptual features of pluralism that scholars

---

[22] For a review, see Gabriel A. Almond with Laura Roselle, "Model Fitting in Communist Studies," in *A Discipline Divided,* ed. G. Almond, pp. 66–116.

[23] Donald K. Emmerson, "Understanding the New Order: Bureaucratic Pluralism in Indonesia," *Asian Survey* 23,11 (1983): 1220–41; and Dwight Y. King, "Bureaucracy and Implementation of Complex Tasks in Rapidly Developing States," *Studies in Comparative and International Development* 30,4 (1995/1996): 78–92.

[24] John Bresnan, *Managing Indonesia: The Modern Political Economy* (New York, NY: Columbia University Press, 1993).

[25] M. Hadi Soesastro and Peter Drysdale, "Survey of Recent Developments," *Bulletin of Indonesian Economic Studies* 26,3 (1990): 3–44.

[26] Emmerson, "Understanding the New Order," p. 1222; and Juan J. Linz, *Totalitarian and Authoritarian Regimes* (Boulder, CO: Lynne Rienner, 2000).

[27] Dahl, "Pluralism Revisited."

[28] Guillermo A. O'Donnell, *Bureaucratic Authoritarianism: Argentina, 1966–1973 in Comparative Perspective* (Berkeley, CA: University of California Press, 1988).

[29] This parallels the general problem of classifying the New Order regime; see Dwight Y. King, "Indonesia's New Order as a Bureaucratic Polity, a Neopatrimonial Regime, or a Bureaucratic Authoritarian Regime: What Difference Does It Make?," in *Interpreting Indonesian Politics: Thirteen Contributions to the Debate,* ed. Benedict Anderson and Audrey Kahin (Ithaca, NY: Cornell Southeast Asia Program Publications, 1982), pp. 104–16.

[30] On diminished versus proper subtypes, see David Collier and Steven Levitsky, "Democracy with Adjectives: Conceptual Innovation in Comparative Research," *World Politics* 49,3 (1997): 430–51.

remove when they employ "bureaucratic" and other modifiers. This problem recalls the earlier critiques of pluralism as a theoretical framework without a coherent set of foundational principles upon which all of its adherents or proponents agreed.

Rescuing pluralism as a tool for understanding Indonesian politics from the analytical morass of slippery definitions and diminished/proper subtypes requires a different strategy than that found in the modified pluralist approach. Rather than describing Indonesian politics as pluralist, modified pluralist, or something else— thereby elaborating the position of the entirety of Indonesian politics within a typological space—the task of pluralism in modern political economy is to provide a tool through which to analyze particular problems in Indonesian politics. That tool is, simply, the analysis of interests and their articulation in the political sphere. The utility of a pluralist approach in one conceptual or empirical domain need not signal its global utility for all questions in Indonesian politics. Proponents of this approach ought to be skeptical of their ability to read interests from observed behavior, or from actors' and groups' economic or social profiles, and will theorize explicitly relationships between interests and particular institutional structures when making claims about the effects of interests on policy or other outcomes. Recalling Lukes's critique of power, critical pluralism will also be sensitive to "recognitional domination," in which the interests of individuals or groups are ascribed to them by external actors, social structures, or state institutions.[31]

Pluralism, then, should not be considered a theory or description of Indonesian politics in the way that modified pluralisms were. It is one framework through which to organize observations about political conflict in Indonesia, and theorize about the origins and consequences of that conflict. Its contribution to the study of material resources and political power is twofold. First, it characterizes the objectives of materially endowed actors. Second, it places material interests alongside non-material interests in order to understand how they interact to shape political action.

Importantly, this is not necessarily an appeal for a more comprehensive or inclusive account of Indonesian politics. For scholars of Indonesian politics who reject oligarchy as a conceptual framework, one strategy for demonstrating the superiority of some alternative conception of Indonesian politics has been to list the facets of Indonesian politics that the concept of oligarchy cannot explain. These are bound to be many, as the oligarchy theorists are clear that there is much that they do not mean to explain—essentially, any source of power that is not material wealth. This "other things matter too" approach is not the strategy adopted here, for it neither addresses the oligarchy approaches on their own terms nor explains the conditions under which material resources *do* have explanatory power. In what follows, I endeavor to hew closely to the perfectly sensible idea that material resources are necessarily at play in all aspects of Indonesia's political economy, from national macroeconomic policy to local resource conflict.

---

[31] Lukes, *Power*, p. 120. Lukes illustrates recognitional domination with reference to Martha Nussbaum's analysis of female identity in India, which is defined only in relation to male interests; see Martha C. Nussbaum, *Women and Human Development: The Capabilities Approach* (New York, NY: Cambridge University Press, 2000).

OLIGARCHY AND PLURALISM: TENSIONS

Understood as an approach to political conflict rather than a type of political order or system of power relations, pluralism is not incompatible with oligarchy as defined in Winters's terms as "the politics of wealth defense by materially endowed actors."[32] Oligarchs may be indifferent to policies or political events that do not affect the security of their material wealth; here, a pluralist lens may clarify what kind of politics follows. Pluralist approaches may explain what exactly the battles among oligarchs are about when oligarchs line up on different sides of a policy debate. Finally, a pluralist analysis could in principle see oligarchs as one group in conflict with one or more other groups, especially in cases of what Winters terms "civil oligarchies," in which oligarchs have surrendered their arms and are constrained by laws.[33]

Robison and Hadiz use a different definition of oligarchy to characterize the Indonesian case. In their analysis, oligarchy is

> Any system of government in which virtually all political power is held by a very small number of wealthy … people who shape public policy primarily to benefit themselves financially through direct subsidies to their agricultural estates or business firms, lucrative government contracts, and protectionist measures aimed at damaging their economic competitors—while displaying little or no concern for the broader interests of the rest of the citizenry. "Oligarchy" is also used as a collective term to denote all the individual members of the small corrupt ruling group in such a system. The term always has a negative or derogatory connotation in both contemporary and classical usage.[34]

This definition is incompatible with conventional pluralism because, in the conventional understanding, interest groups and other collective actors who are not defined by their wealth nevertheless possess and exercise power. Yet it is wholly compatible with the critical pluralism outlined above, *just so long as* there exists identifiable distributional conflict among the "wealthy … people" that forms the basis for political action. Without such conflicts, there is nothing for a pluralist to explain. A critical pluralist analysis, in fact, might conclude that what a naïve pluralist would observe to be conflicting interests groups may really be the manifestations of battles among oligarchs and elites that have been strategically "externalized" onto society (a phenomenon familiar to any observer of the orchestrated *demo* in post-Suharto Indonesia).

---

[32] Winters, *Oligarchy*, p. 7. Elsewhere, Winters and Benjamin Page observe that an oligarchy can exist within a broadly pluralist political landscape, as in the United States. See Jeffrey A. Winters and Benjamin I. Page, "Oligarchy in the United States?," *Perspectives on Politics* 7,4 (2009): 731–51. Any account, pluralist or otherwise, of Indonesian politics that denies the existence (real or potential) of a particular politics that follows from wealth defense would be, trivially, incompatible with Winters's approach to oligarchy.

[33] While this is true *in principle*, I have no clear sense of what such an analysis would look like in practice. Winters and Page are skeptical that treating oligarchs as an interest group makes sense; Winters and Page, "Oligarchy in the United States?," p. 738.

[34] See Robison and Hadiz, *Reorganising Power*, pp. 16–17, note 6. The original source is Paul M. Johnson, "Oligarchy," *A Glossary of Political Economy Terms*, http://www.auburn.edu/~johnspm/gloss/oligarchy, accessed February 13, 2013.

Explaining the political consequences of different configurations of power and interest is central to the pluralist tradition. Yet neither oligarchy nor conventional pluralism is capable on its own of making causal claims. The typology of oligarchy advanced by Winters—in which oligarchies vary by degree of fragmentation, the source of coercion, and whether they are wild or tamed—is instructive in this regard. There are no claims that emerge from this typology of oligarchies about what different oligarchic types *cause*. Instead, these are constitutive statements about what oligarchic types *are* based on theoretically prior claims about how oligarchs relate to one another and to the provision of violence. There are some observations about what oligarchs *do* as a result of the type of oligarchy in which they find themselves. But causal claims about the consequences of oligarchy for policy or political outcomes cannot be drawn from this typology alone. This weakness, of course, is shared by conventional pluralism.

Robison and Hadiz's understanding of oligarchy similarly does not provide causal explanations for political outcomes. But it is not an elaboration of the concept of oligarchy as a theoretical category, but rather of the practice of oligarchy (as defined by the authors) in Indonesia. This description of the Indonesian case is no less theoretical than that of Winters, but it stresses the historical development of a structure of political power and its changes over time.

However, despite the compatibility of both conceptions of oligarchy and what I have described as critical pluralism, it is not true that oligarchy and pluralism are orthogonal theoretical projects. This makes the relationship between oligarchy and pluralism different than the relationship between oligarchy and democracy, which both Hadiz and Robison and Winters hold to be compatible.[35] Critical pluralism makes demands on the analysis of oligarchy, political power, and material inequality in Indonesia. For scholars working in the pluralist tradition, any attempt to study politics without reference to policy and its consequences is incomplete. Here, policy is understood simply as "a principle or course of action adopted or proposed as desirable, advantageous, or expedient."[36] Policy is central to the pluralist tradition because it is the object of political contestation. It can be as broad and substantive as a social democratic party platform, or as narrow and venal as directing a regulator to harass a business competitor.[37] Policies have direct effects (for example, on the business competitor who is harassed) and indirect effects (for example, on the investment decisions of potential market entrants who anticipate being harassed themselves). In the pluralist tradition, a progressive research program in Indonesian

[35] In the conventional understanding, the association between pluralism and democracy is definitional. Dahl is absolutely clear: "all democratic countries are pluralist democracies"; see Robert A. Dahl, *Dilemmas of Pluralist Democracy: Autonomy vs. Control* (New Haven, CT: Yale University Press, 1982), p. 5. While theoretically important for the pluralist tradition, this point is ultimately of little consequence for the current purposes of characterizing politics in countries marked by vast inequality of material resources. A committed materialist might argue that the associations that are relatively autonomous in pluralist democracies like Indonesia are simply those that lie outside of the interests of oligarchs or economic elites.

[36] This is a standard dictionary definition. "policy, n.1," *OED Online* (Oxford University Press, December 2012), http://www.oed.com/view/Entry/146842?rskey=uMAZca&result=1&isAdvanced=false (accessed February 10, 2013).

[37] Note, further, that policies may be coherent or contradictory; that policies may be pursued by politicians, their supporters, or by segments of society that are entirely disenfranchised; and that policies may even be illegal.

political studies would be one that produces theories of political outcomes and policy choices, and that can explain why policies and outcomes vary across time and space through falsifiable hypotheses derived from these theories.

The study of corruption in post-Suharto Indonesia illustrates the differences between typological theory and causal explanation, and, accordingly, the differences between approaches rooted in oligarchy versus the pluralist tradition. Oligarchy theorists have noted that the power of Indonesia's super-wealthy has been "reorganized" rather than reduced since the transition to democracy.[38] In Winters's typology, Indonesian oligarchy is transforming from a sultanistic oligarchy towards an "untamed ruling oligarchy."[39] Related observations about the structure of elite politics and political business relations (the term "oligarchy" is not used) in the early post-New Order period were made separately by Andrew MacIntyre and Ross McLeod, both considered to be working in different theoretical traditions than scholars of oligarchy.[40] Focusing on corruption, each argues that the basic logic of money politics changed after the New Order's demise. MacIntyre and McLeod, however, propose hypotheses to explain how different organizations of elite politics or political business relations affect the overall level and structure of corruption. They imply, following canonical models of the industrial organization of corruption,[41] that without any mechanism for binding the grasping hands of thousands of lower-level politicians and administrators, bribes in post-Suharto Indonesia are smaller in size than they were during the New Order but more frequent in number. As a consequence, corruption in post-Suharto Indonesia has threatened investment more than corruption under the New Order did, at least at the time that MacIntyre and McLeod were writing.[42]

I am not aware of any test of this hypothesis, and the available evidence supporting it is impressionistic and incomplete, supported by anecdotes and blanket pronouncements of what "everybody knows." However, MacIntyre and McLeod's arguments are consistent with a research program that moves from a descriptive account of the changing organization of money politics to a causal account of its effects on investment in post-Suharto Indonesia. This is an argument that can be falsified, though it is true that no systematic attempt to do so has been initiated to date.

In sum, the points of tension between analytical approaches based on oligarchy and critical pluralism lie not in the conceptualization of oligarchy or in the analytical focus on the social foundations of political conflict, but rather in the focus on policy as the object of political contestation and the development of causal explanations for political outcomes. These tensions are consequential for the study of Indonesian

---

[38] Thus the title of Robison and Hadiz, *Reorganising Power*.

[39] Winters, *Oligarchy*, p. 181.

[40] Andrew MacIntyre, "Institutions and the Political Economy of Corruption in Developing Countries," paper presented at the "Workshop on Corruption," Stanford University, January 31–February 1, 2003; and Ross H. McLeod, "Soeharto's Indonesia: A Better Class of Corruption," *Agenda* 7,2 (2000): 99–112. I make no claim that either would be comfortable being labeled as a (critical) pluralist, or even as working in a pluralist tradition or framework. Their insights, however, are wholly compatible with my approach to constructing a pluralist analysis of corruption in Indonesia.

[41] Andrei Shleifer and Robert W. Vishny, "Corruption," *Quarterly Journal of Economics* 108,3 (1993): 599–617.

[42] Both authors saw Indonesia's legal system as completely ineffective.

politics. The following section expands on this theme, presenting two topical studies of political conflict in Indonesia in the context of massive inequality in material wealth and political power.

OLIGARCHY AND PLURALISM AT WORK

To demonstrate that a focus on oligarchy alone occludes fundamental questions of politics and policymaking, I examine here two of the central political issues of the past twenty years of Indonesian history: the economic crisis of 1997–98 and local political economies in decentralized Indonesia. In the case of the crisis, I argue that even ignoring non-material interests entirely, a pluralist approach provides the only theoretical framework that can capture the conflicts concerning policy adjustments within the New Order coalition that set in motion the collapse of the Indonesian economy and, ultimately, of the New Order regime. In the case of decentralization, I show that the effects of material resources on political conflict are always conditional on non-material factors, making it impossible to understand the effects of material inequality in isolation from the conditions under which resources are deployed.

MATERIAL INTERESTS, ADJUSTMENT POLICY, AND REGIME CHANGE

By the early 1990s, most analysts of the New Order had come to agree that Suharto, as an individual, wielded extraordinary political power. In characterizing the system of rule over which Suharto presided, scholars of oligarchy draw attention to a tiny cohort of extremely wealthy businessmen (they were nearly all men) whose economic position depended on their close personal relationships with Suharto and who amassed fortunes of truly staggering size. These scholars, like those working in other traditions, identified these wealthy figures as the movers and shakers of the Indonesian economy during the New Order. The personal lives and business empires of figures such as William Soeryadjaya and Liem Sioe Liong, in fact, could be used to chart the evolution of Indonesia's entire political economy.[43] A central argument in Robison and Hadiz is that many of these powerful individuals were remarkably successful in protecting not only their wealth but also their political position during the course of Indonesia's democratic transition, something that the most Pollyannaish analysts of Indonesia's democratic transition might not have expected. For his part, as noted above, Winters argues that the politics of wealth defense in Indonesia is in the process of moving from a sultanistic oligarchy towards an "untamed ruling oligarchy"[44] in which money is at the core of politics, but in a different way than it had been under the New Order.[45] The approaches therefore agree that Indonesia oligarchy has changed, but not been eliminated, through democratization.

---

[43] Marleen Dieleman and Wladimir M. Sachs, "Coevolution of Institutions and Corporations in Emerging Economies: How the Salim Group Morphed into an Institution of Suharto's Crony Regime," *Journal of Management Studies* 45,7 (2008): 1274–300; and Yuri Sato, "The Astra Group: A Pioneer of Management Modernization in Indonesia," *The Developing Economies* 34,3 (1996): 247–80.

[44] Winters, *Oligarchy*, p. 181.

[45] This "less genteel game of *bagi-bagi*" compares with Aspinall's analysis of the *proyek* (project); see Edward Aspinall, "A Nation in Fragments: Patronage and Neoliberalism in Contemporary Indonesia," *Critical Asian Studies* 45,1 (2013): 27–54.

If interest groups, trade associations, labor groups, and others do not effectively lobby or campaign on enduring issues or coherent platforms, then the conventional pluralist framework of interest group competition is not appropriate for characterizing Indonesian politics, at least at the national level. However, even if analysts stay focused on the national level, careful analysis of distributional politics in the pluralist tradition is necessary to understand the most important events in Indonesia's modern history since the consolidation of the New Order in 1971: the collapse of the Indonesian economy in 1997 and of the New Order in 1998.

As I detail elsewhere, the Asian Financial Crisis did not generate a free-for-all among those who would be labeled as oligarchs, nor a unified rejection of Suharto's regime by oligarchs and political and business elites,[46] nor did it simply disrupt a fundamentally flawed political-economic model.[47] It generated a specific distributional conflict between two fractions of capital owners: those with fixed and mobile capital.[48] At the root of the conflict was a disagreement regarding how to adjust to the crisis, featuring two technically incompatible adjustment policy packages with different distributional implications. The group of individuals who would be labeled as oligarchs were one set of actors, divided between the two fractions, but the fractions included more modest business interests as well. Distributional conflict therefore both divided the oligarchs and created common cause between oligarchs and less spectacularly wealthy actors.

This perspective reveals that the manifestly ineffective policy response of the New Order's final year in office was far from irrational or ideological.[49] Instead, it was fundamentally political—the low politics generated by the oligarchs and small businesses alike trying to avoid going out of business. The problem was of their own making, with firms having become overextended and borrowers having ignored exchange rate risk when obtaining loans denominated in foreign currencies. And the conflict was simple: imposing capital controls was directly contrary to the interests of mobile capital, but the exchange rate peg and expansionary macroeconomic policy

---

[46] This is implied by Winters's quote from Rizal Ramli, "Everyone is piling on now and kicking him because they know he's down … " Winters, *Oligarchy,* p. 178.

[47] For Robison and Hadiz: "We propose that the crisis eroded the financial and political cement that had papered over a profoundly flawed and vulnerable system wholly reliant on the protection of a corrupt and authoritarian system of state power and an unregulated engagement with volatile global capital markets … " Robison and Hadiz, *Reorganising Power,* p. 149.

[48] Thomas B. Pepinsky, "Capital Mobility and Coalitional Politics: Authoritarian Regimes and Economic Adjustment in Southeast Asia," *World Politics* 60,3 (2008): 438–74.

[49] In an otherwise compelling treatment, Robison and Andrew Rosser mistake the nature of policy conflict during the crisis; see Richard Robison and Andrew Rosser, "Contesting Reform: Indonesia's New Order and the IMF," *World Development* 26,8 (1998): 1593–609. Rather than a fundamentally ideological conflict between the IMF and "Suharto, the politico-business families, and the major conglomerates" (pp. 1599–1603), this was a distributional conflict *within* the latter about *how* to escape the crisis without destroying the economic resources of some fraction of capital owners. Robison and Hadiz similarly neglect the basic conflict within Suharto's ruling coalition when describing IMF (International Monetary Fund) programs as "frustrated by resistance from the major politico-business families … " Robison and Hadiz, *Reorganising Power,* p. 157. Managing twin currency and banking crises in any emerging economy requires difficult choices about exchange rate and capital account policy. The fact that the IMF mandated a "neoliberal" policy package did not make this policy conflict any more serious than it would have been without the IMF, as the Malaysian experience shows. See Pepinsky, "Capital Mobility."

stance so desired by local firms rooted in Indonesia would be feasible only with a closed capital account.[50]

The observation that Indonesia's super-wealthy protected their wealth as much as they could during the crisis conveys precisely no information about the nature of that most central policy battle. The distributional coalitions activated by the currency crisis of 1997 were decidedly not interest groups as conventionally understood, and they did not act as coherent actors that aimed to represent some enduring social or economic interest. Yet political conflict in the final months of the New Order was fundamentally conflict over how to distribute the burden of adjustment across various allies of the regime. I further argue that this conflict not only shaped adjustment policy, it ultimately tore the regime apart, explaining not only the collapse of Suharto's rule but also the manner in which the regime fell.[51] But even if the end of the New Order was overdetermined—if the "true" cause of its collapse was actually Suharto's senility, the mobilization of civil society opposition and brave protesters, the rightful resistance of key opposition elites, a revolt within the military, a combination of these, or something else altogether—distributional interests are essential for characterizing policy conflict during the crisis. There is no other coherent explanation for why the regime would pretend to be committed to implementing the IMF's adjustment packages, why oligarchs and lower-level business interests would object (and object for the reasons that they did), how the distributional coalitions would emerge to contest both the IMF and the Suharto regime, and why Suharto or any of his closest cronies would care about any of this.

According to scholars working in the oligarchy tradition, the economic crisis led elites and oligarchs to fight among each other and eventually to abandon Suharto, an analysis that papers over the fundamental conflicts within the regime's coalition. Analyses based in the oligarchy tradition also ignore—because they are not equipped to observe—the basic observation that most brutal dictatorships temporarily insulate themselves from global financial markets when facing unanticipated currency and banking crises, using the breathing space to reflate their economies and crush their opponents.[52] An approach rooted in the pluralist tradition asks, first, what the distributional consequences of different adjustment measures are, and, second, which political coalitions happen to be empowered (for reasons that can be uncovered from the historical evolution of particular regimes). It both explains how adjustment policy battles unfolded in Indonesia, and provides a template for comparative analysis of the Indonesian case, facilitating direct comparison with both Malaysia during the Asian Financial Crisis and certain Latin American dictatorships during the 1980s debt crisis.[53]

The case of adjustment policy conflict and the collapse of the New Order illustrates the power of distributional politics as a framework for understanding the actions of even the most powerful and wealthy economic actors in Indonesia. I do

---

[50] The cases of Malaysia in 1998 and Chile and Mexico in 1982 demonstrate this solution in action, as well as the distributional politics of such a policy response.

[51] Thomas B. Pepinsky, *Economic Crises and the Breakdown of Authoritarian Regimes: Indonesia and Malaysia in Comparative Perspective* (New York, NY: Cambridge University Press, 2009).

[52] The case of Malaysia after September 1, 1998, is one example. The onset of Malaysia's crackdown against its domestic opposition followed by exactly one day the announcement of capital controls and an exchange rate peg.

[53] Pepinsky, *Economic Crises*.

not conclude from this discussion that a pluralist approach to policy conflict in the New Order's final year requires any fundamental rethinking of the *theory* of oligarchy as articulated by either Robison and Hadiz or Winters. Instead, the intensely political struggle over adjustment policy during Indonesia's financial crisis reveals the limits of analyses focused on oligarchy for understanding political conflict among Indonesia's most extremely wealthy and powerful citizens.

MATERIAL INTERESTS, DECENTRALIZATION, AND LOCAL POLITICS

After democratization, decentralization is the second fundamental change to the New Order political economy that occurred after the Asian Financial Crisis. Decentralization has empowered subnational political actors in new ways, and placed new pressures on local politicians to cater to their constituents' demands. The results have been disappointing on a number of fronts: corruption and money politics remains rampant, local reforms have stalled, district governments continue to be ineffective, and other pathologies abound. Hadiz traces most if not all of these pathologies to the basic observation that "predatory" interests at the local level were not disempowered by the collapse of the New Order and the democratization and decentralization that followed.[54] Just the opposite: regime change in Jakarta generated new pressures for local elites to use the new powers delegated to them to protect their own political and economic interests. Even self-styled reformist outsiders must obey the rules of the game of *bagi-bagi* (sharing around) as Hadiz and Robison and Winters all comment when discussing the rise of populist reformer Joko Widodo.[55]

Scholars working in many theoretical traditions have concluded that decentralization has not generated the outcomes that its most strident advocates had promised, in some cases providing empirical cases that anticipated the theoretical analyses that draw on oligarchy.[56] This has been raised in reviews of major critical works on local politics and Indonesian democratization, which have noted that the balance of existing scholarly opinion on democratization and decentralization has always been circumspect in suggesting that the two would produce unambiguously

[54] Vedi R. Hadiz, *Localising Power in Post-Authoritarian Indonesia: A Southeast Asian Perspective* (Stanford, CA: Stanford University Press, 2010).

[55] Vedi R. Hadiz and Richard Robison, "The Political Economy of Oligarchy and the Reorganization of Power in Indonesia," this volume, pp. 35–56; and Jeffrey A. Winters, "Oligarchy and Democracy in Indonesia," this volume, pp. 11–33.

[56] The literature on this topic is now large and developed. Some representative contributions include Iwan Jaya Azis and Maria Monica Wihardja, "Theory of Endogenous Institutions and Evidence from an In-depth Field Study in Indonesia," *Economics and Finance in Indonesia* 58,3 (2010): 30–334; Michael Buehler, "Decentralisation and Local Democracy in Indonesia: The Marginalisation of the Public Sphere," in *Problems of Democratisation in Indonesia: Elections, Institutions and Society*, ed. Edward Aspinall and Marcus Mietzner (Singapore: Institute of Southeast Asian Studies, 2010), pp. 267–85; Blane Lewis, "Tax and Charge Creation by Regional Governments under Fiscal Decentralization: Estimates and Explanations," *Bulletin of Indonesian Economic Studies* 39,2 (2003): 177–92; Michael S. Malley, "New Rules, Old Structures, and the Limits of Democratic Decentralisation," in *Local Power and Politics in Indonesia: Decentralisation and Democratisation*, ed. Edward Aspinall and Greg Fealy (Singapore: Institute of Southeast Asian Studies, 2003), pp. 102–16; and Thomas B. Pepinsky and Maria M. Wihardja, "Decentralization and Economic Performance in Indonesia," *Journal of East Asian Studies* 11,3 (2011): 337–71.

positive outcomes in terms of representation or popular welfare, in Indonesia or anywhere else.[57] So critical political economy does not help much to characterize the disappointing outcomes of Indonesian decentralization. The strong insight offered by a critical analysis of wealth defense and predatory elites, rather, is that institutional reforms may change the character of local politics without disembedding the local elites who occupied positions of power directly prior to the reforms. Those local elites "have a large stake in the localisation of power, thus in decentralisation and democracy,"[58] yet not in popular representation or accountability. I believe that even the most skeptical analysts of Indonesian decentralization failed to anticipate the importance of this argument for Indonesia today.

A conventional pluralist analysis of local politics as competition among interest groups has not been shown to offer much empirical traction in analyses of important topics in Indonesian local politics. However, recalling that a critical pluralism should question why interests are or are not articulated, should move beyond one- and two-dimensional analyses of power and interest, and take history and social structures seriously, then pluralism offers the natural framework through which to build an account of how local politics varies across Indonesia and why this matters.

Begin first with the problem of interest articulation. Conventional pluralist analyses in Indonesia fail because local politics in Indonesia generally does not provide a forum for the articulation of group interests, or of anything resembling the public interest (assuming such a thing exists). However, some interests are articulated—and, indeed, represented—in some contexts. Why? One possibility is that interests are represented when the local political and economic elite has a particular structure, such as what Christian von Lübke has labeled a "contested oligarchy," in which local elites compete, but not too much, allowing some private interests to seek representation.[59] Another possible explanation is that local elites can choose to seek political support from different segments of society, sometimes reaching out to the poor and serving as effective representatives.[60] Alternatively, Ryan Tans argues that despite the ubiquity of money politics in Indonesian local elections, it is possible to identify different types of political coalitions in various local contexts: mafias, machines, and mobilizing coalitions.[61] Mobilizing coalitions are most conducive to interest group representation in the pluralist mode, and machines are more likely to provide public goods than are mafias. Tans proposes that different coalitions emerge in different circumstances depending on the

[57] Michael Buehler, "Review of Nankyung Choi, *Local Politics in Indonesia: Pathways to Power*," *Publius: The Journal of Federalism* 42,4 (2012): e9; and Marcus Mietzner, "Review of Vedi R. Hadiz, *Localising Power in Post-Authoritarian Indonesia: A Southeast Asia Perspective*," *South East Asia Research* 19,3 (2011): 669–72.

[58] Hadiz, *Localising Power*, p. 88.

[59] Christian von Lübke, "Striking the Right Balance: Economic Concentration and Local Government Performance in Indonesia and the Philippines," *European Journal of East Asian Studies* 11,1 (2012): 17–44. Von Lübke's use of "oligarchy" as the basis for an analytical framework does not correspond to either Winters's or Robison and Hadiz's use of the term.

[60] Andrew Rosser, Ian Wilson, and Priyambudi Sulistiyanto, "Leaders, Elites, and Coalitions: The Politics of Free Public Services in Decentralised Indonesia," Developmental Leadership Program Research Paper 16, 2011.

[61] Ryan Tans, *Mobilizing Resources, Building Coalitions: Local Power in Indonesia* (Honolulu, HI: East West Center, 2012).

resources, both material and non-material, that are available to local politicians. Following this approach, any analysis of money politics that ignores non-monetary resources at the disposal of local politicians, or the goals for which monetary resources are used, will fail to account for this variation.[62]

The next step in building a progressive research program from Tans's analysis is to delineate the consequences of coalition types for policymaking and political outcomes. For example, it could be that mobilizing coalitions secure more public goods than do mafias or machines, and that flows of financial resources to constituents are combined with mobilizational efforts that recognize and/or reify existing group identities and interests. Such an analysis in the pluralist tradition would argue that the determinants of interest articulation in Indonesian local politics are only rendered visible by taking into account the interaction of material and non-material resources available to local politicians. The concept of *interaction* is critical: it rejects the presumptive defense by a materialist scholar that non-material resources are outside of his/her theory's explanatory scope. Instead, the importance of material resources always depends on non-material factors. By specifying *ex ante* the determinants of coalition types and the consequences of coalitional politics for policies and political outcomes, moreover, such accounts can easily be falsified, and readily subject to critical comparative analysis.

All pluralist analyses take history and social structure seriously, but a critical pluralism should use history and structure to help understand why interest articulation fails. In the context of decentralized Indonesia, this means understanding the legacies of authoritarian rule, and the ways in which these shape the resources and strategies available to local political actors. Michael Buehler has observed that reform and accountability have been hamstrung by the simple fact that old elites continue to dominate local politics in the era of decentralization.[63] This fact is compatible with an oligarchic approach to local political economies, but it is not demonstrative of any theory. It might instead reflect the continuity of the Indonesian state,[64] which, to use Benedict Anderson's colorful language, has continued to "excrete ... personnel in a continuous, steady process, often over long periods of time."[65] Further complicating this analysis is the extraordinary heterogeneity among New Order elites, a category that is descriptively simple but conceptually broad and unwieldy precisely because the New Order regime so pervaded the public sphere and associational life. This renders nearly all post-New Order elites tainted by their association with the New Order regime, regardless of their backgrounds or interests or resources or actions in the post-Suharto era.[66]

The pluralist approach recognizes that the presence of New Order holdovers in local elections does not convey much information about what they do or how their

[62] Ibid., pp. 56–57.

[63] On the political and administrative backgrounds of candidates for provincial elections, see Buehler, "Decentralisation and Local Democracy"; and Marcus Mietzner, "Local Democracy: Old Elites are Still in Power, but Direct Elections Now Give Voters a Choice," *Inside Indonesia* 17 (2006): 17–18. Based on incomplete data, the pattern appears to be similar in district elections; Michael Buehler, personal communication, January 2013.

[64] Buehler, "Decentralisation and Local Democracy."

[65] Benedict R. O'G. Anderson, "Old State, New Society: Indonesia's New Order in Comparative Historical Perspective," *Journal of Asian Studies* 42,3 (1983): 477–96, p. 478.

[66] See also Tans, *Mobilizing Resources*, pp. 56–57.

presence affects local politics or policy. It may be that the New Order holdovers are unresponsive to the very notion of interest articulation because they were socialized under an essentially corporatist model of interest management. It may be that New Order holdovers have differential access to material resources, which frees them from the need to represent interests in order to ensure their political survival. It may be that some kinds of New Order holdovers do not act in the same way: lifetime politicians may be different from bureaucrats-turned-politicians. These arguments have different implications for variation in local governance across regions, and they have different implications for the prospects for reform. Each of these possibilities recognizes the New Order's historical legacy as being fundamental to understanding contemporary local politics. None follows from the oligarchic approach, or from the observation that decentralization reforms did not themselves purge New Order elites from local politics.

The final directive for a critical pluralist analysis of local politics in decentralized Indonesia is to transcend one- and two-dimensional conceptions of power. Lukes's third dimension of power is the power to shape how others understand their own interests, which is important for pluralist analyses because it rejects the assumption that interests are "real" even if believed to be so by those who claim to be acting upon them. This argument has methodological consequences for any analysis of power and political conflict, applying equally to pluralism as to any materialist approach to social analysis, oligarchy included.[67] For a pluralist analysis, the important challenge is that the mechanism of interest articulation may be broken through the purposive actions of oligarchs and elites, who may not act in the direct sense, by smashing unions or imprisoning activists and other movement entrepreneurs, but, more indirectly, by creating the conditions of domination (ideological or structural) that ensure that those groups that might form common interest associations do not believe it possible or desirable to do so.[68]

This phenomenon has long been a concern for critical political economists—it is at the heart of long debates about ideological domination and class conflict in capitalist democracies[69]—and a critical pluralism must take it seriously. Yet critical pluralism is a framework for social explanation, and so when applied to Indonesia,

---

[67] The Lukes critique reveals a subtle distinction between Winters's and Hadiz and Robison's understanding of power and interest. Winters explicitly understands power in terms of the "power resources" approach; see Winters, *Oligarchy,* p. 6. This approach intends to transcend debates over the nature of power rooted in the behavioralist tradition, such that the third dimension of power is simply an "indirect strateg[y] for the rational deployment of power resources … " Walter Korpi, "Power Resources Approach vs. Action and Conflict: On Causal and Intentional Explanations in the Study of Power," *Sociological Theory* 3,2 (1985): 41. However, the power resources approach makes clear and direct causal claims about the relationship between the strength of the Left and outcomes of interest such as the development of the welfare state; see Walter Korpi, "The Power Resources Approach," in *The Welfare State Reader,* ed. Christopher Pierson and Francis G. Castles (Cambridge: Polity Press, 2006), pp. 76–88. In fact, one logical implication of the power resources approach is that it is not possible to study the power of one type of actor in isolation, for outcomes depend on the relative *distribution* of power among actors (for Korpi: classes). Hadiz and Robison, unlike Winters, make no appeal to power resources theory.

[68] Of course, the entire point of the Lukes critique is that those latent interests can never be observed, making the task of interest attribution (like the concept of power) an "essentially contested" one; Lukes, *Power,* pp. 124, 44–51.

[69] Antonio Gramsci, *Selections from the Prison Notebooks,* trans. Quintin Hoare and Geoffrey Nowell Smith (New York, NY: International Publishers, 1971).

the central endeavor is to theorize the application of power (in all its dimensions) in a way that can explain the variation across time and space in interest articulation. This task can be illustrated in the context of natural resource extraction in the era of decentralization. The exploitation of natural resources by oligarchs is common throughout the Indonesian archipelago. Yet, despite the common interest of oligarchs in discouraging (or suppressing, or eliminating) local resistance to resource exploitation, the local politics of resistance varies in readily apparent ways. Resistance to forest destruction and plantation development in Papua embraces a language of colonial occupation and common armed struggle that is absent in Kalimantan.[70] For the resource extractors, this necessitates a range of different practices in Papua—even if violence, coercion, bribery, and domination are always present in some form in both contexts. The reasons for the differences between Papua and Kalimantan in this case are obvious. The theoretical point is that any critical analysis of resource extraction in contemporary Indonesia cannot be restricted to the interests of economic elites or oligarchs alone. Powerful economic actors with unparalleled wealth and material resources will attempt to shape local communities' understandings of their own interests, but the strategies that they must pursue to do so will vary predictably. That inquiry is squarely within the ambit of the pluralist tradition.

No one working in the oligarchic tradition would deny that there is important variation in politics and policymaking across local contexts in Indonesia. Hadiz has himself analyzed how local politics has developed in very different districts. Yet neither that analysis nor the theoretical apparatus of oligarchy provides a framework for building explanations for why or how politics varies. The historicist observation that politics varies as a result of local conditions is, of course, not falsifiable when so articulated. It is also imprecise. *Which* factors, under *what* conditions, explain *what kinds of* variation in local politics, with *what kinds of* consequences?[71] Analyses following the pluralist tradition should certainly not embrace a conventional pluralist sociology that defines local politics as simple interest group competition, yet they are well placed to build accounts that can answer these questions.

---

[70] For overviews, compare Longgena Ginting and Oliver Pye, "Resisting Agribusiness Development: The Merauke Integrated Food and Energy Estate in West Papua, Indonesia," *ASEAS—Austrian Journal of South-East Asian Studies* 6,1 (2013): 160–82; and Leslie Potter, "Dayak Resistance to Oil Palm Plantations in West Kalimantan, Indonesia," presented at the Seventeenth Biennial Conference of the Asian Studies Association of Australia, Melbourne, July 1–3, 2008, available at http://artsonline.monash.edu.au/mai/files/2012/07/lesleypotter.pdf.

[71] One interesting contrast that is richly described, but not theorized explicitly, is in the different political success in East Java and North Sumatra of various thugs and goons whose power dates to the New Order period. In East Java, the "New Order's former enforcers have notably thrived less in their forays into local politics than their counterparts in North Sumatra." Hadiz, *Localising Power*, p. 116. Some explanations for the relative failure and success of various candidates proposed in this discussion include the traditional strength of Nahdlatul Ulama in East Java (which alters the nature of competition among local thugs by changing the balance of power among paramilitary groups), different histories of youth gangs in Medan versus Surabaya, and different kinds of military involvement in the criminal underworld; see ibid., pp. 133–42 and especially pp. 139–40.

CONCLUDING REMARKS

This essay has traced the development of pluralism as a framework for comparative analysis of political conflict in Indonesia. Mindful of the many trenchant critiques of the conventional pluralism of mid-twentieth-century North Atlantic political science, it has shown that the pluralist tradition has been largely abandoned as a grand theoretical project or paradigm in comparative politics, but that the tradition survives in the analysis of distributional politics. It has further argued that a critical pluralism provides a useful framework for understanding Indonesian politics, even recognizing the striking inequality of material wealth and political power that characterize Indonesia in the post-Suharto era. This argument rejects the typological theorizing of what I have called the "modified pluralisms" of New Order political economy, and places particular emphasis on causal explanation as a central endeavor for Indonesian political studies.

This argument is a challenge to approaches to Indonesian politics that emphasize oligarchy as the central analytical framework. To reiterate the points of tension elaborated above, the challenge is not to Winters's definition of oligarchy as the politics of wealth defense and his conceptualization of how oligarchy varies across time and space, or to Hadiz and Robison's central insight that powerful elites have survived Indonesia's democratization and decentralization and harnessed new institutional arrangements to protect their interests. Rather, critical pluralism challenges the explanatory capacity of these frameworks. In reviewing basic issues confronting scholars of material wealth and political conflict in contemporary Indonesia—the 1997–98 financial meltdown and subsequent collapse of the New Order, money politics and elite continuity in local elections, the exploitation of natural resources, and so forth—I have shown the limits of the oligarchy approach as a framework of analysis and the utility of a critical pluralist approach. These topical areas are precisely those in which an approach based on oligarchy, which is tightly attuned to the effects of material wealth (and its extraordinarily uneven distribution) on Indonesian politics, should be most useful. That oligarchy does not provide the analytical framework to make sense of these problems should be seen as a challenge to those who rely on oligarchy as a focal lens when seeking to understand the Indonesian case. It also has clear implications for the comparative utility of the oligarchy theses.

Critical pluralism does not only challenge oligarchy by providing competing explanations—derived from a close attention to policy as the fundamental object of contestation—for fundamental issues in Indonesian politics. Critical pluralism also embodies a competing practice of knowledge production in which the task of causal explanation is a natural complement to theoretically informed description and conceptual development. Causal explanations require theories that link causal variables to outcomes of interest under properly delineated scope conditions, and which produce arguments that are subject to falsification. In this sense, the critical pluralism I have described in this essay contains a prescriptive statement about what the scientific analysis of power, conflict, and material inequality in Indonesia ought to become. It is not just that critical pluralism interprets Indonesian politics differently than do other approaches. Rather, the study of Indonesian politics must follow broader disciplinary advances in the social sciences, and adopt a more sophisticated toolkit for adjudicating among competing approaches and perspectives.

This conclusion should not obscure the commonalities between the pluralist tradition and oligarchic approaches. Indeed, I have argued elsewhere that the critical political economy approach of Hadiz, Robison, and others in the Murdoch school shares a basic insight with the most rationalist approaches to institutions in political science.[72] That insight is that interests, not institutions, lie at the root of any coherent explanation of politics and policymaking. A progressive research program on the social foundations of Indonesian political economy will build on this common perspective on the root origins of political conflict. It will also take seriously the task of constructing explanations that can demonstrate the utility of interest-based explanations for capturing the great variation in the nature of political conflict and policy outcomes in unequal societies, such as Indonesia's.

---

[72] Thomas B. Pepinsky, "The Institutional Turn in Comparative Authoritarianism," *British Journal of Political Science* (forthcoming 2013). A previous version of that essay circulated under the title "Rochester and Murdoch in Kuala Lumpur." Compare this to the critique of naïve institutionalism in Vedi R. Hadiz, "Decentralization and Democracy in Indonesia: A Critique of Neo-Institutionalist Perspectives," *Development and Change* 35,4 (2004): 697–718.

OLIGARCHS, POLITICIANS, AND ACTIVISTS: CONTESTING PARTY POLITICS IN POST-SUHARTO INDONESIA

Marcus Mietzner

In the discussion about the role of the oligarchy in Indonesia, particularly contentious disagreement has focused on the exact extent to which oligarchs dominate the country's political institutions. For example, Jeffrey Winters has conceptualized post-Suharto Indonesia as an "untamed ruling oligarchy," in which senior political office holders are "almost always oligarchs."[1] According to Winters, this is also true for political parties, where top positions are "disproportionately held by oligarchs or by actors who can capture significant oligarchic resources."[2] While Winters views political engagement as one of many options available to oligarchs, Vedi Hadiz and Richard Robison theorize it as a logical and inescapable consequence of the nature of oligarchy in Indonesia.[3] For them, the Indonesian oligarchy *must* exert hegemonic influence through the state and its institutions. It "cannot rule from outside the apparatus of the state [...] in the same way it does in the United States."[4] As a result, the post-1998 political establishment predominantly consists of a wealthy, rent-seeking mix of "former apparatchiks, military men, entrepreneurs, and assorted political operators and enforcers of Suharto's New Order—at both the national and local level."[5] Opposition to oligarchic rule in Indonesia is consequently considered weak by these authors: Winters asserts that non-oligarchic elites can challenge oligarchs by mobilizing sufficient social capital, but rarely succeed in doing so; Hadiz and Robison, for their part, have described such opposition as

---

[1] Jeffrey A. Winters, *Oligarchy* (Cambridge: Cambridge University Press, 2011). pp. 181, 189.

[2] Ibid., p. 190.

[3] Richard Robison and Vedi Hadiz, *Reorganising Power in Indonesia: The Politics of Oligarchy in an Age of Markets* (London: Routledge, 2004).

[4] Vedi R. Hadiz and Richard Robison, "The Political Economy of Oligarchy and the Reorganization of Power in Indonesia," this volume, p. 38.

[5] Vedi Hadiz, *Localising Power in Post-authoritarian Indonesia: A Southeast Asia Perspective* (Stanford, CA: Stanford University Press, 2010). p. 28.

"piecemeal."[6] While Winters and Hadiz and Robison are the most important authors representing this view, other writings have echoed their sentiments in analyses of the growing dominance of money politics in Indonesian elections,[7] the emergence of wealthy political dynasties,[8] and the exploding costs of politics.[9]

This chapter critically reviews this assumption of oligarchic dominance over Indonesia's political institutions. Using the role of oligarchs in political parties as a case study, the chapter tests the above-mentioned assertion that oligarchs hold an overwhelming percentage of party leadership positions. It argues that while Winters, Hadiz, and Robison describe significant patterns in post-Suharto party politics, they overstate their point. Instead of a clear-cut hegemony of oligarchs over Indonesian parties and their affairs, there is an ongoing and fierce contestation between oligarchs and counter-oligarchic forces, in political parties as well as in other institutions. In this context, I propose an alternative definition of oligarchic actors in order to better grasp the degree of oligarchic influence in Indonesia. This definition also helps to highlight the operations of non-oligarchic forces whose influence is more than just "piecemeal." In doing so, the chapter does not intend to downplay the significance of oligarchic forces and interests. Their power is undeniable. Rather, it delivers a more comprehensive picture of the power distribution between oligarchic and non-oligarchic groups. Based on this picture, I offer an alternative interpretation of post-1998 power relations—one that goes beyond the focus on money as the "most vital power resource in Indonesia since Suharto's removal from office."[10]

My analysis is organized around three points. The first section assesses the degree to which Indonesian oligarchs have gained control over political parties. It finds that while a trend of oligarchization has taken place in the top echelons of some parties, the social capital owned by non-oligarchic politicians has prevented a complete oligarchic takeover. In addition, the section argues that intra-party oligarchization trends have been aggravated—if not caused—by Indonesia's dysfunctional party-financing system, which does not provide meaningful public funding for parties. In this sense, the analysis views oligarchization primarily as an institutional design problem rather than a path-dependent destiny for Indonesia. The second section further disaggregates the category of "oligarch." Identifying five different groups and subgroups of oligarchs, this segment pinpoints the diverse motivations that lead oligarchs to join parties—motives that go beyond the often-cited notion of "wealth defense." The third section focuses on the mobilization of counter-oligarchic forces in Indonesian parties. Besides long-entrenched party cadres who continue to challenge oligarchic newcomers, there has been a significant influx of reformist civil society elements into parties since the mid-2000s. As a result, the leadership and organization of Indonesian parties is more heavily contested than an

---

[6] Hadiz and Robison, "The Political Economy of Oligarchy," p. 54.

[7] Nankyung Choi, "Democracy and Patrimonial Politics in Local Indonesia," *Indonesia* 88 (October 2009): 131–64.

[8] Michael Buehler and Paige Tan, "Party–Candidate Relationships in Indonesian Local Politics: A Case Study of the 2005 Regional Elections in Gowa, South Sulawesi Province," *Indonesia* 84 (October 2007): 41–69; Okamoto Masaaki and Abdul Hamid, "*Jawara* in Power, 1999–2007," *Indonesia* 86 (October 2008): 109–38.

[9] Bima Arya Sugiarto, "Political Business," *Inside Indonesia* 87 (2006), at http://www.insideindonesia.org/weekly-articles/political-business

[10] Winters, *Oligarchy*, p. 181.

exclusive emphasis on oligarchs would suggest. The chapter concludes by introducing an alternative paradigm of post-authoritarian politics in Indonesia that highlights the continued and multi-layered contestation for politico–economic power and remains inherently skeptical of accounts that prematurely declare victory for the oligarchic forces.

OLIGARCHS AND POLITICAL PARTIES IN INDONESIA

Any assessment of the extent to which oligarchs "rule" or dominate Indonesia's political parties is highly dependent on how "oligarchs" are defined. According to Winters, oligarchs "are actors who command and control massive concentrations of material resources that can be deployed to defend or enhance their personal wealth and exclusive social position."[11] Importantly, Winters clarifies that these resources do not necessarily have to be personally owned. Under this definition, popular politicians who attract sizeable donations from sponsors could also be classified as oligarchs, although they may not be themselves massively wealthy. Hadiz and Robison, on the other hand, describe oligarchs as actors who operate "as a system of power relations that enables the concentration of wealth and authority and its collective defense."[12] This definition is even less precise than Winters's, and leads them to describe the entire socio–political system as being collectively involved in oligarchic wealth politics. I propose to address this problem of terminological elusiveness by defining oligarchs more narrowly than either Hadiz and Robison, or Winters, as *actors whose primary power resource is the personal and direct possession of large amounts of capital*. This capital, in turn, is deployed to seek political and/or economic benefit. This definition captures the material privileges of oligarchs in political competition in a more succinct and effective manner, allowing us to focus on personal wealth—as opposed to the financial resources conventional politicians can attract when seeking or occupying public office—as the main political instrument of oligarchs. It also makes it possible to separate analytically personal control of material resources from other political resources, such as social capital, popularity, dynastic lineage, and intra-institutional connectedness.

The problematic nature of imprecise definitions of oligarchic actors is palpable in Winters's analysis of the Indonesian case. The main example he gives in *Oligarchy* for the power of oligarchs in Indonesian party politics is the rise and fall of Akbar Tandjung, the chairman of Suharto's former government party, Golkar (Golongan Karya, Functional Groups), between 1998 and 2004. According to Winters, Akbar was an oligarch who eventually lost out to an oligarch with more resources (Jusuf Kalla). Tellingly, however, even Winters appears doubtful about whether Akbar truly was an oligarch. At the beginning of his discussion, he refers to Akbar as a full *"pribumi* [indigenous Indonesian] oligarch."[13] But as his analysis progresses, Akbar is first downgraded to a "middle oligarch" and, ultimately, to a "minor oligarch."[14] Using the revised definition developed above, Akbar was no oligarch at all. He was affluent, but his wealth was too small to be a decisive political resource. He relied on his unrivaled political connections within Golkar instead. In fact, Akbar felt a deep

---

[11] Ibid,. p. 6.

[12] Hadiz and Robison, "The Political Economy of Oligarchy," p. 37.

[13] Winters, *Oligarchy*, p. 182.

[14] Ibid,. pp. 187, 189.

aversion towards oligarchs such as Kalla. Akbar lamented that "I have attended Golkar congresses since 1973—I have never seen Kalla at any of them."[15] Rather than deploying his own limited wealth for party activities, Akbar "collected funds from sponsors, and when I traveled, I distributed them to the branches."[16] Thus, Akbar's connectedness within Golkar was his primary political resource, which allowed him to attract funds that further consolidated his power. In other words, access to sponsorship funds was the product—rather than the source—of his political influence. In Winters's own terminology, Akbar is, therefore, more appropriately described as an elite actor than as an oligarch.

The classic archetype of an oligarchic party leader is Aburizal Bakrie, the current chairman of Golkar. In the early 1970s, Bakrie had joined the company founded by his father, and he managed to turn it into one of the country's largest conglomerates.[17] While the crisis of 1998 hit Bakrie's interests hard,[18] his company survived—mostly due to a very generous debt restructuring deal. Bakrie subsequently used his economic and political connections to gain access to lucrative coal mining licenses in the Outer Islands. As the price of coal increased drastically (it quintupled between 2002 and 2008),[19] so did the value of Bakrie's shares. With his business flourishing, Bakrie decided to enter politics. In 2004, he unsuccessfully sought Golkar's presidential nomination, and then supported Susilo Bambang Yudhoyono and Kalla's bid and was rewarded with a ministerial post. During his time in government, Bakrie's businesses continued to prosper—in 2007, *Forbes* magazine ranked him as Indonesia's richest man, with a fortune of US$5.4 billion.[20] Although his wealth declined drastically after 2008 as a result of collapsing coal prices, he nevertheless was able to use his political influence to protect his personal business interests. For instance, even though one of Bakrie's drilling companies caused the now infamous mud volcano of Sidoardjo in East Java to flood more than 700 hectares of densely populated land in May 2006, the government did not make Bakrie fully liable for the damage. While Yudhoyono required Bakrie to spend around US$700 million to purchase the destroyed land, the government met all the long-term costs for land remediation and social assistance.

Having introduced paradigmatic examples of non-oligarchic and oligarchic party leaders, it is now possible to measure the degree of oligarchic intervention in Indonesian parties. One effective way of doing so is to establish the number of oligarchs who lead Indonesian parties today. Using this approach, and applying the revised definition above, we find the dominance of oligarchs is far from clear-cut: out of the ten main parties contesting the 2014 elections, five are chaired by oligarchs. The parties dominated by oligarchs are oligarchs are Bakrie's Golkar, Surya Paloh's Partai NasDem (Partai Nasional Demokrat, National Democrats), Hatta Radjasa's

---

[15] Interview with Akbar Tandjung, Jakarta, February 11, 2008.

[16] Ibid.

[17] Richard Robison, *Indonesia: The Rise of Capital* (Sydney: Allen & Unwin, 1986).

[18] Richard Robison and Andrew Rosser, "Surviving the Meltdown: Liberal Reform and Political Oligarchy in Indonesia," in *Politics and Markets in the Wake of the Asian Crisis*, ed. Richard Robison, et al. (London: Routledge, 2000), pp. 171–91.

[19] David Strahan, "The Trouble with Coal," *New Scientist* 197,2639 (January 19, 2008): 40.

[20] "Bumi Row Threatens Indonesian Tycoon's Presidency Bid," *Channel NewsAsia*, 12 (November 2012), at http://news.asiaone.com/News/AsiaOne%2BNews/Asia/Story/A1Story20121112-382895.html

PAN (Partai Amanat Nasional, National Mandate Party), Prabowo Subianto's Gerindra (Gerakan Indonesia Raya, Great Indonesia Movement), and Wiranto's Partai Hanura (Partai Hati Nurani Rakyat, People's Conscience Party). These are cases in which the oligarchs' personal wealth has allowed them either to purchase the chairmanship of an existing organization or to establish a new party from scratch. Without these massive personal resources, it would have been impossible for them to play a significant role in politics. To begin with, Bakrie became chairman of Golkar in its 2009 congress, winning what party insiders described as a "bidding war" against his fellow tycoon and political opponent, Surya Paloh.[21] The latter, a wealthy media entrepreneur who controls Metro TV, a leading news channel, moved on to found his own party in 2011. Hatta Radjasa, for his part, assumed the chairmanship of the National Mandate Party in 2010, replacing another oligarch, Soetrisno Bachir. While reporting a personal wealth of only 14.8 billion Rupiah (US$1.5 million) in 2009, Hatta, an engineer by training and former president director of a drilling company, is widely believed to be involved in several oil firms that are not listed as his personal property.[22] Prabowo and Wiranto, finally, founded their parties in 2008 and 2006, respectively, following controversial careers as senior military leaders under Suharto. Neither general possessed significant social capital (i.e., genuine popularity), so their wealth formed the most important resource in their bids for political power. Prior to the 2009 elections, Prabowo reported a private wealth of 1.57 trillion Rupiah (US$157 million),[23] while Wiranto's officially reported fortune stood at 81 billion Rupiah (US$8.1 million).[24]

By contrast, the other five parties are led by non-oligarchic figures: Megawati Sukarnoputri's PDI-P (Partai Demokrasi Indonesia–Perjuangan, Indonesian Democratic Party of Struggle), Muhaimin Iskandar's PKB (Partai Kebangkitan Bangsa, National Awakening Party), Suryadharma Ali's PPP (Partai Persatuan Pembangunan, United Development Party), Yudhoyono's PD (Partai Demokrat, Democratic Party), and Hilmi Aminuddin's PKS (Partai Keadilan Sejahtera, Prosperous Justice Party). The primary political resource of these party leaders is not money, but diverse forms of social capital. For example, Megawati's primary power resource is her dynastic heritage and charisma. As the daughter of Indonesia's founding president, Sukarno, she was able to mobilize dissatisfaction with the New Order regime in the later periods of its rule. Having gained further societal support from that achievement, she went on to win the first post-authoritarian elections in 1999 and became president in 2001. Obviously, her massive popularity and electoral success attracted donations and other forms of support from oligarchs but this does not mean that she was or is an oligarch herself. Winters has described Megawati as a "hidden" oligarch,[25] without explaining what, exactly, that entails. Under the

---

[21] Confidential interview, Jakarta, February 10, 2010.

[22] Hatta led PT Arthindo Utama from 1982 to 2000, after which he formally left the oil business to become a politician.

[23] Prabowo's campaign was also supported by his businessman brother, Hashim Djojohadikusomo, who was ranked thirty-ninth on the *Forbes* list of Indonesia's forty richest persons in November 2012, with an estimated fortune of US$750 million. See http://www.forbes.com/indonesia-billionaires/#page:4_sort:0_direction:asc_search, accessed October 18, 2013.

[24] "Total Kekayaan Wiranto Rp 81 Miliar," *VivaNews*, May 20, 2009.

[25] Jeffrey A. Winters, "Oligarchy and Democracy in Indonesia," this volume, p. 28 (Table 3).

definition offered in this chapter, however, Megawati is not an oligarchic actor in her own right. Similarly, Muhaimin Iskandar owes his standing within PKB to his lineage and personal links within Nahdlatul Ulama (NU), Indonesia's largest traditionalist Muslim group. As the nephew of Abdurrahman Wahid—NU's leader in the 1980s and 1990s and Indonesia's president from 1999 to 2001—Muhaimin had significant advantages when he began his organizational career in NU in the 1990s. As chairman of PKB since 2008, he has attracted financial support from sponsors, but he cannot be classified as an oligarch. Suryadharma Ali, the chairman of PPP, is not an oligarch, either. Like Muhaimin, he worked his way up the ranks of NU-affiliated organizations before occupying a number of key positions in the hierarchy of his party. His appointment as minister in the Yudhoyono cabinet in 2004 provided him with patronage opportunities, but did not give him direct and personal possession of large amounts of capital.

Susilo Bambang Yudhoyono, Indonesia's president between 2004 and 2014, is also a non-oligarchic actor. Unlike Prabowo and Wiranto, Yudhoyono did not rely on massive capital resources to launch his political career. Yudhoyono's popularity grew rapidly in the early 2000s because of his well-crafted media appearances and his projection of a calm, measured style of politics that reassured an anxious Indonesian electorate. His unprecedented electoral appeal raised interest from oligarchs but Yudhoyono did not owe his rise to them. Winters describes Yudhoyono as a mixture between a full and a hidden oligarch[26]—revealing both the difficulties inherent in his definition of oligarchy and its proper application to the Indonesian case. In the same vein, despite Hilmi Aminuddin's notorious predilection for brokering lucrative business deals, his rise in the PKS was not due to his ownership of, or access to, big bank accounts. Rather, he managed to establish himself as the undisputed religio–political authority in the party, building on his Saudi Arabian education, his founding of a Brotherhood-style movement in the 1980s, and his subsequent arrest by the New Order regime. Thus, to the younger generation in the party, he appeared as a battle-scarred leader with unquestionable religious credentials and a unique commitment to the movement. There is no doubt that Hilmi used his position to increase his personal wealth.[27] But as in the case of Megawati, Muhaimin, Suryadharma, and Yudhoyono, it was Hilmi's social capital that facilitated the mobilization of monetary resources. In clear-cut cases of oligarchic actors gaining political power, this relationship between social capital and money is reversed.

Nevertheless, the prominence of five massively wealthy party leaders—Bakrie, Surya Paloh, Hatta Radjasa, Prabowo, and Wiranto—highlights the fact that oligarchs have acquired half of the Indonesian party leaderships. This trend is the result of two key developments in Indonesian democracy since 2004. First, there has been a dramatic explosion of campaign and other operational costs for political parties. In the period between 1999 and 2004, Indonesia witnessed only one election for which parties had to mobilize financial resources. In the five-year electoral cycles since then, more than 550 elections have had to be paid for at both the national and local levels. In addition, the increasing professionalization of Indonesian elections introduced opinion polls, consultancy firms, and media advertisements as standard elements of electoral campaigning, replacing traditional in-house and low-cost

---

[26] Ibid.

[27] "Dari NII Jadi Godfather," *Majalah Detik*, March 3, 2013.

methods.[28] Second, Indonesia failed to develop new institutions and mechanisms to accommodate the costs of modern campaigns. While many advanced and new democracies offer significant state funding to parties in order to reduce the influence of oligarchs,[29] Indonesia all but abolished state subsidies for central party boards in 2005—ironically, at the very moment that political costs rose exponentially. Before 2005, the central boards of Indonesian parties received Rp. 1,000 (US$0.10) per vote every year in subsidies. After 2005, that allocation shrank to a miniscule average of Rp. 108 (US$0.01).[30] With costs increasing, membership fees non-existent, and donors mostly sponsoring individual politicians rather than party treasuries, parties turned to oligarchs as an easy and quick fix to their financial troubles.

It is tempting to interpret the abolition of state subsidies for parties as a conspiracy by oligarchs to expand their power. Indeed, the institutionalized financial weakness of parties is the *conditio sine qua non* for oligarchs who aspire to intervene in party politics. But the drivers behind the 2005 reduction in subsidies were not the oligarchs. Instead, the move was initiated by a peculiar coalition involving the Ministry of the Interior, the president's office, civil society, and public opinion. To begin with, the Ministry of the Interior—which manages the subsidies—had argued as early as 2002 that parties should not be funded by the state.[31] This was despite the fact that the total allocation was a tiny fraction of state expenditure, and, by international standards, a comparatively small investment. There were also individuals in the presidential office—which holds the authority to determine the amount of money that parties receive per vote—who strongly advocated for abolishing the subsidies. Most prominent among these anti-subsidy advocates was Andi Mallarangeng, then President Yudhoyono's spokesman and highly influential domestic policy adviser. Justifying the 2005 presidential decree that cut the subventions, Andi said "parties should not be funded by the state—subsidies only attract political entrepreneurs who want to establish a party to make money."[32] As a US-trained political scientist, his word carried significant weight in Yudhoyono's circles. Moreover, the majority of civil society groups opposed the subsidies as well, insisting that the money could be used more effectively for social development programs. Finally, most ordinary Indonesians also believed that the monetary flow between parties and society should be one-way only—that is, from the former to the latter.[33] Thus, the main institutional change that has benefited party oligarchs was

[28] Marcus Mietzner, "Political Opinion Polling in Post-authoritarian Indonesia: Catalyst or Obstacle to Democratic Consolidation?" *Bijdragen tot de Taal-, Land- en Volkenkunde* 165,1 (2009): 95–126.

[29] Jonathan Hopkin, "The Problem with Party Finance: Theoretical Perspectives on the Funding of Political Parties," *Party Politics* 10,6 (2004): 627–51.

[30] Marcus Mietzner, "Party Financing in Post-Soeharto Indonesia: Between State Subsidies and Political Corruption," *Contemporary Southeast Asia* 29,2 (2007): 238–63. While provincial, district, and municipal governments also pay subsidies to parties, their size differs greatly from territory to territory. Thus far, it has been impossible to calculate the total amount of subsidies paid at the local level. In any case, much of this money was quickly absorbed by local party boards trying to pay for the costs of local elections, and therefore could not be used to build strong central party organizations.

[31] "Bantuan untuk parpol ditinjau ulang," *Media Indonesia*, March 26, 2002.

[32] Interview with Andi Mallarangeng, Jakarta, September 28, 2006.

[33] In 2012, President Yudhoyono was reportedly prepared to reintroduce substantial state subsidies for parties, but then decided against it because his advisers warned him of a possible public backlash. Confidential interview, November 15, 2012.

not devised by them, but by forces that would later bitterly complain about the oligarchs' political rise.

Overall, then, a detailed assessment of the role oligarchs play in Indonesian parties delivers a more nuanced picture than Winters or Hadiz and Robison suggest. First, "only" half of Indonesia's party leaderships are in the hands of oligarchs, with the other half controlled by more conventional politicians with alternative political resources. Thus, key political actors are not "almost always oligarchs."[34] This in itself is not only empirically, but also analytically significant. It suggests that continued contestation rather than oligarchic domination is the main feature of power relations within Indonesian parties. Second, the trend of oligarchization in some party leaderships was fueled by the failure of Indonesia's institutional designers to respond adequately to the rising cost of political operations after 2004—the year direct presidential and local elections were introduced. Instead of strengthening the existing institutional barriers against oligarchic influence and erecting new ones, Indonesia almost completely abolished the most important of these barriers: namely, public funding for the central boards of political parties. Hence, the growing power of Indonesian oligarchs after 1998 was not simply the result of their being released from the shackles Suharto had imposed on them, as Winters suggests,[35] but was rather the consequence of a major institutional deficiency for which oligarchs were not responsible.

OLIGARCHS AND THEIR MOTIVATIONS: ONLY WEALTH DEFENSE?

The previous section demonstrated that portrayals of Indonesian party politics as being dominated by oligarchs are rather overstated. Equally important, however, is the fact that these portrayals do not sufficiently explore the differences among the various types of Indonesian oligarchs who engage in party politics. As a result, most authors representing the oligarchization school imply that all oligarchs who engage in politics are part of the oligarchy's quest to "rule." To be sure, Winters distinguishes between indigenous Malay and ethnic Chinese oligarchs, emphasizing that the former have focused strongly on "holding top party positions, and having strategic party affiliations,"[36] while the latter typically do not. However, the entry of the ethnic Chinese tycoon Hari Tanoesoedibjo into party politics in the early 2010s has shown that these distinctions are no longer as relevant as they used to be.

A more useful typology of Indonesian oligarchs—and a better understanding of their political involvement—can be drawn from analyzing their motivations for engaging in politics. For Winters, the overarching goal of oligarchic operations is "wealth defense," defined as consisting of two components: "*property defense* (securing basic claims to wealth and property) and *income defense* (keeping as much of the flow of income and profits from one's wealth as possible under conditions of secure property rights)."[37] According to Winters, in Indonesia, the primary focus of

---

[34] Winters, *Oligarchy*, p. 181.

[35] Jeffrey Winters, "Who Will Tame the Oligarchs?" *Inside Indonesia* 104 (2011), at http://www.insideindonesia.org/feature-editions/who-will-tame-the-oligarchs

[36] Winters, *Oligarchy*, p. 189.

[37] It is important to note that in Winters's model, political engagement is only one avenue for oligarchic wealth defense. The massive wealth of oligarchs allows them to pursue a wide range of alternative pathways. At the same time, Winters clarifies that not everything that oligarchs do with their money is related to wealth defense—they can "engage their material

oligarchs is on property defense, because secure property rights are not yet established. For Hadiz and Robison, the ultimate goal of (necessarily political) oligarchs is "the concentration of wealth and authority and its collective defense."[38] This excessive concentration on "wealth defense" distracts analysts from acknowledging the broad range of motivations that have driven Indonesian oligarchs into party politics. The development of a motivation-based typology of Indonesian oligarchs reveals that not all oligarchs are in politics for the purpose of wealth defense. In other words, there are a significant number of oligarchs who are not in the service of the "untamed ruling oligarchy" that Winters sees in control of Indonesia.

Five subgroups of oligarchs can be identified. The first contains politically active oligarchs who seek to advance their politico–economic interests by holding public office. In essence, this is the type of oligarch described by Winters as well as by Hadiz and Robison. Bakrie is the main example of this category. The other four subgroups, however, are not theorized by Winters or by Hadiz and Robison. The second subgroup features oligarchs who enter politics primarily out of personal vanity, spending much of their fortunes to gain recognition beyond the business world. In many cases, individuals in this group of oligarchs exhaust rather than expand their power while in politics. Sutrisno Bachir is one such case. A batik entrepreneur from Central Java, he was unknown on the national stage when he was elected to chair PAN in 2005. There are no indications that he profited financially from entering politics, but he could proudly proclaim that "now the president of Indonesia sometimes gives me a massage."[39] Indeed, after funding the party for almost five years, he had to watch helplessly as former chairman Amien Rais, a non-oligarch, pushed him aside in 2009 to take direct control of coalition negotiations with Yudhoyono.[40] Bitter, Bachir surrendered the chairmanship and left party politics altogether. Clearly, it is vital to separate tycoons like Bachir from oligarchs such as Bakrie—while the former are prepared to lose much of their money in politics, the latter are focused on personal wealth expansion.

The third category in the typology of oligarchs consists of wealthy entrepreneurs who seek to represent the interests of private capital as a whole. Representatives of business play a legitimate and important role in economic policy formulation in Indonesia, as in any other society. In fact, scholars of democratization have frequently credited entrepreneurial forces with attacking authoritarian state structures and promoting political liberalization in the name of removing hurdles to economic growth. While these theories on the link between entrepreneurship and democracy have been mostly developed in the Western European context,[41] some authors have found similar patterns in East Asia.[42] In Indonesia, a significant number

resources across a range of political issues about which they care deeply." Nevertheless, Winters's chapter on Indonesia is heavily focused on the political engagement of oligarchs as a key strategy of wealth defense. See: Winters, *Oligarchy*, pp. 6–8.

[38] Hadiz and Robison, "The Political Economy of Oligarchy," p. 37.

[39] Interview with Sutrisno Bachir, Jakarta, January 16, 2008.

[40] Bachir caims to have spent 180 billion Rupiah (US$18 million) of his own money on the party in the first two years alone. Ibid.

[41] Nigel Harris, "New Bourgeoisies?" *Journal of Development Studies* 24,2 (1988): 237–49; Barrington Moore, *The Social Origins of Dictatorship and Democracy* (Boston: Beacon Press, 1966).

[42] Kanishka Jayasuriya, "The Political Economy of Democratization," in *Towards Illiberal Democracy in Pacific Asia*, ed. Daniel A. Bell et al. (New York, NY: Palgrave, 1995), pp. 107–33;

of business leaders have become active in party politics largely in order to voice the concerns of the business community rather than to protect their individual wealth. For instance, Golkar's Airlangga Hartarto, the chairman of AEI (Asosiasi Emiten Indonesia, Indonesian Association of Publicly Listed Companies), has been widely considered a competent representative of professional business interests in the parliament. Similarly, members of HIPMI (Himpunan Pengusaha Muda Indonesia, Indonesian Young Entrepreneurs Association) have joined political parties, and they have advanced proposals for further institutional change. Thus, while these entrepreneurs qualify as oligarchs simply because their primary political resource is capital, they differ vastly from their counterparts who use it to advance their personal interests and/or that of their companies.

The fourth group of oligarchs comprises opportunists whose primary goal is to make money from political connections. Unlike the massively wealthy tycoons of the first category who buy their way into politics, these second-rung entrepreneurs often seek political office first to gain funds as a basis for further self-enrichment. Once they have amassed sufficient monetary resources, they spin an ever-increasing web of connections that produces further wealth, eventually turning into brokers of state contracts and positioning themselves in the center of a vast patronage network. A good example of this kind of oligarch is Muhammad Nazaruddin, the former treasurer of PD and a legislator for his party from 2009 to 2011. Initially an unknown regional politician-cum-businessman, Nazaruddin offered himself to PD functionary Anas Urbaningrum as a fund-raiser in the mid-2000s. Promoted by Anas to increasingly influential party positions, Nazaruddin eventually controlled contracts worth hundreds of millions of dollars, mostly obtained through kickbacks and influence-peddling. At the time of his arrest in August 2011, the PD treasurer was under investigation for 131 cases involving five ministries and a total project value of 6 trillion Rupiah (US$600 million).[43] While on the run and in detention, Nazaruddin laid out intimate details of his money-making scheme, through which he was able to enrich himself while supplying Anas with operational funds. In February 2013, Anas was indicted for corruption as well. In contrast to the second category of oligarch, the Nazaruddin-type operators are utterly indifferent towards politics as a way of gaining publicity. Indeed, taking a back seat and avoiding the public's attention is an essential key to their success.

The final but highly important category is located at the intersection between oligarchic and non-oligarchic actors. This category consists of politicians who run businesses to finance their political operations. These politicians are not oligarchs, since their command of personal funds is usually not their primary power resource and the businesses involved are too small to be described as oligarchic. However, the money generated by these enterprises is crucial in determining the politicians' standing in party politics. One example of this type of entrepreneurial politician is Maruarar Sirait, a deputy chairman of PDI-P. As the son of Sabam Sirait, one of PDI-P's most respected leaders, Maruarar always understood he would eventually pursue a career in politics. But he also knew that he would have to build up his own

Richard Robison, Garry Rodan, and Kevin Hewison, *Transplanting the Regulatory State in Southeast Asia: A Pathology of Rejection* (Hong Kong: City University of Hong Kong, 2002); and Andrew Wyatt, *Party System Change in South India: Political Entrepreneurs, Patterns and Processes* (Abingdon: Routledge, 2010).

[43] "Total Nilai Proyek 'Ditangani' Nazaruddin Rp 6.037 Trilyun," *Republika*, August 14, 2011.

businesses in order to fund his political aspirations. Pointing to his belly, Maruarar stated that "you have to take care of this before you go into politics; if you don't, you'll become corrupt—politics is expensive these days."[44] Mostly, such politicians leave their businesses in the hands of relatives or professional managers once they enter fully into party politics, drawing from the profits of their businesses to finance their political activity. "I know it's unavoidable, but I could get sick sometimes if I think about how much of my business earnings I have spent on politics," said Alvin Lie, then a member of the PAN caucus in the DPR (Dewan Perwakilan Rakyat, People's Representative Council, or parliament).[45] For this category of politicians with income-generating businesses, oligarchic "wealth defense" is not their primary goal—neither in terms of Winters's definition nor in the revised one offered above.

But even for those oligarchs whose most important goal is wealth defense, political interventions do not always deliver the expected results. Bakrie, for instance, saw his net worth shrinking from US$5.4 billion in 2007 to below US$1 billion in 2012.[46] Remarkably, this decline occurred during a period in which he became chair of Golkar, controlled several cabinet positions, and enjoyed a famously good relationship with Yudhoyono. Bakrie's case points to the circumstance that, at a time during which most Indonesian tycoons have their companies publicly listed in domestic and international stock exchanges, political power is no longer sufficient to protect them. Fluctuations in the world economy, changes in the price of key commodities, and bad business decisions can affect a tycoon's economic fate more decisively than the extent of his or her political access. In October 2008, for example, when the share prices of Bakrie's flagship company Bumi Resources plunged dramatically, Bakrie could initially use his political power to achieve a suspension of its share trade at the Jakarta Stock Exchange. But Finance Minister Sri Mulyani Indrawati immediately overturned the decision, causing Bumi's shares to fall further.[47] While Bakrie subsequently led a campaign against Sri Mulyani that contributed to her resignation from the cabinet, this did not protect Bakrie from similar declines in Bumi Resources's share values in October 2011 and throughout 2012. In neither of these cases did Bakrie get help from the state; instead, he had to enter into humiliating bailout deals with offshore and domestic investors. Of course, the inability of some oligarchs to defend their wealth through political engagement does not contradict the oligarchic model developed by Winters and Hadiz and Robison, but it is notable that discussions of such failures are almost completely absent from their writings.

In sum, not only do Winters and Hadiz and Robison overemphasize the influence that oligarchs have on Indonesian politics and the parties that shape it, they have also paid scant attention to the important differences *between* politically active oligarchs. Winters's description of the Indonesian case identifies wealth defense as the main motivation of oligarchs to engage in party politics,[48] while Hadiz and Robison's systemic view of oligarchy and their intense focus on the state assumes

---

[44] Interview with Maruarar Sirait, during a trip to his legislative constituency in Subang, October 22, 2006.

[45] Interview with Alvin Lie, Jakarta, December 8, 2006.

[46] "Bakrie out of Rich Men's Club," *Jakarta Post*, November 10, 2012.

[47] "Mulyani, SBY at Odds over Bumi Trading," *Jakarta Post*, November 7, 2008.

[48] Winters, *Oligarchy*, p. 189.

that political oligarchs are inherently involved in wealth defense.[49] The above analysis, however, has pointed to fundamental differences among the oligarchs who engage in politics. Indeed, it has shown that only two subgroups of oligarchs are in politics to pursue an exclusive agenda of personal wealth protection and expansion: tycoons such as Bakrie, who have a clear track record of intervening in the political process to gain financial benefit; and the political brokers like Nazaruddin, who develop patronage networks with the single goal of increasing their wealth. The other categories are more diverse, including tycoons who spend much of their fortunes to purchase a place in the limelight, entrepreneurs interested in good economic policy, and "traditional" politicians who set up companies to fund their political careers. While the first section has shown that the process of oligarchization has affected some, but not all parties, the discussion here has questioned the notion of oligarchs as a coherent political entity with the common goal of wealth defense.[50] In the following final section, the discussion turns to the counter-oligarchic forces in Indonesian politics that have challenged the increasing influence of money and tycoons over the political process.

COUNTER-OLIGARCHIC FORCES IN INDONESIAN PARTIES

Given their focus on the overwhelming oligarchic dominance over Indonesia's state and society, it is understandable that Winters and Hadiz and Robison downplay the significance of opposition to that dominance. To be sure, both Winters and Hadiz and Robison acknowledge the existence of oppositional politics that challenges the oligarchs—they just do not believe that this opposition is important. For Winters, "Indonesia has decisively moved in the direction of a ruling oligarchy as *pribumi* oligarchs have increasingly captured and dominated the open democratic process."[51] Hadiz and Robison note the "widespread rise of reformist movements" but question "the larger transformative significance of these forms of oppositional politics."[52] Ultimately, they contend, "incremental demands for reform by individuals or groups can only be piecemeal."[53] What is needed, by contrast, is nothing less than "the disintegration of the old order and its social underpinnings and the forging of a new social order with its political forces."[54]

Consequently, Winters and Hadiz and Robison choose not to address the counter-oligarchic response by many civil society activists who have joined political parties since the mid-2000s. However, the influx of activists into parties is significant because it signals a strategic watershed in the relations between civil society and formal political institutions. Immediately after Suharto's fall in 1998, many reformist

---

[49] Hadiz and Robison, "The Political Economy of Oligarchy," pp. 36ff.

[50] While Winters recognizes conceptually that oligarchs can have diverse political interests and agendas, his work on Indonesia hardly engages with such intra-oligarchic differences. In *Oligarchy*, he introduced the *pribumi*–Chinese dichotomy as the only typological difference between oligarchs. As demonstrated above, there are many more fundamental differences among individual actors within the oligarchic category.

[51] Winters, *Oligarchy*, p. 192.

[52] Hadiz and Robison, "The Political Economy of Oligarchy," p. 54.

[53] Ibid.

[54] Ibid.

civil society activists were reluctant to join parties.[55] Some activists insisted that it was the task of civil society to monitor the conduct of political institutions, not to become part of them. Others argued that the pro-democracy segments of civil society should found their own issue-oriented parties. But by the mid-2000s, both camps had to rethink their positions. The initial supporters of party absenteeism realized that their unwillingness to engage had surrendered the political arena to established elites, including oligarchic forces. At the same time, the camp that had favored the establishment of issue-oriented parties had to admit the failure of such parties at the ballot box—in the 1999 and 2004 elections, the combined vote share of those parties had been minuscule. As a result, both groups came to agree that joining existing mainstream parties was not only an acceptable option, but a necessary one. Veteran journalist and activist Daniel Dhakidae eloquently summarized the rationale for this move, telling a younger NGO leader in 2010 that "we can't leave Indonesian democracy only to the hellhounds [*anjing neraka*], that is, the rich and powerful; if we want democracy to work, we must participate in its institutions."[56]

Of course, many Indonesian politicians claim a civil society background, and not all of them are interested in advancing a counter-oligarchic agenda. Thus, the pro-democracy activists discussed here are only those who have a strong track record in advancing a socio–political reform agenda that collides with the interests of established, affluent elites. By this definition, there were 37 pro-democracy, counter-oligarchic activists among the 560 national legislators in 2009—or 7 percent of the total DPR membership. Their number in key political party positions is more difficult to establish, but the influence of such reformers has been particularly visible in three areas: women's affairs, labor issues, and human rights.

To begin with, some activists became concerned in the early 2000s that democratization could damage rather than promote women's rights. For example, the proportion of women elected to the first post-Suharto parliament in 1999 declined to 8.8 percent, from 10.8 percent in the last New Order legislature of 1997.[57] According to women's rights activists, one of the reasons for this decline was that low-profile female candidates were losing out to well-funded male candidates. As a consequence, prominent feminists decided to seek seats in parliament themselves. One of them was Nursyahbani Katjasungkana, the former secretary-general of the Coalition of Indonesian Women (Koalisi Perempuan Indonesia), who became a PKB legislator in 2004, and was later appointed deputy chair of the party. Once in parliament, Nursyahbani demanded more credible quotas for women in parties and on electoral lists.[58] Mobilizing women's rights activists in and outside of parliament, Nursyahbani played a key role in the passing of regulations to that effect in 2008. The

[55] Mikaela Nyman, *Democratising Indonesia: The Challenges of Civil Society in the Era of Reformasi* (Copenhagen: Nias Press, 2006); A. E. Priyono, Willy Purna Samadhi, and Olle Toernquist et al., *Making Indonesian Democracy Meaningful: Problems and Options in Indonesia* (Jakarta: Demos—Lembaga Kajian Demokrasi dan Hak Asasi, 2007).

[56] Interview with Usman Hamid, Jakarta, November 30, 2010.

[57] Sharon Bessell, "Increasing the Proportion of Women in the National Parliament: Opportunities, Barriers, and Challenges," ed. Edward Aspinall and Marcus Mietzner, *Problems of Democratisation in Indonesia: Elections, Institutions, and Society* (Singapore: Institute of Southeast Asian Studies, 2010), p. 219.

[58] Interview with Nursyahbani Katjasungkana, Jakarta, November 25, 2010.

percentage of women in the 2009 legislature subsequently rose to an unprecedented 18 percent.[59]

The continued pressure from women's rights activists in political parties led in 2013 to the exclusion of several smaller parties from the 2014 elections. For the first time since Suharto's fall, the KPU (Komisi Pemilihan Umum, General Election Commission) treated the stipulation that each party's national *and* regional boards must have 30 percent women as a binding threshold. Hence, when it announced the participants of the 2014 elections in early 2013, only parties that met the threshold were included. "We know that this is a legal breakthrough, but we decided in the KPU that this needs to be done to ensure better participation of women in parties, elections, and parliaments," said Hadar Gumay, a KPU Commissioner.[60] Besides being crucial in overcoming religious prejudices and antiquated social perceptions, the goal of increasing the level of female participation in politics also had a distinctively counter-oligarchic impetus. Women candidates have always found it difficult to compete with their financially stronger male counterparts. The provision of guaranteed positions on electoral lists meant that women could avoid paying large fees for their nominations—instead, parties actively sought female candidates. Some parties tried to circumvent the new regulations by including the wives, daughters, nieces, aunts, and other female relatives of male party bosses on their candidate lists. But despite this phenomenon, there remains sufficient room for reformist women's rights activists as well.

Women's rights activists were not the only counter-oligarchic forces to enter Indonesian party politics. Labor leaders also began to populate mainstream parties. While the former had been driven into party politics by the disappointing gender composition of the 1999 parliament, the latter changed their strategy largely because of the electoral collapse of the leftist splinter parties they had supported in 1999 and 2004. Thus, when parties such as Golkar, PKS, PKB, and PDI-P started to approach labor activists to represent them as legislative nominees in the 2009 elections, many of them were open to the idea. In her study on the engagement of trade unions in the local legislative elections in Batam in 2009, Michele Ford has described the remarkable extent to which labor union officials stood as candidates in the polls. In fact, their involvement was so extensive that the pro-labor vote was split among the many candidates, and eventually none of them was elected.[61] However, some of their national colleagues did better. In 2009, for example, Budiman Sudjatmiko, a former leader of the pro-labor PRD (Partai Rakyat Demokratik, People's Democratic Party) and political prisoner under Suharto, was elected as a legislator for PDI-P. Other labor activists aligned themselves directly with senior party executives, particularly those holding high public office. Among them has been Dita Indah Sari, a labor leader also imprisoned under Suharto.[62] Having run for parliament in 2009 for the Reformasi Star Party (Partai Bintang Reformasi, PBR), in 2010 Dita accepted the

---

[59] *Kompas, Wajah DPR dan DPD, 2009–2014: Latar Belakang Pendidikan dan Karier* (Jakarta: Kompas Penerbit Buku, 2010).

[60] Interview with Hadar Gumay, Jakarta, December 10, 2012.

[61] Michele Ford, "Learning by Doing: Trade Unions and Electoral Politics in Batam, 2004–2009," *South-East Asia Research* (in press).

[62] Max Lane, *Unfinished Nation: Indonesia Before and After Suharto* (London and New York, NY: Verso, 2008), p. 149.

invitation of PKB chairman and Minister of Manpower and Transmigration Muhaimin Iskandar to become his close aide and spokesperson.

Since the late 2000s, the increased presence of labor activists in party politics—and the generally improved organization of the workers' movement—has been reflected in better conditions for labor.[63] Most importantly, there has been a dramatic increase in the minimum wage in 2011 and 2012, with many governors and district chiefs giving in to the pressure of labor advisors in their political and electoral assistance teams.[64] In Jakarta, for instance, a 15 percent increase in the minimum wage in 2011 was followed by a whopping 44 percent rise in 2012.[65] Minister Muhaimin supported the shift, hoping to mobilize political support for his party. Indonesia's business elite, however, were furious. Sofyan Wanandi, the billionaire chairman of Apindo (Asosiasi Pengusaha Indonesia, Indonesian Employers' Association), launched a passionate campaign against the wage hikes. "The government forgets that by taking a populist decision, employers will suffer losses," Wanandi said, adding that "as a consequence, employers will have to lay off workers."[66] Wanandi was also highly critical of the increasing frequency of workers' strikes, which, according to Wanandi, cost Indonesian employers US$100 million on a single day. But the labor advocates—some now deeply entrenched in parties and the bureaucracy, as well as in traditional grassroots movements—did not back down. In addition to the minimum wage increases, labor activists achieved key changes to the outsourcing regime in 2012. Importantly, they also managed once again to prevent an initiative to revise the country's 2003 labor law, which is widely viewed as one of the most worker-friendly pieces of legislation in the developing world.

Human rights activists have also increasingly joined political parties. Rachland Nashidik, for example, who led the human rights NGO Imparsial in the late 2000s, became a member of Yudhoyono's PD in 2010 and was immediately appointed the secretary of the human rights department. When making the decision to enter party politics, Rachland was fully aware that he would face an uphill battle against the country's oligarchic and conservative forces. "I had no illusions," Rachland said, "I knew that the political system is corrupt; but that's no reason to stay outside and watch [...] I wanted to push for small but meaningful reforms in human rights."[67] Based on Rachland's accounts, he appears to have been at least partially successful. As an NGO figure, he explained, "I would often call up a senior police or military officer to complain about this or that case, and if I was lucky, he picked up the phone; but he couldn't care less about what I said." Now, by contrast, "these officers have changed their attitude—they believe that there is a possibility, however small, that Yudhoyono could have instructed me to call them."[68] Obviously, Rachland has had to put up with a large number of oligarchic and anti-reformist figures in his own

---

[63] For a discussion of labor's involvement in the social security movement of 2010–11, see Edward Aspinall, "Popular Agency and Interests in Indonesia's Democratic Transition and Consolidation," *Indonesia* (October 96): 101–21.

[64] For an extended analysis of this link, see Teri L. Caraway and Michele Ford, "Labor and Politics under Oligarchy," this volume, pp. 139–55.

[65] "Massive Layoffs Inevitable: Businesspeople," *Jakarta Post*, February 22, 2013.

[66] "Apindo Says a 44% Wage Increase in Jakarta Means Lay-offs," *Jakarta Globe*, November 16, 2012.

[67] Interview with Rachland Nashidik, Jakarta, December 8, 2010.

[68] Ibid.

party—many of its members are affluent retired military officers opposed to any scrutiny of the past or present human rights record of the security forces. But the contest between reformers such as Rachland and the conservatives mirrors more general patterns in Indonesian party politics: rather than exhibiting features of domination by oligarchs, the political arena is contested by a variety of forces.

It is important to neither romanticize nor understate the role of counter-oligarchic forces in Indonesian parties. It would be inaccurate to suggest that the influx of reformist and counter-oligarchic elements into party politics since the mid-2000s has neutralized the power of oligarchic actors. Indeed, as long as Indonesia's party and campaign financing system remains unchanged, this is unlikely to happen. In a system in which the state does not provide substantial subsidies to political parties (and in an era in which party membership fees are small and declining around the world), parties are almost certain to turn to wealthy patrons for financial support. Thus, oligarchic influence on parties and policy-making is set to remain an inherent phenomenon of the post-Suharto polity. But it would be equally wrong to ignore the impact that counter-oligarchic forces have had on the dynamics of Indonesian politics. As the examples of women's rights, labor, and human rights activists have shown, counter-oligarchic forces have left a noticeable imprint on the post-authoritarian polity. Women's rights activists initiated measures that have reduced the economic and political marginalization of women, directly challenging the dominance of rich and well-connected patriarchs; union leaders have pushed through wage increases and worker-friendly policies, infuriating large-scale entrepreneurs; and human rights advocates have—for the first time—made their influence felt from within the system, increasing the scrutiny placed upon security forces and their individual officers. To ignore these successes would mean to overlook a significant segment of the political mosaic that is post-Suharto Indonesia.

CONCLUSION: OLIGARCHY OR PLURALIST CONTESTATION?

This chapter has tested the claim by oligarchy theorists that the post-Suharto polity is dominated by oligarchs (Winters) or an oligarchic system of power relations (Hadiz and Robison). Focusing on the role of oligarchs in political parties as a case study, the chapter has demonstrated that while oligarchic forces are strong in Indonesian parties, their influence is far from monopolistic. Using a more specific definition of oligarchs than the broad classification proposed by Winters and the systemic definition advanced by Hadiz and Robison, the discussion has shown that the current power constellation in Indonesian party politics is characterized by high levels of fragmentation, involving both oligarchic and non-oligarchic elements. Moreover, it has pointed to the diversity of interests pursued by oligarchs who engage in party politics. While wealth defense is the primary goal of some plutocrats, others not only refrain from using parties as an instrument of wealth advancement, but, in fact, spend much of their fortunes in order to satisfy their personal vanity or drive for publicity. Thus, the number and influence of oligarchs in Indonesian parties is not as overwhelming as suggested, nor are those who do engage in party politics necessarily part of a "ruling oligarchy" (Winters) or a "system of power relations of wealth and authority and its collective defence" (Hadiz and Robison). In other words, Indonesian parties witness both contestation between oligarchic and non-oligarchic forces as well as divergent agendas *within* the very heterogeneous class of politically active oligarchs.

Most importantly, the chapter has shed light on the operations of counter-oligarchic groups in Indonesian parties and legislatures. Women's rights, labor, and human rights activists have all left a noticeable imprint in the architecture of post-authoritarian party politics. Observers may rightfully disagree about the exact extent of their influence, but it would be empirically and analytically problematic to ignore or belittle them.[69] In addition to facing resistance from these reformist activists, oligarchs often have to compete with conventional politicians, branch leaders, religious figures, small-town entrepreneurs, student groups, and other elements for hegemony over party positions. Accordingly, an approach focused on just one kind of actor—even one as powerful as the oligarchs—fails to grasp the pluralism of players in post-authoritarian politics. In an attempt to redress this imbalance, this chapter has advanced an alternative understanding of politics after Suharto's fall: a paradigm that highlights the ongoing struggles among a wide variety of forces, with the outcome far from certain. The equilibrium between oligarchic and non-oligarchic forces in party leaderships is a reflection of the current balance of power in parties and in Indonesian political affairs more generally. Arguably, it is this equilibrium that has caused the current stagnation in Indonesia's democratic consolidation. On the one hand, oligarchic and conservative forces have not been strong enough to cause a democratic reversal (i.e., a roll-back of reforms that, in their view, have excessively empowered individual voters over elites); on the other hand, non-oligarchic elements have failed to advance further democratic reforms—their success in preventing a full-blown reversal of Indonesian democracy notwithstanding.[70]

Besides adopting a pluralist interpretation of post-Suharto party politics, this chapter has also taken a distinctively institutionalist approach. In contrast to Hadiz and Robison, who downplay the importance of institutions, it has identified Indonesia's dysfunctional party system as the main source of the partial oligarchization of party politics. Winters appears to agree with this conclusion, stating that "except for countries where public funds are a major source of finance for political campaigns, finding the money needed to be a political contender is always a challenge."[71] As Winters rightly notes, in Indonesia "no public funds are available and [...] small-donor funding is almost non-existent."[72] In the vast majority of cases, polities that fail to provide significant state subsidies for central party boards tend to create conditions in which conventional politicians can't mobilize the funds necessary to compete for public office and thus have to surrender the political arena to oligarchs. It seems only logical, then, that the introduction of substantial state subsidies for parties could help in mitigating the oligarchic problem. Arguably, increasing the proportion of state subsidies *vis-à-vis* party expenditure from currently less than 1 percent to around 30 percent (as in other new democracies) would go a long way towards reducing the influence of oligarchs.[73] Therefore, the political taming of the oligarchs may not require the complete overthrow of Indonesia's social

---

[69] Edward Aspinall, "The Triumph of Capital? Class Politics and Indonesian Democratization," *Journal of Contemporary Asia* 43,2 (2013): 226–42

[70] Marcus Mietzner, "Indonesia's Democratic Stagnation: Anti-reformist Elites and Resilient Civil Society," *Democratization* 19,2 (2012): 209–29.

[71] Winters, *Oligarchy*, p. 189.

[72] Ibid.

[73] Marcus Mietzner, *Money, Power, and Ideology: Political Parties in Post-authoritarian Indonesia* (Singapore: NUS Press/KITLV/Hawaii University Press, 2013).

order—as Hadiz and Robison propose—but it certainly necessitates a number of fundamental reforms to the way post-Suharto politics is financed.

For theorists of oligarchy, the findings generated by the Indonesian case suggest that any analysis of the power of oligarchs must focus on oligarchic *and* non-oligarchic forces in equal measure. Winters, Robison, and Hadiz deserve credit for highlighting an important feature of Indonesian politics—and political affairs in post-authoritarian states more generally. Indeed, oligarchic actors and networks are crucial elements of the story of Indonesia's post-Suharto transition and consolidation. But because Winters, Robison, and Hadiz focus so intensely on oligarchs and their support infrastructure, they lose sight of non-oligarchic segments of society. As a result, they are unable to measure the extent of oligarchic power against the influence of non-oligarchic or counter-oligarchic actors and groups. Theories of oligarchy can only grasp the social and political realities of a particular society if they refrain from exaggerating the power of oligarchs for the sole purpose of sharpening or strengthening a theoretical argument. In order to assess the degree to which oligarchs have penetrated a state's socio–economic and political structures, the resistance posed by rival groups needs to be explored in-depth—and not ignored or declared insignificant without proper investigation. With such an approach (one that balances the focus on oligarchy with an equally strong emphasis on non-oligarchic politics), the power of oligarchs—and the damaging effects it can have on democratic societies—can be theorized in a more compelling and empirically satisfying manner.

Popular Agency and Interests in Indonesia's Democratic Transition and Consolidation

Edward Aspinall[1]

A review of the last decade's worth of writing on Indonesia's democratic transition and consolidation reveals that a consensus seems to be emerging, at least among writers who emphasize the primacy of class and other social structures. At the risk of doing a disservice to many authors and the subtleties of their work, that consensus goes something like this. In the mid-1990s, the New Order regime, with Suharto at its apex, was very strong. There were tensions within the regime and sections of the middle classes were increasingly alienated from it, but these problems were second order; the authority of the regime was not seriously threatened. A managed succession to a post-Suharto order, in which the basic elements of the regime would remain intact, was in the offing. That the regime fell in 1998 was not a result of popular mobilization per se. Instead, it was due to the exogenous shock of the 1997–98 economic crisis and tensions within the regime, triggered by the increasingly centralizing dynamic around Suharto, his children, and Suharto's inner circle. The economic shock set off protests that heightened political unrest, but these mobilizations were secondary to the economic crisis and the regime's internal tensions. The subsequent transition to electoral democracy was thus ersatz, or at least severely compromised. Forces representing genuine liberal reform or the interests of the lower classes were too poorly organized, or too dominated, to influence the regime change or character of the successor regime. This weakness of progressive forces was a legacy of the military's violent destruction of the PKI (Partai Komunis Indonesia, Indonesian Communist Party) and the rest of the Left in 1965–66, a legacy that continues to disable popular forces to this day. As a result, it was the very social and political forces that were nurtured by the New Order regime that were best placed to capture the institutions of formal democracy during and after the

[1] I thank Eve Warburton for her excellent research assistance, and the participants in the Sydney University workshop who offered feedback. My thanks also go to the *Indonesia* reviewers and the editors of this volume, Michele Ford and Thomas Pepinsky, and to Takuya Hasegawa for their very useful feedback on earlier drafts of this article. I am grateful to the Australian Research Council, which, through two grants (DP098550404 and DP120103181), provided support to conduct part of the fieldwork upon which this article is based.

transition, and stamp their interests on policy formulation and implementation at all levels. Now, as a melancholy consequence of this confluence of factors, the oligarchs rule Indonesia, progressive forces are dispersed, and Indonesia suffers from an illiberal or stunted democracy as a result.[2]

There is much that is persuasive about this analysis, and I have myself articulated aspects of it in previous works.[3] However, it is my contention in this essay that this approach, even if we adopt a class analytic framework, suffers from a major deficiency and misses critical dimensions of contemporary Indonesian politics. Accordingly, the article proceeds through three steps.

First, I propose that the conventional view writes popular agency too blithely out of the transition and the post-authoritarian dispensation. My view is that Indonesia's democratic transition was essentially driven from below, but that certain features of popular political forces—notably their organizational fragmentation—meant that key political institutions were thereafter captured, if not by former New Order incumbents, at least by former "semi-opponents" who had existed in an ambiguous relationship with state authority during the authoritarian period.[4] I am increasingly convinced, however, that many analysts moved too quickly to write off lower class political agency and influence in the post-New Order period as well.

Indeed, much writing on such matters in Indonesia is defined by an absence that lurks, as it were, just off stage. Many writers, whether explicitly or not, seek in Indonesia models of popular agency and representation derived from earlier

---

[2] The picture of a standard narrative presented in this paragraph is, of course, a composite, and it is possible to find many works that argue against all or some aspects of it. Nevertheless, I contend that this narrative dominates scholarly interpretations of post-Suharto politics, either directly or indirectly (so that most authors writing on relevant topics at least feel compelled to respond to its key propositions). Key texts articulating the narrative are the major expositions of the oligarchy thesis discussed in this volume, notably Richard Robison and Vedi R. Hadiz, *Reorganising Power in Indonesia: The Politics of Oligarchy in an Age of Markets* (London: RoutledgeCurzon, 2004); Vedi R. Hadiz, *Localising Power in Post-Authoritarian Indonesia: A Southeast Asia Perspective* (Stanford, CA: Stanford University Press, 2010); and Jeffrey A. Winters, *Oligarchy* (Cambridge: Cambridge University Press, 2011), but also other works by these authors as well as later elaborations by scholars who explicitly adopt their oligarchy framework (most recently Yuki Fukuoka, e.g., "Oligarchy and Democracy in Post-Suharto Indonesia," *Political Studies Review* 11,1 [2013]: 52–64). But key elements of the standard narrative, especially emphases on elite continuity in government office, exclusion of interests of subordinate groups in policymaking and implementation, and the detrimental effects of these phenomena on democratic quality, are found much more widely. Such arguments are, for example, pervasive among most early writings on post-Suharto local politics, and can be found in many chapters in major edited works on the topic, such as Edward Aspinall and Greg Fealy, eds., *Local Power and Politics in Indonesia: Democratisation and Decentralisation* (Singapore: Institute of Southeast Asian Studies, 2002); Henk A. Schulte Nordholt and Gerry van Klinken, eds., *Renegotiating Boundaries: Local Politics in Post-Suharto Indonesia* (Leiden: KITLV Press, 2007); and Maribeth Erb and Priyambudi Sulistiyanto, eds., *Deepening Democracy in Indonesia? Direct Elections of Local Leaders (Pilkada)* (Singapore: Institute of Southeast Asian Studies, 2009), as well as in full-length treatments of the topic, such as Nankyung Choi, *Local Politics in Indonesia: Pathways to Power* (London and New York, NY: Routledge, 2011).

[3] See especially Edward Aspinall, "The Irony of Success," *Journal of Democracy* 21,2 (2010): 20–34.

[4] Edward Aspinall, *Opposing Suharto: Compromise, Resistance and Regime Change in Indonesia* (Stanford, CA: Stanford University Press, 2005); "Semi-Opponents in Power: The Abdurrahman Wahid and Megawati Soekarnoputri Presidencies," in *Indonesia: Soeharto's New Order and its Legacy: Essays in Honour of Harold Crouch*, ed. Edward Aspinall and Greg Fealy (Canberra: ANU E-Press, 2010), pp. 119–34.

historical epochs in other countries. Basically, authors have been searching for evidence of powerful, formalized, and permanent lower-class political parties and alliances of the sort that were associated with the extension of suffrage and democratic rights early in the European and Latin American democratic eras, especially in the form of a social democratic party based on a powerful labor union movement.[5] Finding such forms absent, we conclude that popular agency is inconsequential and that Indonesian politics are entirely dominated by a reconstituted elite. Despite the descriptive accuracy of the account—there are no permanent, powerful, lower-class coalitions or parties—it misses many avenues for lower-class political agency and influence that have been open throughout the transition, and that are now experiencing greater and increasingly productive traffic. In short, observers have been looking for forms of agency and influence that do not exist, and missing those that do exist before our eyes.

Second, the article makes an initial attempt to identify key avenues for lower-class political influence that have emerged in post-authoritarian Indonesia. Two such avenues are proposed: fragmented activism and electoral populism. With regard to the first, the main reason observers have discounted the influence of organizations representing workers, farmers, and other subordinate groups is that such organizations have been splintered and have failed to build political parties with significant voter support. Here it is proposed that although fragmentation poses challenges to the capacity of such groups to wield influence, it does not mean that such influence has been absent or insignificant. In particular, political pressure exerted directly through mobilization occupies a prominent place in Indonesia's new political order, and policymakers are often responsive to it. Electoral populism locates the driving force for subaltern influence in the rise of competitive elections themselves, and the incentives they provide to contestants for political office to offer redistributive policies and other concessions to their lower class constituents. Much has been written about the dominance of forces nurtured in New Order circuits of power in post-Suharto governments, but this emphasis misses how many politicians have endeavored to reinvent themselves by offering policy concessions to poor voters.

Third, to illustrate the preceding argument, the article explains how over the last half decade Indonesia has begun to see policy outcomes that do not fit with the narrative of a devastated Left and a democratic transition lacking organized representation of social interests. It would be possible to illustrate that point by analyzing a number of policy areas, but I focus on labor rights and healthcare, where we see significant advances and the continued maintenance of gains achieved early in the transition. I argue that changes in healthcare policy are primarily an outcome of electoral populism, while labor's continued prominence illustrates the ongoing power of fragmented activism.

As we shall see, my argument is not that scholars who emphasize political inequality in Indonesia, particularly proponents of the "oligarchy thesis," such as Richard Robison, Vedi Hadiz, and Jeffrey Winters, are entirely incorrect either in their underlying premises or in their diagnosis of Indonesian political power. With

---

[5] Richard Robison and Vedi Hadiz, for example, describe one critical weakness of Indonesian democracy as the absence of "a genuinely social democratic party … with an agenda based on social justice," a prospect that they say is "currently implausible given the weakness of organized labor." See *Reorganising Power*, p. 259.

these authors, I accept the proposition that material inequality produces political inequality, including in democratic settings. I also do not question that there has been significant continuity in the composition of Indonesia's ruling elite, or that oligarchs are disproportionately powerful actors in the new regime. Such matters are beyond dispute. The more interesting questions are about the degree to which these oligarchs and other elites face challenges, and the degree to which other social interests, notably those of lower class groups, are also able to influence political outcomes. It is argued here that by focusing single-mindedly on the character and mechanisms of oligarchic dominance, structuralist scholars have lost sight of the bigger picture of contention among social groups that, it hardly needs to be said, has been central to materialist analyses of politics for over a century. My goal in this short piece is thus to place lower class groups and their interests back at the center of analysis of Indonesian politics. This suggests it is first important to review briefly the new structuralist orthodoxy, not simply about oligarchs and elites, but also about lower class political agency.

POPULAR POLITICS AND REGIME CHANGE IN INDONESIA

The downplaying of the role of popular politics in analyses of post-authoritarian Indonesia has roots that can be traced back to analyses of Indonesia's democratic transition itself, if not before. The irony is that it has consistently been writers on the Left, especially those most influenced by Marxist and structuralist perspectives, who have been most dismissive of social agency.[6] Perhaps in reaction against the optimism generated early in Indonesia's transition by liberal commentators, and wanting to demonstrate continuity in oligarchic power, their analyses emphasize internal conflict within the ruling bloc, exacerbated by the 1997 Asian financial crisis, as the main factor in Indonesia's transition. Space limitations prevent a thorough literature review, but there are a few samples worth consideration.

Among the starkest formulations is that advanced by Jeffrey Winters in his recent, masterly comparative book on oligarchy. Winters locates the trigger for regime change at the apex of the political and social structure rather than further down:

> This breach among powerful actors at the top—which involved not just oligarchs, but also elements in the armed forces, party elites, leaders of Islamic mass organizations, and even members of Suharto's cabinet—created a vital political space for a mobilization of the last minute that could be reasonably secure against frontal retribution and thus gain enough momentum to overwhelm the regime.[7]

He is equally clear in his assessment of popular forces and their capacity to bring about political change at this time:

---

[6] There are exceptions, such as Max Lane, *Unfinished Nation: Indonesia Before and After Suharto* (London: Verso, 2008); and A. E. Priyono, W. P. Samadhi, and O. Törnquist, ed., *Making Democracy Meaningful: Problems and Options in Indonesia* (Jakarta: Demos, 2007).

[7] Winters, *Oligarchy*, p. 178.

[...] anger and resentment from below was a constant across the entire New Order. However, there are no indications that capacities and opportunities to organize civil society had improved significantly since the massacre of the PKI in 1965 and the shutting down of independent student organizations in the 1970s. There are no indications, moreover, that the regime had softened its approach in the 1990s to dissent, activism, organizing, and resistance from below [...] On the other side of the ledger, what did change dramatically was the degree of unity and coherence at the level of elites and oligarchs [...] By the onset of the 1997 financial crisis, [Suharto] had been abandoned.[8]

Such analyses by major scholars have now been taken up and reproduced in blunter form by more junior analysts who, presumably, did not witness the tumultuous street politics that accompanied the downfall of Suharto. It is hard to imagine how otherwise one could come to an assessment that "the fall of the Suharto regime took place even in the absence of an assertive civil society."[9]

Such analyses systematically and unjustifiably diminish the role of societal organization and mobilization in the decade leading to the downfall of Suharto, and of social groups' critical influence in the regime change itself. Contrary to Winters's assessment, civil society capacities had increased steadily in the decade leading to Suharto's fall. Though they still faced formidable government repression, almost every sector of social activism (human rights, environmental activism, labor, the peasantry, to name a few) developed new organizations, forms of protest, communication networks, and other initiatives through the 1990s that had been entirely absent in earlier decades. Indonesia's pro-democracy civil society organizations were not as unified or forceful as in some authoritarian settings, such as apartheid South Africa or military-ruled South Korea, but the public sphere was certainly not denuded, and activist groups were far less cowed than in earlier decades.

It is also important to be clear about the relationship between societal mobilization and elite disunity in the events leading to the downfall of Suharto. Rather than seeking an explanation that attributes the collapse of the regime to a single factor, we need to diagnose carefully the interactions among the various competing forces. Even so, reconstruction of the chronology of events shows that, as Indonesia's political crisis began in late 1997, it was not elite fragmentation that triggered societal mobilization, but precisely the reverse. In the early 1990s, a significant fissure had opened within the regime, especially in the army. But by 1997, Suharto was again firmly in control: potential opponents had been excised from parliament, the cabinet, and other state organs, and the ruling elite had fallen in behind him once more (rather than having been abandoned by Suharto, as Winters would have it). No doubt, some senior regime figures were privately disgruntled with Suharto's continuing dominance, and many oligarchs were unhappy about the depredations of his children, but such discontent was contained, and entirely failed to find open political expression. What broke the political deadlock, and dramatically altered the calculus of senior regime leaders, was the wave of massive student and other demonstrations that began in February 1998, remaking the political landscape

---

[8] Ibid., p. 177.

[9] Yuki Fukuoka, "Indonesia's 'Democratic Transition' Revisited: A Clientelist Model of Political Transition," *Democratization*, iFirst (2012): 1.

and confronting regime leaders with new dilemmas (e.g., whether to authorize the security forces to shoot protestors). Accordingly, the critical breaks in the regime were initiated not by people who had been uncomfortable with Suharto's dominance, but by individuals who counted as his most ardent loyalists, such as Harmoko, the speaker of the House of Representatives. To be sure, after the mobilizations began, we saw the beginnings of what Alfred Stepan has called the "complex dialectic" between elite disunity and public protest, as students and others took heart from every sign of hesitation, vacillation, or disunity within the regime.[10] There was thus ultimately a two-way interaction, but the forces that finally cracked open the regime were triggered more by popular mobilizations than elite friction. Indonesia's democratic transition was society-initiated.[11]

However, it was certainly not a society-dominated transition. Scholars such as Hadiz and Robison are correct in highlighting the organizational fragmentation and co-optation of large parts of civil society and the effects this had on the nature of the transition. Indonesia went into its transition while the opposition was in certain respects disorganized. In my own past work, I attributed the fragmentation and fluidity of organizational forms among opposition groups to the effects of New Order repression and the strategies opponents adopted to sidestep it.[12] However, as this pattern of fragmentation has persisted into the post-authoritarian setting, I have come to see it as having other sources as well—including the influence of neoliberalism, and the persistence of patronage as a mode of organizing political life—and to see fragmentation as the defining feature of virtually all aspects of contemporary Indonesian social and political affairs, not just civil society.[13] Whatever its source, the fact remains that the organizational, as opposed to the mobilizational, weaknesses of Indonesian pro-democracy groups allowed forces incubated under the New Order to reassert their leadership, so that the oligarchs and other elites captured the institutions of national and local state power, as has been exhaustively covered in the literature.

What about the role of lower class agency after the transition proper? Many structuralist writings on Indonesian politics in the post-Suharto period simply write popular forces out of the frame, without attempting to evaluate their influence seriously. Vedi Hadiz is one exception. In his assessment, "The main benefit of democratization for marginalized and formerly suppressed social groups is that they can now organize more freely and with less fear of direct repression from the state's security apparatus."[14] Overall, however, he argues this "greater scope for political participation has resulted in little discernible empowerment of people who had already been marginalized under centralized authoritarianism."[15] He elaborates:

---

[10] A. Stepan, *Rethinking Military Politics: Brazil and the Southern Cone* (Princeton, NJ: Princeton University Press, 1988), p. 39.

[11] A more complete version of the basic argument presented in this paragraph can be found in Aspinall, *Opposing Suharto*, especially chapter eight.

[12] Ibid., p. 240.

[13] Edward Aspinall, "A Nation in Fragments: Patronage and Neoliberalism in Contemporary Indonesia," *Critical Asian Studies* 45,1 (2013): 27–54.

[14] Hadiz, *Localising Power*, p. 144.

[15] Ibid.

In a nutshell, the experience of organized labor in general and that of some peasant movements in the post-authoritarian period shows that democratisation and decentralisation have not produced an environment in which the interests of those who had been suppressed in the first place under authoritarian rule can now thrive. Although a certain amount of euphoria accompanied the fall of the New Order, workers and peasants have found that the institutions of decentralization and democracy—parties, local parliaments, and the like—continue to be inhabited by the kinds of powerful interests with few organic links to peasant or labor movements. Instructively, similar to post-authoritarian Thailand and the Philippines, there is no major political party that claims to represent the interests of the working class or the peasantry. Indeed, those presiding over mutually competing local predatory coalitions have few reasons to set a course for social and political reforms entailing a substantial degree of redistribution of economic and political resources. Consequently, the new salience of electoral politics has been of only limited use to lower-class interests and social movements in post-authoritarian Indonesia.[16]

Hadiz's assessment is carefully qualified (e.g., "little discernible empowerment," rather than "no empowerment"; "limited use," rather than "no use"; and so on). In many respects, it is therefore difficult to disagree with it. But in seeking to assess the continuing influence of the fragmented and fractious political forces that transformed Indonesian politics in the final decade of Suharto's rule and drove the events leading to his regime's downfall, it is worth starting with three points.

First is the continuing ability of groups representing lower class interests to take advantage of the greater space afforded to them to organize and mobilize in defense of their interests, a point recognized by Hadiz. This has not been a trivial change. In the cacophony that is contemporary Indonesian democracy, as anyone who even glances at daily news reports would know, popular protest has become a well-established mode of political expression, despite the fragmented nature of the organizations responsible.[17] Time and again, we see the policy goals and aspirations of business interests and other elite players being frustrated by protests or other forms of popular resistance, a point I illustrate in the next section.

Second, although formal politics have been dominated by oligarchs and former New Order powerbrokers, the influence of other forces and actors inside the formal political system is far from trivial. In fact, one of the problems for the Left in Indonesia is not that it is isolated and oppressed (as the standard, still-to-survive-from-the-cataclysm-of-1965 narrative would have it), but that its members face too many pathways for entry and absorption into mainstream politics, preventing their consolidation as a distinctive oppositional force.[18] With official politics dominated by populist and economic nationalist discourse, the boundary between official politics and the world of activism is highly porous. As a result, the failure of NGOs and left-

---

[16] Ibid., p. 160.

[17] One recent compilation of reports of protests from the national media, put together by Anom Astika, records a total of 1,114 demonstrations for the period January 5–25, 2013: https://www.evernote.com/   shard/s208/sh/54ed5263-919c-4f14-a164-a6c8dacaf964/7f6c9d741bb739bfa3666a92c681ce54 . Accessed April 15, 2013.

[18] This point is developed at greater length in Edward Aspinall, "Still an Age of Activism," *Inside Indonesia* 107 (2012), http://www.insideindonesia.org/weekly-articles/still-an-age-of-activism.

wing social movements to form their own parties does not mean such forces are alienated from formal politics. On the contrary, over the last decade most mainstream political parties have been eager to recruit former activists and use their networking skills and populist credibility for the party's benefit. Both the national parliament and regional legislatures contain many former activists. As Marcus Mietzner has demonstrated, while former activists-turned-politicians have not been able to dominate Indonesia's parliament, their role has been significant and, often cooperating with NGO lobbyists and protestors outside parliament, they have been able to promote legislative change in a host of areas, such as military reform, women's right, and labor law.[19] Thus, despite the image of an unreconstructed New Order elite still holding sway in the literature, the real picture is more complex, with many networks and clusters of actors that connect that ruling elite with activist groups and coalitions, providing not only mechanisms for co-optation from above, but also conduits for policy influence from below.

Third, we should not let the standard narrative of continuity in Indonesia's oligarchy and ruling elite make us miss the extreme internal heterogeneity, fragmentation, and competitiveness of that elite. Admittedly, the oligarch theorists concede this point in the abstract, but they tend to overlook the many opportunities elite fragmentation has afforded in practice to social movements and other forces to extract policy concessions from the new ruling caste. One of the defining features of the post-Suharto order is elite competition, with a highly varied array of bureaucrats, businesspeople, brokers, and others constantly rising to the surface of district, provincial, and national politics, forever remaking their political alliances as they shoulder each other aside in the competition for positions of political authority and control over resources. This fractiousness, ultimately a product of the decentered organization of patronage and of the new politics of electoral competition, is demonstrated by such phenomena as the continued internal conflict, splintering and remaking of political parties at the center, and the constant churning and replacement of local government leaders in the regions.[20] Such elite competition means that electoral strategies produce at least some elites who try to strengthen themselves politically by reaching out to poor constituents via political networks or by offering concessions, as an increasing number of accounts of local electoral dynamics reveal.[21] In short, the fragmentation and competitiveness of the ruling elite multiplies the opportunities for groups representing more marginal social interests to engage in strategic cooperation with, and wring concessions from, elite politicians, even if the compromises and coalitions so formed rarely take stable or institutionalized form.

As a result of these three factors—the liberalization of politics and resulting flourishing of mobilization, the penetration of official politics by groups linked to social movements, and intra-elite competition—Indonesian democracy is beginning to deliver not simply greater space for organization, but also some social gains for

[19] Marcus Mietzner, "Fighting the Hellhounds: Pro-Democracy Activists and Party Politics in Post-Suharto Indonesia," *Journal of Contemporary Asia* 43,1 (2013): 28–50.

[20] Aspinall, "A Nation in Fragments." Note that this internal conflict within the oligarchy, and between oligarchs and other elites, is also a critical component of Winters's account in *Oligarchy*.

[21] See, for example, Ryan Tans, *Mobilizing Resources, Building Coalitions: Local Power in Indonesia* (Honolulu, HI: East–West Center, Policy Studies No. 64, 2012).

the poor. The following pages illustrate this basic proposition by way of two examples, each representing one of the two main mechanisms of non-elite political leverage identified at the outset of this paper: fragmented activism and electoral populism. These examples do not demonstrate that oligarchs are insignificant in politics. But they do suggest that mono-tonal characterizations of Indonesian politics as being simply about elite capture of state power need to be qualified significantly.

FRAGMENTED ACTIVISM AND THE POLITICS OF LABOR

Organized labor is the political force that, arguably, is seen as being the most marginalized in post-authoritarian Indonesia. Its role in the political transition itself, in contrast to groups like students or the urban poor, was minimal.[22] As numerous authors have pointed out, the rapid dismantling of many of the most restrictive anti-union laws and regulations in the aftermath of the collapse of the regime was followed by a flourishing, but also a fragmentation, of labor activism.[23] Two years after the collapse of the Suharto regime, twenty-four national unions and more than ten thousand enterprise unions had registered with the government.[24] A couple of years later, there were more than sixty union federations and three significant confederations, and by 2012 six confederations and ninety-one federations.[25] By late 2012, labor activists themselves were lamenting the "localism and sectoralism" that defines their movement: "lots of trade unions are formed at the level of just one city … or at the level of just one factory or company."[26] These have not been propitious circumstances for the rise of labor as a powerful political force. Attempts to form electorally successful labor-based political parties and to seek governmental power through workers' support have failed. Yet, for all its apparent marginalization, labor exercises surprising leverage via industrial and street power, and through informal linkages to electoral politics.

Take, for example, national regulations. In the view of one observer, the post-Suharto period has seen a "major shift in government policy towards greater support of labour rights and standards."[27] This was partly related to the appointment of several ministers of manpower who had backgrounds as former leaders of the corporatist labor organization of the New Order. Particularly important was the role

---

[22] Edward Aspinall, "Democratisation, the Working Class, and the Indonesian Crisis," *Review of Indonesian and Malaysian Affairs* 33,2 (1999): 1–32.

[23] Teri L Caraway, "Protective Repression, International Pressure, and Institutional Design: Explaining Labor Reform in Indonesia," *Studies in Comparative International Development* 39,3 (2004): 28–49; and Michele Ford, *Workers and Intellectuals: NGOs, Trade Unions, and the Indonesian Labour Movement* (Singapore: Singapore University Press, 2009).

[24] Ford, *Workers and Intellectuals*, p. 161.

[25] Chris Manning, "The Political Economy of Reform: Labour after Soeharto," in *Soeharto's New Order and Its Legacy: Essays in Honour of Harold Crouch*, ed. Edward Aspinall and Greg Fealy (Canberra: ANU E Press, 2010), p. 157; and "Gerakan Buruh Kian Mandiri," *Kompas*, December 3, 2012.

[26] Interview with Dita Indah Sari, Jakarta, September 14, 2011. Note, however, that according to Benny Juliawan, the picture of fragmentation is often exaggerated: "As a matter of fact, there are only three confederations, whose combined membership in 2008 covered almost 80 percent of all union members." Benedictus (Benny) Hari Juliawan, "Playing Politics: Labour Movements in Post-Authoritarian Indonesia" (PhD Dissertation, Oxford University, 2011), p. 152.

[27] Manning, "Political Economy of Reform," p. 158.

of the Suharto-era SPSI (Serikat Pekerja Seluruh Indonesia, All Indonesia Union of Workers) leader Jacob Nuwa Wea as minister under Megawati Soekarnoputri (Nuwa Wea retained his SPSI presidency while serving as manpower minister). Under his stewardship, and demonstrating the importance of highlighting political variation among leaders "incubated" under the New Order, Law No. 13 of 2003 was passed:

> This law covers a wide range of labour protection issues, bringing together previous legislation scattered in a range of Ministerial and Presidential Decrees and government laws, as well as setting new standards in areas such as protection of female workers and procedures and compensation for layoffs and dismissals.[28]

Though the law was not an unqualified victory for trade unions (for example, unionists subsequently criticized it for allowing outsourcing of labor services), in certain respects it is significantly pro-labor. In particular, the provisions on severance pay, which set rates at fifteen to twenty months' salary for workers with five to ten years of employment, were much higher than in most countries.[29]

The pro-labor aspects of the law were a result both of labor's mobilizational efforts and its policy lobbying, and of the greater openness of elements within the new ruling elite to labor demands. When the plans for a new labor bill were first announced, there were massive protests at the national parliament, or DPR (Dewan Perwakilan Rakyat, People's Representative Assembly), in September 2002, leading to the bill's postponement, "the first time since the controversy around the 1974 Marriage Law that a social group had forced the parliament to postpone the promulgation of a law."[30] Members of the relevant parliamentary commission (especially several from the PDI-P, Partai Demokrasi Indonesia-Perjuangan, the Indonesian Democratic Party of Struggle) subsequently invited a number of worker representatives to contribute their input to the law's design.[31] Minister Nuwa Wea also personally intervened at a critical moment in the negotiations, securing for workers the very generous severance pay conditions that later caused so much criticism by employers.[32]

In addition to the significant input that organized labor had in the formulation of this legal framework, it is worth noting labor's mobilizational power in defending those aspects it saw as beneficial to its interests. In the mid-2000s, employer organizations and Yudhoyono's first manpower minister, Fahmi Idris, called for revisions to the law, bemoaning in particular the severance pay conditions it mandated, saying that these were a major disincentive to investment.[33] When the government sent amendments to the DPR, a major wave of worker mobilizations

---

[28] Ibid., p. 158.

[29] Ibid, p. 160, fn. 14.

[30] Jafar Suryomenggolo, "Labour, Politics, and the Law: A Legal–Political Analysis of Indonesia's Labour Law Reform Program," *Labour and Management in Development* 9 (2008): 4.

[31] Ibid, pp. 4–6. See also Teri L. Caraway, "Explaining the Dominance of Legacy Unions in New Democracies: Comparative Insights from Indonesia," *Comparative Political Studies* 41,10 (2008): 1371–97.

[32] Dinna Wisnu, "Governing Social Security: Economic Crisis and Reform in Indonesia, the Philippines and Singapore" (PhD dissertation, Ohio State University, 2007), p. 193.

[33] "Labor Factor Seen as Hindering FDI," *The Jakarta Post*, July 15, 2005.

began. There were massive strikes on May Day 2005, and also a huge rally that ended with violent clashes outside the DPR building in Jakarta. Notably, as these protests gained steam, parts of the official political establishment expressed support, keen to burnish their populist image. PDI-P and PKS (Partai Keadilan Sejahtera, Prosperous Justice Party) leaders were particularly vocal in endorsing the demands of protesting workers, and eventually the DPR stated it would refuse to consider the amendments.[34] Finally, the government backed down and shelved the revisions. As Chris Manning concludes, "Fear of union and wider community backlash against any reforms which appeared to be against the interests of labour ... meant that reforms aimed at reducing hiring costs and rigidity in employment and wages were too sensitive a subject for political leaders."[35]

This capacity for influential street politics is based on what has become a deeply entrenched subculture of protest action among sections of labor at the local level. According to Benny Juliawan, although the "plethora of alliances, coalitions, and forums or fronts that exist among small trade unions and their overlapping constituencies can look chaotic to an unsuspecting observer, fragmentation is only half of the story."[36] Labor unions, NGOs, and other groups, he argues, have a great capacity for alliance building and cooperative action, even though "tactical alliances [often] last only for one particular collective action."[37] This pattern of both fragmentation and propensity to alliance-building is itself a legacy of the last decade of the authoritarian period, when the combination arose as part of an attempt to minimize repression while maximizing political effect.[38] Much of the new labor activism is, by necessity, extremely fragmented, occurring in a single factory, focusing on wage rises in one particular district, or otherwise taking place at a local level. Nevertheless, Juliawan sees in the proliferation of local street protests by workers the embryo of an Indonesian "movement society," in which the representation of claims by social movements has become normalized.[39]

Moreover, in recent years, organized labor has increasingly taken the political offensive. Another wave of major mobilizations occurred through 2011 and 2012, particularly in the industrial heartland of Bekasi to the east of Jakarta, but also in other areas.[40] While some of these protests focused on traditional issues, such as wages, others were more proactive, for example, demanding the end of outsourcing and contract work. Major labor mobilizations have also occurred in support of social issues, such as to defend fuel subsidies and promote social security reform. Unions have pioneered increasingly militant forms of action, including general rather than single factory-based strikes, blockades of roads leading in and out of industrial estates, and the practice of "sweeping," in which militant workers invade factories and enable or force those workers inside to join them. The recent wave of

---

[34] "House Tells SBY to Drop Labor Law Revisions," *The Jakarta Post*, June 5, 2006.

[35] Manning, "Political Economy of Reform," p. 163.

[36] Juliawan, "Playing Politics," p. 155.

[37] Ibid.

[38] See, for example, Aspinall, *Opposing Suharto*, pp. 97, 132.

[39] Benny Juliawan, "Street-level Politics: Labour Protests in Post-authoritarian Indonesia," *Journal of Contemporary Asia* 41,3 (2011): 367.

[40] See Teri L. Caraway and Michele Ford, "Labor Unions and Electoral Contests in Democratic Indonesia," paper presented at "Beyond Oligarchy? Critical Exchanges on Accountability and Representation in Indonesia," the University of Sydney, December 14–15, 2012.

mobilization, which included a national strike of two million workers in early October 2012, is the greatest in modern Indonesian history and reflects remarkable confidence on the part of labor. In 2012, labor militancy became so widespread that spokespersons of the Employers' Association, APINDO (Asosiasi Pengusaha Indonesia), spoke of it as representing a major impediment to investment, said that companies were considering relocating overseas, and threatened a production strike.[41]

Even organized labor's marginalization from electoral politics may be changing. Some sectors of the workers' movement formed labor parties early in Indonesia's democratic transition, but recorded poor results. At the same time, some of the more effective and militant labor organizations, such as the metalworkers' federation, FSPMI (Federasi Serikat Pekerja Metal Indonesi), abstained from the electoral arena, reflecting a broader activist hostility toward representational politics in the early transition.[42] Yet, as Michele Ford and Teri Caraway note, the mood began to change as Indonesian democracy consolidated, and as major parties recognized the mobilizational power of labor.[43] Ford explains that there have been "substantial and repeated overtures made to prominent labor activists in the industrial heartlands of Java and Sumatra, which began shortly after the 2004 general election and subsequently strengthened in the lead-up to the electoral contests of 2009."[44] Few successes have been achieved by the ensuing coalitions, but they point to deeper and less formal interactions among organized labor and electoral politics. Thus, in many other cases, labor activists work as members of *tim sukses* (campaign teams) of non-labor candidates, wresting concessions from them in the process; other candidates in local and national elections sign "political contracts" with labor groups.[45] In the 2009 presidential election, for example, "the Megawati–Prabowo pair promised to institute May Day as a national holiday and to abolish contract work, the Jusuf Kalla–Wiranto pair pledged to abolish contract work and outsourcing practices."[46]

Although such flirtations with electoral politics have not translated into embedded institutional power for labor, the desire of mainstream politicians to court workers' support has nevertheless produced concrete gains. In particular, the fact that local governments now have a role in setting regional minimum wages has made officials in industrial regions eager to court labor support, especially in periods leading to elections. Thus, for example, the West Java government, in a year leading to a *pilkada* (direct local elections), authorized a 16 percent minimum wage increase in Bekasi, in excess of the 10 percent recommended by the National Wages Council and prompting the employers' association to sue.[47] In Jakarta in 2011, approaching another election year, Governor Fauzi Bowo raised the minimum wage for Jakarta by

---

[41] See, for example, "Pengusaha Ancam Mogok Produksi," *Koran Tempo,* November 6, 2012.

[42] Michele Ford, "Towards Issue-Based Politics: Trade Unions and Elections in Batam, 2004–2010," paper presented at "Decentralization and Democratization in Southeast Asia," Freiburg University, June 15–17, 2011, p. 8.

[43] Caraway and Ford, "Labor Unions and Electoral Contests." See also Caraway and Ford, "Labor and Politics under Oligarchy," this volume, pp. 139–55.

[44] Ford, "Towards Issue-Based Politics," p. 3.

[45] Juliawan, "Playing Politics," p. 264.

[46] Ibid., pp. 264–65.

[47] "Labor Row Rages on as Court Decides to Hear Apindo," *Jakarta Post*, January 25, 2012; and "Mekanisme Pengupahan Dilanggar Elite Lokal," *Kompas*, February 3, 2012.

15 percent, three times higher than the local inflation rate and twice the recommendation of the independent mediation body.[48] His successor, Joko Widodo, increased the minimum wage by 43 percent, amidst a rash of large wage increases in other regions, earning the condemnation of employers' organizations for doing so.[49] Such increases have produced a dramatic increase in real wages, even if labor costs are still far less than in some relevant comparison regions, such as Southern China. The increases certainly have been unwelcome to, and condemned by, employers, many of whom have sought exemptions.

Indonesia has not seen a radical expansion of the political power of labor. It has not embarked on the path blazed by early industrializing countries one hundred years ago, with large labor-based parties or electoral coalitions able to wrest governmental power directly from their class rivals. But we do not need to set the bar so high in assessing the changing balance of class forces in post-Suharto Indonesia. Organized labor has made gains that have gone beyond greater freedom of organization and expression. Democratization has generated significant space to mobilize for improvements in terms of wages, workplace conditions, and other social benefits, and labor has recorded many achievements in this sphere. Labor's influence has been gained primarily in two ways: first, by the street power it has won, enabled by democratic space to organize and, second, by informal interactions with the world of formal politics. And this increasing influence has been achieved despite the fragmentation of labor organizations.

We could make similar analyses of other sectors where, despite fragmented organizational patterns and uneven progress, social and material gains have been recorded by lower-class groups. For example, in many parts of the country disenfranchised peasants achieved significant victories in the immediate aftermath of *reformasi*. In places where land disputes between local communities and state agencies or private developers had stretched for years, or even decades, farmers occupied hundreds of thousands of hectares of land, with these informal occupations leading to permanent victories in many places in the form of title to the land being subsequently granted to the occupiers. Business groups and officials frequently complain vociferously about the difficulties and expense of acquiring land for their activities as a result of residents' protests and recalcitrance, and the country is littered with failed projects where land acquisition has come to nothing.[50] This is a critical change from the Suharto period, when conflicts over land expropriation invariably ended with victory for the developers and when compensation to the losers was often extremely meager, if given at all. In a few cases, such as parts of the province of Bengkulu, or the district of Batang, in Central Java, farmer groups have

---

[48] Liam Gammon, "Voters, Elites, and Urban Planning in an Asian Megacity: A Case Study of the 2012 Gubernatorial Elections in Jakarta" (honors thesis, Australian National University, 2012), p. 45. See also "Upah Minimum Provinsi: Pekerja dan Pengusaha Kaget Kenaikan Upah," *Kompas*, November 26, 2010.

[49] See, for example, "UMP Naik Sofjan Salahkan Jokowi," *Koran Sindo*, April 9, 2013. These increases were not the first time Jakarta had seen large wage rises linked to elections: in 2001, another election year (though at that time governors were still elected by provincial legislatures), Governor Sutiyoso raised the minimum wage by 40 percent, the largest such increase in Indonesian history up to that time; see Manning, "Political Economy of Reform," p. 10.

[50] For one recent example, see "Land Acquisition a Big Problem for Infrastructure Projects," *Jakarta Post*, December 3, 2012.

been able to achieve greater electoral success than their equivalents in the labor movement, wresting significant influence in local legislatures and executive governments.[51]

As with organized labor, it would be possible to point to many exceptions and to list numerous qualifications. The patterns are often messy and there are many forms of bargaining and compromise between lower class constituents and the traditional elites who occupy political office. Brokerage and clientelism more often mediate connections between the two groups than do social movements and political mobilization. This, in many ways, is the point: social struggles and advances are now happening in highly fragmented ways, reflecting the patterns of splintered activism that constitute contemporary Indonesia's social-movement landscape, and its enmeshment in fractured clientelistic and electoral politics. Such a fragmented pattern may not constitute a decisive shift in the balance of class forces, but it does suggest that significant social gains are possible, a topic we turn to now.

ELECTORAL POPULISM AND THE POLITICS OF HEALTH

Since about 2005, a near-revolutionary shift in the nature of Indonesian politics has taken place, though few observers have noticed it. During early post-Suharto elections, many analysts derided the empty populism of the campaigning: parties and candidates, it was all but universally agreed, offered little to the electorate except vague slogans. Programmatic politics were virtually absent and voters could expect little concrete improvement in their life situations from voting for particular candidates or parties. Such was the conventional assessment.

This situation has changed significantly. Throughout Indonesia, candidates for political office, especially in local elections, are responding to electoral incentives and competing with one another to offer increasingly elaborate and generous social programs. In particular, promises of free and improved healthcare and education have become all but ubiquitous in local executive government head elections. At the national level, too, successive governments have offered increasingly ambitious and generous social programs. True, many of these promises are not implemented fully after the votes are counted, but it is impossible to deny the new political salience of social welfare in Indonesian politics. The tentative beginnings of an Indonesian welfare state are becoming visible.

The remainder of this section examines the rise of social welfare in Indonesian politics by focusing on healthcare. The recent history of the expansion of public healthcare programs in Indonesia is complex, and begins with the financial crisis of 1997–98, when the central government, with assistance from the World Bank, established a "Social Safety Net" that included healthcare cards that granted free access to health services for the poor, and increased funds for those services. A series of new schemes was introduced under successive governments, culminating in 2008 with a scheme called Jamkesmas (Jaminan Kesehatan Masyarakat, Community Health Insurance). Jamkesmas provided "basic healthcare in public health clinics and

---

[51] One excellent overview is Dianto Bachriadi, "Between Discourse and Action: Agrarian Reform and Rural Social Movements in Indonesia, Post-1965" (PhD dissertation, Flinders University, 2011).

hospital inpatient care" for the poor and informal sector employees.[52] By 2012, the scheme was covering approximately 76.4 million beneficiaries, with a budget allocation of Rp 7.29 trillion (approx. US$750 million).[53]

But reform did not stop there. Framing these schemes and other measures, the national parliament passed two laws setting out an ambitious agenda to provide universal social insurance: Law No. 40 of 2004, on the National Social Security System; and Law No. 24 of 2011, on the National Social Security System Provider Bodies. The first of these laws established a plan to provide universal social insurance to cover healthcare, workplace accidents, death, old-age care, and pensions; the second law provides the framework for the institutions that administer the scheme. Under the system, insurance for private and public sector employees is covered by mandatory contributions shared between employers and employees; contributions are for the first time also made obligatory for informal sector workers. The government pays the premiums on behalf of the poor. The scheme began to be implemented at the start of 2014 and is expected to be fully operational by 2019. By this time, social insurance coverage will have become universal.

Overall, welfare policies have had an important, but seldom remarked upon, role in national politics. Before the 2009 election, the government invested heavily in various social programs; in the aftermath, President Susilo Bambang Yudhoyono's poll figures improved significantly. According to one assessment:

> [I]t was the introduction of massive cash programs for the poor that triggered Yudhoyono's meteoric rise from electoral underdog to almost unassailable frontrunner. Between June 2008 and April 2009, the government spent approximately US$2 billion on compensation payments for increased fuel prices, schooling allowances, and micro-credit programs.[54]

In healthcare, it has, however, been at the local level where most of the political action has taken place. Decentralization reforms passed responsibility for managing public health to Indonesia's district governments. Beginning with a few celebrated cases, such as the Jaminan Kesehatan Jembrana, in Jembrana, Bali, over the last decade, local health insurance and protection schemes spread like wildfire across Indonesia's regions, such that there were at least six at the provincial level and hundreds in the districts, with 2011 national data suggesting that 32 million persons were covered by such schemes.[55] Since early 2014, these schemes have, at least theoretically, been subsumed by the new National Social Security Scheme.

---

[52] Robert Sparrow, Asep Suryahadi, and Wenefrida Widyanti, *Social Health Insurance for the Poor: Targeting and Impact of Indonesia's Askeskin Program* (Jakarta: SMERU Working Paper, 2010), p. i.

[53] Elly Burhaini Faizal, "Government to Spend Rp 25 trillion for BPJS," *The Jakarta Post*, August 2, 2012.

[54] Marcus Mietzner, "Indonesia's 2009 Elections: Populism, Dynasties, and the Consolidation of the Party System," an analysis for Lowy Institute for International Policy (May 2009), p. 4.

[55] *Profil Data Kesehatan Indonesia 2011* (Jakarta: Kementerian Kesehatan Republik Indonesia, 2012), table 5.34. A 2012 survey conducted by the SMERU Research Institute found that 245 of 262 districts that provided information had some sort of local health financing scheme; see SMERU, "District Health Care Financing Study: Descriptive Statistics and Initial Results," PowerPoint presentation, 2012.

There was much variation in the coverage these schemes provided. Some of the most generous, especially those in cashed-up resource-rich regions, such as the province of Aceh or the district of Musi Banyuasin, in South Sumatra, provided universal coverage, with access to all manner of healthcare services for all residents. These schemes covered a fuller range of treatments and paid for longer periods of care than what was provided under Jamkesmas. In Aceh, for example, under Jaminan Kesehatan Aceh (JKA, Aceh Health Insurance program), there was no limit on the variety of illnesses that could be treated. Patients who required care that could not be provided in Aceh—neurological or heart surgery, for example—could be flown to hospitals in Jakarta, in chartered airplanes, and accompanied by medical staff if necessary. In Aceh, the scheme was very popular, and its introduction produced a sudden spike in the number of patients using the public health system, such that demand outpaced supply, and many patients had to sleep on hospital floors due to a shortage of beds.[56]

Most schemes provided less comprehensive coverage than did Aceh's. For instance, in Solo, a "gold card" for poor residents did not limit the amount of care provided; a silver card was provided to "almost poor" residents whose benefits were capped at Rp. 2 million per year.[57] Other schemes, especially in poor regions, were even more restricted. For example, in Central Lombok, the newly elected *bupati* did not promise comprehensive coverage, but instead promised that there would be free maternity coverage.[58] The fact that candidates even in resource-poor regions promised such services during elections, however, points to how widespread the model was becoming, and to the power of electoral competition to drive policy change.

How are we to explain healthcare's newfound political salience? What does it say about the balance of social power in Indonesia's new democracy? Guidance can be found in studies of other cases in the region. In examining new healthcare regimes in South Korea and Taiwan, Joseph Wong has persuasively argued that conventional structural explanations fail to account for the emergence of wide-ranging social programs in both countries since the 1980s. He discounts class mobilization theories that see welfare programs as a product of the "balance of class power."[59] Instead, Wong argues, the key factor was democratization itself, whereby universalization of healthcare was a "strategic response to the new logic of political competition," especially by incumbents.[60] A similar dynamic has been apparent in Indonesia, though the time lag between democratic breakthrough and universalization of healthcare has been longer, and it is more challenging to establish social protection in a country that is poorer than either Taiwan or South Korea was at the time of their

---

[56] "RSU di Aceh Booming. Pasien JKA Tidur di Lantai," *Serambi Indonesia,* September 30, 2009. The latest province to experience such an upsurge in patient demand was Jakarta, after the introduction in late November 2012 of a free healthcare scheme by the new governor, Joko Widodo. See, for example, "Free Healthcare Overwhelms Depok, Jakarta," *Jakarta Post,* February 23, 2013.

[57] Interview with Asep Suryahadi, SMERU Research Institute, September 12, 2011.

[58] http://lomboktengahkab.go.id/index.php?option=com_content&view=article&id=531:7-komitmen-bupati-loteng-segera-dilaksanakan&catid=1:berita&Itemid=36, accessed March 1, 2013.

[59] J. Wong, *Healthy Democracies: Welfare Politics in Taiwan and South Korea* (Ithaca, NY: Cornell University Press, 2004), p. 11.

[60] Ibid., p. 15.

transitions. In Indonesia, as in South Korea and Taiwan, the spread of new social welfare schemes is not dependent on structural coalitions among labor and other social groups, though there was significant mobilization by labor unions and NGOs in favor of the passage of the national social security legislation.[61] Instead, welfare schemes have been promoted by mainstream, elite politicians, eager to present themselves as champions of social reform for electoral gain.

This logic is clearest at the local level, where access to affordable healthcare has been promoted by the new governing elite in the regions, the very force identified in much of the literature as representing social exclusion and oligarchic domination. Rosser, Wilson, and Sulistiyanto argue that the *bupati* who have adopted free education and healthcare policies have tended to be those who are "relatively autonomous of predatory interests."[62] Adopting policies that appeal to the poor, they argue, allows such politicians to bolster their chances of reelection and confront potentially hostile legislatures. Accordingly, some of the *bupati*, mayors, and governors who initiated new healthcare schemes had backgrounds in public health, links with NGOs, or some other aspect in their personal biography that inclined them toward universalizing healthcare. The lead example here is Gede Winasa, the former *bupati* of Jembrana, Bali, and the best-known pioneer of local health insurance in Indonesia. He had worked in the health system for many years as a dentist, academic, and civil servant, but also had a history of political activism, notably in the post-1998 movement to abolish the caste system in Bali.[63] The governor of Aceh responsible for the JKA scheme, Irwandi Yusuf, was not only a former separatist rebel, he was also a university-trained veterinarian sympathetic to the ideas of European social democracy.

While the personal qualities of leaders may have been important in the early take up of local healthcare schemes, in subsequent years it appears that this policy strategy became modular, with programs being copied and adapted from region to region with great rapidity and variety. Indeed, some of the politicians identified with the new policy approach were the epitome of old-style politics, being local bosses long-entrenched in the bureaucracy and adept at playing patronage politics. Among these were Alex Noerdin, the former *bupati* of Musi Banyuasin and then governor of South Sumatra; and Fauzi Bowo, governor of Jakarta in 2007–12. In Jakarta, Fauzi, a notorious old-style patronage politician, launched an 800 billion rupiah "health card" program, which provided free healthcare up to 100 million rupiah per person in 2012, which happened to be an election year in Jakarta.[64] Fauzi made healthcare and education policies central to his bid to win re-election. Alex Noerdin, who also ran in the Jakarta election, campaigned on his success in providing free healthcare and

---

[61] Rachelle Peta Cole, "Coalescing for Change: Opportunities, Resources, Tactics, and Indonesia's 2010–11 Social Security Campaign" (honors thesis, University of Sydney, 2012).

[62] Andrew Rosser, Ian Wilson, and Priyambudi Sulistiyanto, "Leaders, Elites, and Coalitions: The Politics of Free Public Services in Decentralised Indonesia," Developmental Leadership Program Research Paper 16, 2011, p. 15. For another important, and early, article that anticipates some of the arguments presented in this chapter, see Andrew Rosser, Kurnya Roesad and Donni Edwin, "Indonesia: The Politics of Inclusion," *Journal of Contemporary Asia* 35,1 (2005): 53–77.

[63] Ibid., p. 19.

[64] "Kartu Sehat: Tahap Pertama Diberikan di 6 Wilayah Kumuh," *Kompas,* November 1, 2012.

education in South Sumatra.[65] The winner was Joko Widodo, the mayor of Solo, who owed part of his own populist appeal to the effective healthcare program he had introduced while running the administration of that central Javanese city.

The centrality of social welfare to the 2012 Jakarta election campaign is just one example of a broader pattern of electoral competition driving policy change throughout Indonesia's regions. Many local government head elections have become virtual bidding wars, in which rival politicians offer ever more generous health insurance schemes (alongside other inducements) to entice voters. At the national level, too, it is all but impossible to identify clear differences in party positions over the National Social Security System; instead, there is virtual unanimity of support for the basic outline. In short, democratization has created strong incentives for all political players to design policies that will appeal to the poor, and over the last half decade or so we have seen adroit politicians adjusting their policies accordingly. Electoral competition has become a key vector through which social welfare policies are being introduced.

It would be naïve to suggest that these changes have ushered in an era of high quality or universal healthcare for Indonesia's poor. The level of investment made by Indonesia in public healthcare remains low even by Southeast Asian standards, though it is rising rapidly. The quality of the services that are provided to poor people is appallingly bad, and certainly miserable in comparison to those provided under universal schemes in rich countries. Staff absenteeism and poor training, misdiagnosis, inadequate treatments and equipment, and other shortcomings are all rampant.[66] Moreover, even ostensibly "free" healthcare often ends up costing users. As Andrew Rosser has cogently argued, illegal fees remain pervasive in healthcare because of the continuing influence of the coalition of politico-bureaucrats and corporate interests that pervades the sector, as elsewhere.[67] There are also major questions about the affordability of these programs; many local programs simply fail to deliver the benefits promised to residents, while others have been driven into debt as they fail to keep pace with their commitments.

Such problems suggest that, if we are witnessing the creation of an Indonesian welfare state, it is still in the early stages of what is likely to be a slow process of formation (though, of course, all welfare states took many decades to construct). On the other hand, the apparent breadth of support for social protection policies across a broad range of Indonesia's parties and local politicians suggests that such policies are arising as a result of a powerful political logic. And, indeed, it would be possible to point to many other areas where the logic of electoral competition is reconfiguring policy. The trend to finance public education is virtually identical to that in healthcare, with a rash of initiatives at the center (not least, a constitutional requirement mandating 20 percent of the state budget be spent on education) and in the regions (a proliferation of free-education policies, subsidies, and scholarship schemes). A less obvious example concerns communities in remote rural and

---

[65] See, for example, "Fauzi Launches Populist Programs as Runoff Nears," *The Jakarta Post*, August 2, 2012; and "Free Healthcare, Education Not Essential," *The Jakarta Post*, July 4, 2012.

[66] For an excellent overview of such problems, see Elizabeth Pisani, "Medicine for a Sick System," *Inside Indonesia* 111 (2013), http://www.insideindonesia.org/write-for-us/medicine-for-a-sick-system, accessed August 15, 2013.

[67] Andrew Rosser, "Realising Free Health Care for the Poor in Indonesia: The Politics of Illegal Fees," *Journal of Contemporary Asia* 42,2 (2012): 255–75.

forested areas that were long neglected by state development programs (e.g., Dayak communities in Kalimantan) and that now find themselves able to leverage their voting power to attract desired development projects that had for decades eluded them: new roads, bridges, community buildings, and the like. Very often these come in the form of "club goods" that are awarded to particular communities by political candidates in exchange for votes; but even if the distribution is clientelistic, such projects are often strongly desired by local communities. Elections have shifted, at least in some places and to some degree, the balance of policy preferences in favor of previously marginalized voters. As a result, even if many occupants of political office are drawn from the same stock as the old New Order elite, some now act according to a new political logic.

CONCLUSION

My main interest in making this analysis has not been to advance a new theory of political power and its relationship to material inequality, or to defend an old one, but to provide a more accurate assessment of the influence of popular forces in Indonesian politics. The phenomena described in this essay suggest that when we consider evidence in the form of policy outcomes, some of our assumptions about the political marginalization of lower class interests in Indonesia require modification. I have thus argued for an analysis that places at its center a wider array of social interests than the oligarchs and elites who have consumed so much scholarly attention. In particular, I have argued we should no longer write subordinate groups out of the frame, but, rather, should pay closer attention to the ways that they express themselves politically and, in doing so, challenge, contend with, or are conciliated or incorporated by, oligarchic power. We have become over-used to viewing Indonesia as a site of political domination; it remains equally a place of contestation—in the contentious politics of street protests and social movements that have become central to political life, and in the perpetual frictions that occur between oligarchic, popular, and other interests within arenas like parliaments, parties, and electoral politics. That these struggles are complex, and take place in contradictory and fragmented ways, involving ever-shifting political coalitions and conflicts, reflects the complexity of Indonesian democracy and the kaleidoscopic patterns of social interest that underpin it.

But, setting this basic message aside, does the analysis presented in the preceding pages fundamentally challenge the oligarchy thesis advanced by authors such as Hadiz, Robison, and Winters (even if it disagrees with the empirical assessment they have made so far of the political influence of subordinate groups)? If we interpret that thesis in its most basic form, as a theoretical proposition that links political authority to material wealth, and as an assessment of Indonesian politics that sees oligarchs as disproportionately influential politically, then the answer is no. Both the growing organizational power on the part of labor described above, and the halting emergence of local healthcare schemes, can be compatible with a society marked by extreme inequalities of wealth and, consequently, political power. Arguably, neither phenomenon challenges the core interests of oligarchs, though big business has been generally hostile to demands advanced by workers, and local healthcare programs presumably divert funds from purposes that might more readily be subject to oligarchic capture. But in such a perspective, what phenomena would constitute a true challenge to oligarchy? In Jeffrey Winters's analysis, for example, oligarchy is all but a universal characteristic of contemporary human society, including in countries like Sweden that are normally considered to be exemplars of social–democratic equality. If all contemporary capitalist societies are marked by extreme inequalities of wealth, and therefore political influence, it is not surprising that Indonesia should be afflicted by the same malady. Simply recognizing the power of oligarchy in Indonesia, therefore, does not get us very far analytically.

Of course, these authors have gone further than merely making such a basic diagnosis of class power; they also suggest that the character of oligarchic dominance contributes particular features to Indonesia's regime form, and its trajectory. For example, Winters writes of Indonesia as being an "untamed" oligarchy in which oligarchic power is all but unconstrained by mediating political institutions or an impartial rule of law. Oligarchs themselves confront "a proliferation of lateral threats and predation from above," but conditions for other actors are even more subject to the caprice of a system virtually without a rule of law.[68] Robison and Hadiz have suggested that the reassertion of forces nurtured under the New Order created an "illiberal form of democracy [that is] already consolidated and entrenched."[69] These authors' works are, to put it bluntly, not optimistic about the prospects for political reform or social progress.

If we broaden our assessment of Indonesia's new democracy in the way suggested in this essay, we may look at some of these issues in a different light. One topic that needs more serious consideration is the consequences of democracy itself for the balance of power between oligarchs and other forces. As Stephan Haggard and Robert Kauffman have suggested, "Democratic politics has long been associated with pressures for redistribution, through mechanisms that are basic, constitutive features of democratic rule itself."[70] These mechanisms include not only the opening of democratic space for organization and mobilization of lower class interests, but also electoral competition itself and its placing of "institutionalized uncertainty" at the heart of political life.[71] We do not need to adopt an extreme pluralist interpretation to note the many ways in which organizations representing subordinate groups in Indonesia are trying to influence policy outcomes, sometimes with considerable success, and the ways in which traditional politicians, including those with links to oligarchic power, are driven to make policy concessions in order to attract electoral support.

More broadly, the analysis presented in this article suggests the need for a wider reconsideration of the nature of Indonesia's democratic transition, its post-authoritarian dispensation, and its future trajectory. Political contestation and the mobilization of subordinate groups were central to the fall of the Suharto regime. They did not end with the consolidation of Indonesia's current political order. The form of Indonesia's current regime distills many of the goals and achievements of

---

[68] Winters, *Oligarchy*, p. 181.

[69] Vedi R. Hadiz and Richard Robison, "Neo-Liberal Reforms and Illiberal Consolidations: The Indonesian Paradox," City University of Hong Kong, Southeast Asia Research Centre Working Papers Series No. 52, 2003, p. 9.

[70] S. Haggard and R. Kauffman, *Development, Democracy, and Welfare States* (Princeton, NJ, and Oxford: Princeton University Press, 2008), p. 13.

[71] On institutionalized uncertainty, see A. Przeworski, *Democracy and the Market: Political and Economic Reforms in Eastern Europe and Latin America* (New York, NY: Cambridge University Press, 1991).

oppositional social movements that were dismissed and marginalized in the period leading to 1998, just as it embodies new forms of influence for oligarchic forces first incubated under the New Order. Oligarchic power is a critical part of the current political dispensation, but so, too, are continuing efforts by subordinate groups to represent themselves and achieve social goals, as well as efforts by politicians, oligarchic or otherwise, to accommodate at least some of their demands.

The emergence over time of a more liberal democracy, of a more tamed oligarchy, or, indeed, of a more effective welfare state, will depend on the outcomes of such contests, not just of internal conflicts among the wealthy and powerful. In particular, lower class groups are likely increasingly to find that many of the formal victories they achieve through policy concessions and legal reform will amount to very little if not backed up by effective rule of law and consistent implementation.[72] The achievement of such reform goals in advanced democracies—to the extent that they have been achieved—was typically the product of multigenerational struggles over long time periods. There is every indication this will be the case in Indonesia, too, and plenty of evidence from the first decade of Indonesian democracy that we need not be morbidly pessimistic about the eventual outcome.

---

[72] One specific example concerns severance pay, generous provisions for which were one of the signal achievements of labor activism in the post-Suharto period. Yet one recent report suggests very low compliance, with only a third of workers entitled to severance pay actually receiving it, and workers receiving only about 40 percent of the payments due to them. See Vera Brusentsev, David Newhouse, and Wayne Vroman, "Severance Pay Compliance in Indonesia," World Bank, Policy Research Working Paper 5933, Social Protection Unit, 2012.

LABOR AND POLITICS UNDER OLIGARCHY

Teri L. Caraway and Michele Ford

In recent years, working-class actors have become a more visible presence in Indonesian politics than in the past. Sustained political mobilization since 2009 has resulted in numerous policy victories for organized labor. Unions have broken free of the confines of Suharto-era ideologies that stressed apolitical unionism and that encouraged labor to focus its energy exclusively on workplace issues.[1] Now, even avowedly apolitical unions incorporate large-scale collective protest as an integral element of their activities. More overtly political unions have gone even further and are engaging actively in electoral politics, making political contracts with political parties and candidates for local executive office. Political parties and local executives, in turn, have shown increasing interest in wooing working-class voters by making political compacts with unions and running union cadres as candidates for legislative seats. The question for this volume, then, is how to make sense of these phenomena within the context of oligarchic theory? As a consequence of their analytic focus on how the extremely rich use the political process to defend their wealth, theorists of oligarchy pay scant attention to working-class actors. This is not to say that they have nothing to say about organized labor. They do, and their theoretical apparatus provides some insight into why unions are disadvantaged in Indonesia's money-driven democracy. Moreover, both Jeffrey Winters and Vedi Hadiz and Richard Robison acknowledge that the disruptive power of labor has at times in Indonesia's modern history posed a significant threat to the country's power structures.[2] It is uncontroversial to say that the post-*Reformasi* period is not one of these revolutionary eras.

Aside from relatively convulsive and episodic revolutionary moments, oligarchic theorists do not consider labor's prospects in contemporary Indonesian politics to be good. For Winters, the rise of oligarchy has diminished labor's relative power. Faced

---

[1] For an account of such workplace issues, see Michele Ford, *Workers and Intellectuals: NGOs, Trade Unions, and the Indonesian Labour Movement* (Singapore: NUS/Hawaii/KITLV, 2009).

[2] Jeffrey A. Winters, "Oligarchy and Democracy in Indonesia," this volume, pp. 11–33; Vedi R. Hadiz and Richard Robison, "The Political Economy of Oligarchy and the Reorganization of Power in Indonesia," this volume, pp. 35–56; Jeffrey Winters, *Oligarchy* (Cambridge: Cambridge University Press, 2011); and Richard Robison and Vedi Hadiz, *Reorganising Power in Indonesia: The Politics of Oligarchy in an Age of Markets* (London: Routledge, 2004).

with the overwhelming power of wealth, organized labor faces an uphill and probably losing battle.[3] Hadiz and Robison emphasize labor's fragmentation, which they argue makes the working class an ineffective force against a dominant politico–bureaucratic elite that controls both wealth and political office. Consequently, "[i]ncremental demands for reform by individuals or groups can only be piecemeal … a transformation of substance … requires both the disintegration of the old order and its social underpinnings and the forging of a new social order with its political forces."[4]

The implication of these perspectives is that Indonesia's democracy is a fundamentally uneven playing field upon which organized labor struggles even to register its presence, let alone present any meaningful challenge to the political order. We find little to disagree with in the assertion that material power gives oligarchs enormous political advantage in Indonesia. Indeed, we take as given that vast disparities in wealth necessarily lead to extreme political inequality. Despite this unfavorable structural position, however, it is evident that working-class actors in Indonesia have been significantly more successful in achieving their collective goals since the advent of democracy than in the Suharto years. The sustained nature of these accomplishments suggests that workers have found ways to create greater political space than would be expected given the disadvantages that workers face in a context characterized by vast disparities in wealth.

These working-class achievements do not necessarily invalidate the oligarchy thesis: theorists of Indonesia's oligarchy acknowledge that oligarchs do not win every battle. But, as Thomas Pepinsky observes, oligarchic theory cannot explain specific political outcomes.[5] The theory operates on a macro level to provide the broad structural backdrop in which politics takes place, aligning actors by their comparative power resources. Oligarchic theory, in other words, does not explain the everyday trench warfare of politics. As a consequence, theorists of oligarchy not only leave the incremental change wrought by non-oligarchic actors unanalyzed empirically, they also dismiss it theoretically. In doing so, they overestimate the difficulties of mobilizing Indonesia's fragmented workers, and to some extent mischaracterize the potency of mobilizational power.

As Winters observes, "most manifestations of mobilizational power are episodic and very difficult to sustain due to the great personal demands mobilization places on participants"—the exception being when mobilizational power is "well institutionalized."[6] Both Winters and Hadiz and Robison rightly note that Indonesian trade unions have struggled to maintain the size and level of militancy required to pose a serious threat to the oligarchy (understood respectively as the greatly wealthy or the politico–bureaucratic elite). Yet, though deeply fragmented, Indonesia's unions come together routinely to pursue collective goals through inter-union alliances that have proven to be formidably effective in achieving a subset of labor's political goals. When workers prove their capacity to mobilize repeatedly, such power generates a latent effect, as other actors come to know that trade unions' *threat* to mobilize is credible. Just as material wealth can be a silent presence, the credible

[3] Winters, "Oligarchy and Democracy in Indonesia."

[4] Hadiz and Robison, "The Political Economy of Oligarchy and the Reorganization of Power in Indonesia," p. 54.

[5] Thomas Pepinsky, "Pluralism and Political Conflict in Indonesia," this volume, 79–98.

[6] Winters, "Oligarchy and Democracy in Indonesia," p. 14.

threat of massive mobilization plays a similar role. In other words, once unions prove that they can deliver on their threats to mount massive protests, they may not actually have to exercise their mobilizational power in order to achieve desired policy outcomes. It is therefore not only wealth that can exert its power in a latent fashion—as Winters rightly claims—but also labor mobilization.

In addition, in analyzing how oligarchs engage in electoral competition as a means of wealth defense, theorists of oligarchy pay insufficient attention to the fissures opened by intense inter-oligarch competition, which can be exploited by subaltern groups. In a situation where oligarchs back many parties, money alone is not decisive in determining who wins any given election. In Indonesia's democracy, money buys parties and individual oligarchs a chance to compete for power. Money is thus a vital precondition for electoral victory. It does not, however, guarantee it. In the context of intensely competitive elections, candidates must also garner votes. And in such a context, the prospect of an alliance with an organized constituency is alluring. In union-dense districts, labor is one of, if not *the*, largest organized interest group. Candidates for executive office and political parties have, therefore, increasingly looked to labor to give them a leg up in their competition with each other.

In this essay, we show how these two dynamics—mobilization and inter-oligarch/elite competition—have combined to enhance labor's political power. We do so through an analysis of the Manpower Act of 2003, minimum wage negotiations and elections for local executives in Bekasi and Tangerang, and the running of union cadres as legislative candidates. In demonstrating how unions have leveraged their mobilizational power to carve out domains of influence within Indonesia's polity, we provide an explanation of the capacity of non-oligarchic forces to act in the national and local political domains to achieve change and, in doing so, challenge some of the fundamental assumptions of the oligarchy thesis as it pertains to contemporary Indonesia.[7]

MOBILIZING AROUND THE MANPOWER ACT OF 2003

Indonesia's unions have secured numerous policy victories at the national level since 1998. The Manpower Act of 2003 substantially increased severance pay for laid-off workers and set numerous restrictions on non-permanent work contracts. With its passage, Indonesia's labor laws became among the strongest in East and Southeast Asia.[8] In the following years, unions beat back successive efforts by the Susilo Bambang Yudhoyono government to weaken these provisions of the law. Unions have also scored other important policy wins at the national level. The Social Security Act of 2011, a top priority for many unions, required employers to make higher contributions for an array of social benefits.[9] In 2012, protests by thousands of

---

[7] This essay was written as part of an ARC Discovery Project entitled "The Re-emergence of Political Labor in Indonesia" (DP120100654). In-depth interviews were conducted in Bekasi and Tangerang in the first half of 2012 with representatives of all major unions, union candidates, party administrators, and members of local and national legislatures.

[8] Teri L. Caraway, "Labor Rights in Asia: Progress or Regress?" *Journal of East Asian Studies* 9,2 (2009): 153–86.

[9] See Edward Aspinall, "Popular Agency and Interests in Indonesia's Democratic Transition and Consolidation," this volume, pp. 117–37; and Rachelle Cole, "Coalescing for Change:

workers were integral in delaying the increase in fuel prices and in persuading the Department of Manpower to issue a new implementing rule for the Manpower Act that limited outsourcing to five types of work.

These victories are surprising, as Indonesia's national legislature is a particularly challenging political arena for unions. Since legislation is generally hammered out in the parliament's various commissions,[10] unions must convince multiple legislators on key commissions to support a piece of legislation. Most legislators do not represent union-dense districts. Even those who do probably have little reason to fear future punishment from voters since individual legislators or even parties cannot be identified as opposing or supporting specific pieces of legislation unless they make public statements to that effect. Moreover, battles over legislation are irregular and take place in Jakarta, which means that most voters do not follow them. Finally, since legislation is typically very complex, its effects are not immediate and apparent to voters. All of these factors make legislative politics the perfect venue for oligarchic domination. Unions also do not have the financial resources to purchase the support of individual legislators, whereas oligarchs do. The incentives for representatives in the national legislature to pacify labor with pro-worker policy are thus weak.

The passage of the Manpower Act and contests around subsequent efforts to revise it show that mobilizational power has been a surprisingly effective means of securing desired policy outcomes at the national level.[11] The Manpower Act was the second major piece of labor legislation enacted after the fall of Suharto. Both employers and workers rejected government drafts of the bill. After unions took to the streets to oppose its passage, Commission VII authorized Indonesian Democratic Party of Struggle (PDI–P, Partai Demokrasi Indonesia–Perjuangan) legislator Herman Rekso Ageng to bring unions and employers together in bipartite discussions to develop a mutually acceptable piece of legislation. The commission agreed to accept the version of the bill formulated in these discussions. While both sides made concessions, the final bill included many protective provisions, such as restrictions on outsourcing, limitations on contract labor, higher pay for workers suspended during the labor dispute-resolution process, and higher severance pay for most categories of dismissal.[12]

By bringing labor to the table, the government prevented another major wave of street protests.[13] This was a vital achievement in a context where local and foreign investors had become increasingly vocal about the threat posed by trade union militancy to the viability of their Indonesia operations. Indonesia had witnessed a series of massive strikes in the late 1990s and early 2000s, which analysts blamed for

Opportunities, Resources, Tactics, and Indonesia's 2010–11 Social Security Campaign" (Honours thesis, University of Sydney, 2012).

[10] Stephen Sherlock, "Decade of Democracy: People's Forum or Chamber of Cronies?" in *Problems of Democratisation in Indonesia: Elections, Institutions, and Society*, ed. Edward Aspinall and Marcus Mietzner (Singapore: Institute of Southeast Asian Studies, 2010).

[11] This paragraph draws on Teri L. Caraway, "Protective Repression, International Pressure, and Institutional Design: Explaining Labor Reform in Indonesia," *Studies in Comparative International Development* 39,3 (2004).

[12] Some unions rejected the law, but since many unions participated in its drafting, labor was split and the worker protests that followed its passage were relatively small and ineffective.

[13] This paragraph draws on Michele Ford, "A Challenge for Business? Developments in Indonesian Trade Unionism after Soeharto," in *Business in Indonesia: New Challenges, Old Problems*, ed. M. Chatib Basri and Pierre van der Eng (Singapore: ISEAS, 2004), pp. 221–33.

destabilizing the business climate. Investors also felt that workers were exerting undue influence over government policy, going as far as to argue that it had become clear that "the government's policy could be dictated by 'terror.'"[14] The policy instrument referred to was Ministerial Decision No.150/2000 on Employment Termination, which employers argued provided too much protection for workers. When employers succeeded in having the decision modified, violent protests ensued, forcing the government to revoke the amendments in June 2001.[15]

In the case of the Manpower Act, employers accepted the bill at the time of its passage, but subsequently pushed for revisions. The Yudhoyono government obliged, making at least three attempts to revise the Manpower Act. The first, beginning in 2005 and ending in 2006, was a response by the administration to complaints by foreign investors and domestic employers.[16] Among other things, the revisions aimed to reduce severance pay and restrictions on outsourcing and contract labor. Predictably, labor opposed these proposed amendments and mounted a series of escalating protests in major industrial areas throughout Indonesia, beginning in March 2006.[17] Rattled by the protests, which were especially disruptive in Jakarta, the government promised not to send the bill to parliament until a tripartite forum agreed to proposed revisions.[18] Unmollified, unions renewed their threat to mount a national strike on May Day unless the government called off plans to revise the law.[19]

On May 1, 2006, tens of thousands of workers from across the archipelago participated in rallies rejecting revisions to the Act.[20] Thousands more returned to the streets on May 3, blocking the toll road and pushing down the three-meter-high gate to the national House of Representatives, prompting the police to fire tear gas to quell the demonstrations. That evening, the leaders of the House announced that they would reject the government's plans to revise the labor law.[21] By September, the

---

[14] "Labor 'Terror' a Blow to Investor Confidence," *Jakarta Post*, June 18, 2001.

[15] For a more general discussion of violent protest in Indonesia, see Michele Ford, "Violent Industrial Protest in Indonesia: Cultural Phenomenon or Legacy of an Authoritarian Past?" in *New Forms and Expressions of Conflict at Work*, ed. Gregor Gall (New York, NY: Palgrave, 2013).

[16] Apindo (Asosiasi Pengusaha Indonesia, Indonesian Employers Association) publicly endorsed the proposed revisions and considered them a step forward in correcting perceived imbalances in the law that unfairly favored workers. See, for example, "Indonesia Dangles Pro-Investor Incentives," *The Straits Times*, March 4, 2006; "Tussle Ahead over Labor Law," *The Jakarta Post*, March 29, 2006; Heri Susanto et al., "Back to Zero," *Tempo Magazine*, April 11–17, 2006. For a discussion of the attempted revision, see Benny Hari Juliawan, "Extracting Labor from Its Owner," *Critical Asian Studies* 42,1 (2010).

[17] For example, on March 24, about ten thousand workers protested in Bandung, five thousand in Cimahi, and thousands more in Bekasi. In the ensuing weeks, tens of thousands more protested in Semarang, Pasuruan, Jakarta, Medan, Surabaya, Riau, and South Sumatra. See "Bandung Workers Protest Revised Law," *The Jakarta Post*, March 24, 2006; "Workers Protest in Major Cities," *Jakarta Post*, April 4, 2006; "Workers Oppose Labor Law Changes," *The Jakarta Post*, March 28, 2006; Ridwan Max Sijabat, "Labor Rallies Spread, Business Counts Cost," *The Jakarta Post*, April 6, 2006.

[18] Salim Osman, "Jakarta Puts Off Changes to Labour Bill," *The Straits Times*, April 9, 2006; Susanto et al., "Back to Zero."

[19] Ridwan Max Sijabat, "Major Labor Unions Renew Opposition to Amendment," *The Jakarta Post*, April 19, 2006.

[20] "Around 100,000 Workers Take to the Streets for May Day," *The Jakarta Post*, May 1, 2006.

[21] "Police Fire Tear Gas as Workers Push Down Gate of House Building," *The Jakarta Post*, May 3, 2006.

Yudhoyono administration had largely given up.[22] Further attempts were made to change the law in 2011 and 2012, when the government again tried to revise the law, but pro-labor lawmakers reminded their colleagues of the body's decision not to revise the law in 2006, and it was struck from the legislative agenda both times.[23]

Despite these victories in the national legislature, the Manpower Act achieved less for workers than unions had hoped. Employers violated the provisions on contract labor and outsourcing with impunity, largely in order to evade paying the law's generous severance payments. The spread of contingent work in turn posed a serious threat to unions, since most of their members are permanent workers. Local governments tasked with enforcing labor laws looked the other way as employers fired permanent workers and replaced them with fixed-term contract workers or temporary workers from labor-supply companies.[24] In the view of unions, one problem was that the implementing legislation was full of loopholes, which allowed employers to violate the spirit of the law. They demanded that the Ministry of Manpower and Transmigration issue a new regulation that more clearly defined the types of work that could be outsourced.

To increase the pressure, hundreds of thousands of workers throughout the country returned to the streets in a national strike on October 3, 2012. They promised additional mass strikes if the government failed to respond.[25] Negotiations in the national tripartite forum were tense, with Apindo (Asosiasi Pengusaha Indonesia, Indonesian Employers Association) rejecting attempts to limit outsourcing to certain categories of work.[26] In mid-November, the ministry nevertheless issued a new regulation that restricted outsourcing to five types of work. Frustrated, Apindo

---

[22] Shawn Donnan, "Indonesia Drops Plan for Labour Reform," *Financial Times*, September 13, 2006.

[23] Sandro Gatra, "Agenda Revisi UU Ketenagakerjaan Dihapus," *Kompas*, December 16, 2011. In late 2011, sympathetic lawmakers leaked to unions the information about government plans to revise the law; in response, union representatives reminded legislators of what would happen if they cooperated with the government.

[24] Juliawan, "Extracting Labor from Its Owner"; Caraway, "Labor Rights in Asia"; Indrasari Tjandraningsih and Hari Nugroho, "The Flexibility Regime and Organised Labour in Indonesia," *Labour and Management in Development* 9 (2008); Indrasari Tjandraningsih, Hari Nugroho, and Surya Tjandra, *Buruh vs. Investasi? Mendorong Peraturan Perburuhan yang Adil di Indonesia* (Bandung: Akatiga, 2008).

[25] Fusk Sani Evani, Bayu Marhaenjati, and Arientha Primanita, "Indonesian Workers Demand an End to Outsourcing," *The Jakarta Globe*, October 4, 2012; Ben Otto and I Made Sentana, "Indonesia Strikers Turn Out in Force," *The Wall Street Journal*, October 4, 2012; "Pekerja Siapkan Aksi Lanjutan Tolak Outsourcing," *Hukumonline*, October 17, 2012; "Pekerja Berencana Gelar Kembali Demonstrasi Massal," *Hukumonline*, November 14, 2012.

[26] "Pekerja Berencana Gelar Kembali Demonstrasi Massal." Apindo is headed at the national level by Sofyan Wanandi, a prominent oligarch. It would be an overstatement to claim that Apindo represents oligarchs as a unified group, but its role as the voice of capital *vis-à-vis* labor should also not be underestimated. In the early transition years, Apindo was an ineffective organization. The main figures in Apindo were usually heads of personnel departments; prominent industrialists ignored it. But after a round of significant minimum wage increases and the issuance of a ministerial regulation in 2000 that increased firing costs, Sofyan Wanandi took over Apindo's reins and transformed it into a more effective voice for capital. Since then, Apindo has been a vocal advocate for the collective interests of capital in its confrontation with labor on matters of wages and other labor-related policies. It strives to limit the size of wage increases, to increase the flexibility of Indonesia's labor markets, and to oppose social welfare programs that require sizable contributions from employers—all of which play an obvious role in wealth defense.

threatened to withdraw from the national tripartite commission and filed a request for a review of the new regulation with the Supreme Court, claiming that it violated the Manpower Act.[27]

The battles over the Manpower Act demonstrate the means through which working-class actors have used their mobilizational power to achieve their national policy goals despite the unfavorable political terrain. This power comes from their capacity to shut down production and to mobilize in the streets, wreaking economic havoc in industrial areas and the capital. Crucially, their success depended not on constant mobilization but rather on the ability to exert pressure strategically and to make credible threats of future action if their demands were not met. Thus far, unions have not made revolutionary demands. Rather, they have fought for a fairer distribution of the pie and some decommodification of labor. Their ability to achieve these goals indisputably demonstrates that workers' mobilizational power is more influential in contemporary Indonesia than suggested by theorists of oligarchy.

Mobilizational Power and Local Executive Elections

Minimum wage negotiations and local executive elections vividly demonstrate the combination of inter-oligarch competition and strategic mobilization that have allowed unions to achieve some of their goals. Despite labor's fragmentation, candidates for local executive office have actively cultivated union support and made political deals with unions. In these deals, candidates have both promised and delivered policies that benefit workers. In this section, using case studies of local elections and minimum-wage-setting in two localities, Bekasi district and Tangerang municipality, we analyze how unions have been able to achieve these gains despite a political process that so dramatically disadvantages them. Before we present the case material, however, some background information about local executive elections and how it opens avenues for labor influence is necessary.

In 2006, Indonesia transformed its process of electing local executives from one of indirect to direct elections. Previously, the parties elected to the local legislature chose local executives, which meant that the selection of the district or municipal head was entirely the result of horse-trading among parties in the legislature, lubricated by copious amounts of cash. Soon after the onset of direct elections for local executive office, the Constitutional Court ruled in 2007 that independent candidates must be permitted to run for executive positions at the district, municipality, and provincial levels.[28] As a consequence of this ruling, local power brokers can now run for office without the backing of a political party, meaning that a larger number of candidates can contest elections. As before, parties often combine in coalitions to back pairs of candidates, but direct elections and the possibility of

---

[27] "Ancam Hengkang dari Tripartit, Apindo Dipanggil DPR," www.hukumonline.com/berita/baca/lt50ed5b2fc0c13/ancam-hengkang-dari-tripartit--apindo-dipanggil-dpr, January 9, 2013, accessed February 4, 2014; and "Pengusaha Harap MA Batalkan Permenaker *Outsourcing*," www.hukumonline.com/berita/baca/lt512f71998afd7/pengusaha-harap-ma-batalkan-permenaker-ioutsourcing-i, February 28, 2013, accessed February 4, 2014.

[28] Michael Buehler, "Decentralisation and Local Democracy in Indonesia: The Marginalisation of the Public Sphere," in *Problems of Democratisation in Indonesia: Elections, Institutions, and Society*, ed. Edward Aspinall and Marcus Mietzner (Singapore: Institute of Southeast Asian Studies, 2010).

independent candidacies have heightened competition in these elections, creating more of a winner-take-all approach.

Intense competition in these races has created incentives for candidates to develop links to organized constituencies rather than to party representatives in the legislature. In union-dense districts, an obvious constituency is labor. Deal making between unions and candidates for local executive office does not obviate the claim of theorists of oligarchy that material power is a determining factor in winning Indonesian elections. But candidates must find ways to tap into constituencies via local networks that can deliver votes. Here, it is also important to note that political elites in political parties and mass organizations—we follow Winters in designating elites as those with political influence that does not stem from material wealth—often provide an essential conduit between wealth and votes. Unions are one possible conduit between candidates and voters,[29] and their leverage increases as races become closer.

Of course, deal cutting between unions and candidates also fits well within analyses that emphasize Indonesia's transactional model of politics. The process that unions typically follow, however, differs from typical transactional politics because unions have insisted on policies that benefit workers alongside conditions that benefit unions organizationally, or union cadres personally (for example, support for training and secretariats, or raising honoraria for those who serve on tripartite committees). More often than not, the policy payoff at stake has been a significant increase in the minimum wage.

Mobilizing around the Minimum Wage

In Indonesia, minimum wage negotiations take place annually. Tripartite committees—comprising unions, employers, and the government—at the district (*kabupaten*) or municipality (*kota*) level set minimum wages. Raises for most workers depend more on these negotiations than on collective bargaining at the plant level. By law, minimum wages apply to all employees regardless of the size of the firm and the sector of employment, so the impact of this wage-setting mechanism extends beyond unionized workers.[30]

Localities vary in terms of how they determine worker representation on these committees, but typically the largest unions dominate. Which unions sit on the committees depends on the dominant industries in a particular locality. In most places, the federations affiliated with the former state-backed union, the Confederation of All-Indonesia Workers Unions (Konfederasi Serikat Pekerja Seluruh Indonesia, KSPSI), hold a number of seats on the committee, but they rarely have the majority of seats in union-dense areas. Unions affiliated with the Confederation of Indonesian Trade Unions (KSPI, Konfederasi Serikat Pekerja Indonesia)—including the powerful Metalworkers Federation (FSPMI, Federasi Serikat Pekerja Metal Indonesia) and the Chemical, Energy, and Mining Federation (KEP, Kimia, Energi dan Pertambangan)—as well as federations affiliated with the

---

[29] See Michael Buehler, "Elite Competition and Changing State–Society Relations: *Shari'a* Policymaking in Indonesia," this volume, pp. 157–75, for a discussion of the influence of Islamic elites in South Sulawesi, which provides another example of non-oligarchic influence.

[30] Of course, many employers violate the minimum wage laws, and they are more likely to do so if workers are not represented by a union.

Confederation of Indonesian Prosperous Workers Unions (KSBSI, Konfederasi Serikat Buruh Sejahtera Indonesia) and a number of independent federations, including the National Workers Union (SPN, Serikat Pekerja Nasional) and the Indonesian Prosperous Workers Union–92 (SBSI–92, Serikat Buruh Sejahtera Indonesia–92), are frequently represented. Some localities, such as the city of Medan in North Sumatra, also allow small unions to participate. Essential to labor's success in these negotiations is presenting a unified labor voice. Unions that sit on the committees, therefore, usually coordinate prior to the annual round of negotiations to agree on a targeted wage and negotiating tactics.

The process of setting a minimum wage creates multiple opportunities for horse-trading within the committee structure and with executive officers at the *kabupaten/kota* and provincial levels, both for members of Apindo, who can offer financial rewards for a favorable outcome, and for unions, which can threaten to bring their members out into the streets. Given that labor and capital seldom agree on wages, the government's vote on tripartite committees is decisive. Government representatives on the committee are drawn from a variety of local offices (for example, Manpower and Trade and Industry), but all are accountable to the district or city head, not to the local legislature. Knowing that they are unlikely to convince each other, both Apindo and the unions concentrate on convincing government representatives to side with them. Apindo's strength lies behind the scenes, where money can be used to influence government representatives. Unions, knowing this, typically mount protests warning the government that there will be more trouble if wage increases are too stingy. The number and intensity of the protests depends on the extent to which unions think the government is accommodating their wishes. Ultimately, the district head or mayor makes the final call in the form of a minimum wage recommendation, which is forwarded to the provincial governor for approval. There, unions and employers have one last chance to affect the outcome. If unions are disappointed with the results at the local level, the governor typically becomes the target of protests.

Minimum Wages and Local Executive Contests

When wage negotiations take place close to the date of a local executive election (*pilkada*), they present an opportunity for unions to exert political pressure on local executives, especially when candidates expect a tight race. While the links between the actions of particular elected officials and particular policy outcomes are largely illegible in Indonesia, this is not the case when it comes to the minimum wage. Given the executive's control over the local budget and its key role in determining minimum wages, it is not surprising that wage negotiations more often than not become the focus of pre-election bargaining—there are definite incentives for candidates for executive office to trade commitments on wages for political support.

Although unions have yet to prove their capacity to deliver votes consistently, candidates for local executive positions have two reasons for cutting deals with them in union-dense districts. First, the specter of a tight executive race encourages incumbents to woo workers, who are unlikely to vote for an incumbent who refuses to sign off on a substantial wage hike. Minimum-wage-setting is an issue that union members follow closely; the process happens at the same time every year and the results are highly anticipated. The effects of the policy are immediately apparent to workers. If wage increases are disappointing, voters know whom to blame: the mayor or district head in the region concerned. But if the increases are healthy, workers may remember the fatter paycheck when they enter a voting booth. Second, in union-dense districts where unions have proven their capacity to paralyze industrial areas with massive actions, mayors and district and provincial heads have an interest in accommodating some wage demands to preserve industrial peace. Even if the candidate does not deliver in the end, the candidate may buy a period free of industrial conflict while unions give the newly elected executive a chance to fulfill campaign promises.

The links between minimum wage negotiations and *pilkada* are nowhere more evident than in Bekasi and Tangerang, two major industrial areas adjacent to Jakarta. To the east, in the province of West Java, Bekasi has an industrial base dominated by heavy industries such as chemicals and metal. Tangerang, to the west in Banten province, has a lighter industrial base, with the production of footwear and textiles predominating. In late 2011 and early 2012, minimum-wage-setting in both localities involved a direct confrontation between employers and unions. In both, unions emerged victorious. Although the chronologies vary slightly, in both cases unions utilized their mobilizational power and exploited inter-oligarch competition in the political arena to achieve significant increases in minimum wages.

In Bekasi, negotiations for the 2012 minimum wages took place in the last quarter of 2011, just months before the *pilkada* for Bekasi district. The incumbent district head, Prosperous Justice Party (PKS, Partai Keadilan Sejahtera) member Sa'dudin, was up for reelection in March. Facing what looked to be a close election in this union-dense district, Sa'dudin made a last ditch effort to win labor votes. Although he had not been an especially close ally to labor during his tenure, his administration supported workers in the 2012 minimum wage negotiations. Ignoring the protests of Apindo, which walked out of the negotiations and refused to sign the committee's wage recommendation, Sa'dudin forwarded a minimum monthly wage recommendation of Rp. 1,491,866 (US$157)—the figure demanded by unions—to the governor, Ahmad Heryawan, who, like Sa'dudin, was a member of PKS. The governor approved the district head's recommendation.

Having lost the battle locally, Apindo went to the courts, where money mattered more than votes. Suspecting that Apindo would bribe the judges, unions mounted a series of protests, with the largest occurring on January 27, 2012, after the court in Bandung ruled against them. They shut down production in all seven of Bekasi's industrial zones and blocked the toll road between Jakarta and Bandung. Proximity to Jakarta and the scale of economic disruption captured the attention of the national media and central government. In effect, workers succeeded in shifting the conflict to a third arena, from the courts to national politics, where their mobilizational power could be exerted more effectively. The central government quickly moved to facilitate a settlement. Unions agreed to accept a tiny reduction of Rp. 1,000 to the minimum wage set by the tripartite committee, a face-saving gesture for Apindo. Once again, workers had prevailed.

The *pilkada* took place almost immediately after the massive protests in January 2012. A number of candidates approached unions asking for their support. Despite Sa'dudin's support for unions in the minimum wage negotiations, none of them opted to back his candidacy. Given his weak track record on labor issues in the district, they interpreted his siding with unions late the previous year as an insincere attempt to capture worker votes. Unions therefore looked to strike deals with other candidates. One union, SPN, formalized its backing of PDI-P in a political contract that promised operational support for the union if the PDI-P candidates won.[31] Bekasi's largest federation, FSPMI, was reluctant to risk backing a losing candidate, fearing that the winner would punish them once elected. Since no clear leader had emerged in public opinion polls, FSPMI hedged its bets by adopting a two-track strategy. While it placed union activists on the campaigns of all of the candidates, behind the scenes it concluded an unwritten political deal with the candidate who ultimately won, Golkar's Neneng Hasanah Yasin, and her Democrat Party (PD, Partai Demokrat) running mate, Rohim Mintareja. No official announcement or written commitment was issued by either side, but union leaders agreed to speak favorably about her to members, and Neneng indicated that she would be amenable to issuing a moratorium on outsourcing, tightening up labor law enforcement, and building a more permanent home for Omah Buruh, a makeshift gathering place for workers that FSPMI had erected in one of Bekasi's industrial zones. In the subsequent minimum wage negotiations for 2013, the government sided with unions and signed off on a minimum wage increase of nearly 35 percent.

In Bekasi, then, we see that an incumbent facing an imminent reelection bid tried to win labor's support by backing unions in the minimum wage negotiations. Labor's victory, however, might have been undone if unions had not again exerted mobilizational power. Having lost at the local level, Apindo tried to shift the arena to the courts. The lawsuit provoked massive protests that led to the intervention of the national government, which also sided with workers. These mobilizations, in turn, demonstrated to all of the *pilkada* candidates that unions were a force to be dealt with in Bekasi, and the eventual winner reached a tacit political deal with them.

The means through which workers secured a sizable increase in the minimum wage for 2012 in Tangerang was more serpentine. But, once again, the decisive factors were intense political competition and massive, disruptive protests. In Tangerang, the *pilkada* preceded the 2012 wage negotiations, which also took place in the last quarter of 2011. In this case, it was the gubernatorial race in Banten in October 2011 that shaped the outcomes of the wage-setting process. In the gubernatorial race, the two top candidates were the mayor of Tangerang, Wahidin, and the incumbent, Ratu Atut Chosiyah.[32] In exchange for support in the 2008 mayoral race, Wahidin had made commitments that Tangerang's minimum wages would not be lower than Jakarta's, that he would work toward establishing sectoral minimum wages in the city, and would take action on outsourcing. Although Wahidin had largely accommodated these demands, the large unions that sat on the provincial tripartite committee in Banten province ultimately backed Atut in the gubernatorial race. Unions chose her for pragmatic reasons. They surmised that,

---

[31] This deal was of little political consequence because SPN has few members in Bekasi. The agreement was shepherded by Waras, who had been expelled from SPN for running a labor outsourcing business. The existence of this political contract was leaked to the press, causing much embarrassment, since it was perceived to be a crass attempt by local SPN leaders to feather their nest by exchanging votes for an organizational payoff. Even so, the striking of the deal demonstrates that political candidates are eager to secure support from unions.

[32] Atut is the daughter of local strongman Tubagus Chasan Sochib, a feared and respected martial arts champion whose family's business and political interests run deep in the province. Although Chasan Sochib himself is now deceased, his family continues to run Banten in classic strongman fashion. Atut and a number of her close family members are members of Golkar, but she has allies in all the major parties, most of which formally supported her candidacy in 2011. In addition, several other members of the clan have held executive or legislative positions.

given her strong provincial network and incumbency advantage, she was the candidate most likely to win. Many of the large unions that sat on the provincial tripartite council subsequently signed a political contract with Atut. In this agreement, concluded in May 2011—prior to the election—the incumbent governor, Atut, pledged to side with them when unions and Apindo split during wage negotiations.

In the 2012 negotiations, which followed soon after Atut's victory, Tangerang municipality's tripartite wage council agreed to a minimum monthly wage of Rp. 1,379,000 (US$145), which the governor approved. With the governor's approval, the wage-setting process should have ended for the year. But when neighboring Jakarta announced that its minimum wage would be set at Rp. 1,529,000, an alliance of smaller unions that did not participate in the wage council demanded that Wahidin raise the municipality's minimum wage, since he had promised that it would not be lower than Jakarta's. However, union representatives on the municipal wage council were reluctant to ask for more money. Their unions, which dominated both the municipal and the regional tripartite committees, had prioritized negotiations for sectoral minimum wages, which are set above the general minimum wage. They had finally succeeded in setting sectoral minimum wages in the 2012 negotiations, but the price for doing so was that they had accepted a relatively small increase in the general minimum wage. Small unions, which benefited less from sectoral wages, were unhappy with this trade-off, and their dissatisfaction ultimately drove them to the streets.

Politicians, meanwhile, had overestimated the extent to which the labor representatives on the wage council spoke for Tangerang's diverse unions, and the deal unraveled when the smaller unions began to pressure Wahidin to raise the minimum wage to the same level as Jakarta's. They mounted protests in front of his office, even at his residence. By this time, Wahidin knew that his attempt to contest in court the outcome of the gubernatorial election had failed, and that he would have to finish his term as mayor. Possibly out of spite, Wahidin issued a new minimum wage recommendation, setting it at the same level as Jakarta's, and sent it to the governor for approval. In doing so, he redirected the swarm of protestors outside his office to Atut's provincial headquarters in Serang. The large unions remained reluctant to renege on their promise to Atut that they would assure labor peace if she sided with unions during wage negotiations. But by this time, they could no longer exert control over their members, who joined in protests against the governor.

Workers by the tens of thousands made their way to Atut's office by motorcycle, causing a complete shutdown of the toll road on December 29, 2011. Facing a membership revolt, the large unions now urged Atut to agree to the higher minimum wage. When the alliance of smaller unions threatened to mount further protests at her inauguration, she reluctantly agreed to raise the minimum wage. But the saga was to continue. As in Bekasi, after losing in local politics, Apindo tried to shift the conflict to the courts. In response, workers from all unions in Tangerang returned to the streets. As in Bekasi, these protests attracted the attention of the national government. Representatives of Yudhoyono's administration persuaded Apindo to withdraw its lawsuit and to accept the revised minimum wage, which it finally did in early February 2012.

In both Tangerang and Bekasi, then, tight elections led candidates for local executive positions to enter into political bargains with unions in which candidates promised support in wage-setting in exchange for a combination of political support and labor peace. In this context, labor's mobilizational power had two critical effects. First, it is this power that captured the attention of candidates in the first place, providing evidence that workers were a significant political force and could unleash mayhem when vital interests were threatened. Second, when executives were reluctant to support unions, or when employers tried to shift the conflict outside of local politics, unions effectively mobilized large numbers of protesters to increase the pressure on local executives or to persuade the national government to intervene on the side of labor. It was this combination of openings provided by political competition and unions' ability to mobilize in the streets that was, in the end, decisive.

These case studies illustrate two dynamics that we believe point to ways that oligarchic theory could sharpen its analysis of contemporary Indonesian politics. First, the local minimum wage struggles in Bekasi and Tangerang show that inter-oligarch conflict—a dynamic that is highlighted in both versions of the oligarchy thesis—provides political space that working-class actors can exploit to their advantage. Theorists of oligarchy have thus far focused primarily on the role that inter-oligarch contests for power play in the oligarchs' efforts to defend their wealth from lateral threats (from other oligarchs) and threats from above (from the state). These dynamics are undoubtedly crucial to an understanding of Indonesia's politics. But so, too, are the ways that this bruising political competition opens avenues for political bargaining by materially disadvantaged groups with strong mobilizational capacities. This political bargaining is substantively important because it illuminates a facet of oligarchic politics under-analyzed by theorists of oligarchy. It demonstrates that, in order to capture the state, oligarchs or the parties that they support may have to form alliances with organized constituencies from below. The need to capture these constituencies, in turn, has implications for the evolution of oligarchic politics.

Second, these case studies also suggest that the mobilizational power of unions has been stronger than anticipated by theorists of oligarchy in their commentary on post-Suharto Indonesia. The labor movement has found ways to mobilize effectively despite its fragmentation into many competing unions; it has sustained a steady stream of mobilizations for many years and secured significant policy victories. Key to the ability of unions to coalesce effectively is the annual rite of minimum wage negotiations, which has led to the formation of networks of unions at the local level. Many different unions sit on wage committees, and cooperation in this forum has facilitated the development of local and even regional networks of unions. In Tangerang, there are even rival networks that sometimes work at cross-purposes, but also come together when employers threaten to undercut policy victories, as occurred when Apindo challenged the increased minimum wage in court. These networks generally lie dormant for most of the year but are revived annually during wage negotiations.

Importantly, unions' exercise of mobilizational power has not depended on workers being in a state of constant mobilization. Instead, it has leveraged periodic massive actions that demonstrate the credible threat of further disruptive actions. In other words, unions did not have to exercise constantly their collective mobilizational power in order to achieve these gains; rather, they used mobilization selectively and strategically both to demonstrate their collective power and to make threats of further disruptive mass protest credible. These credible threats of future mobilizations in turn caused executives to seek out political deals to stop or to prevent mass protest. Mobilizational power, then, has been critical to labor's policy victories at both the national and local levels. This mobilizational power, in turn, has attracted the attention of some of Indonesia's political parties.

ENGAGING IN ELECTORAL POLITICS

There is also a demonstrable link between the mobilizational power of unions and party recruitment of union leaders as candidates in legislative elections. Political parties began to approach leading union figures as the 2004 legislative elections drew near.[33] Their interest intensified in the lead-up to the 2009 legislative elections, when large parties like PKS, Golkar, PDI-P, and the United Development Party (PPP, Partai Persatuan Pembangunan) wooed trade unionists in the hope of securing the labor vote in union-dense districts. Numerous smaller or newer parties, including the Great Indonesia Movement Party (Gerindra, Partai Gerakan Indonesia Raya) and the People's Conscience Party (Hanura, Partai Hati Nurani Rakyat), have also courted prominent union cadres. One party, PKS, concluded agreements with two of Indonesia's largest unions, FSPMI and SPN, under which they agreed to place numerous union cadres as legislative candidates at the *kabupaten/kota*, provincial, and national levels.[34]

Although initially suspicious of what they call "practical politics,"[35] within a few short years a number of influential union leaders had embraced this model of political engagement. The reasons why unions have agreed to partner with political parties are obvious. Political parties are central in most democracies, since they are the main vehicles through which political actors compete in elections. In Indonesia, political parties are especially powerful gatekeepers because its electoral system prohibits independent candidacies from running for legislative office and for the presidency. Individuals who wish to run for these offices must therefore do so through a political party. It is possible to establish new parties, but onerous registration requirements make it difficult, and electoral thresholds mean that most first-time entrants are excluded after competing in just one election. In the absence of an effective labor party, unions have thus had little choice but to turn to mainstream players.

The question is, then, why did parties reach out—however tentatively—to unions? It goes without saying that in Indonesia, as in all democracies, those seeking to control government offices must win elections. Vast sums of cash are a necessary condition for competing in Indonesia's elections, but money alone does not guarantee victory. Parties must therefore find the means, in addition to money, to persuade voters to select particular candidates. Unsurprisingly, parties therefore also

---

[33] For examples of this cooperation, see Michele Ford and Surya Tjandra, "The Local Politics of Industrial Relations: Surabaya and Batam Compared," paper presented at the Indonesia Council Open Conference, Melbourne, September 24–25, 2007.

[34] PKS signed a formal political contract with SPN. Its agreement with FSPMI neither bound the union exclusively to the party nor was backed up by a formal contract. The deal with FSPMI nevertheless resulted in the placing of several trade union candidates with the party in Tangerang municipality and elsewhere, including West Java, Banten, and the Riau Islands.

[35] Michele Ford, "Economic Unionism and Labour's Poor Performance in Indonesia's 1999 and 2004 Elections," in *Reworking Work: Proceedings of the Nineteenth Conference of the Association of Industrial Relations Academics of Australia and New Zealand, February 9–11, Sydney, 2005, Volume 1 Refereed Papers*, ed. Marian Baird, Rae Cooper, and Mark Westcott (Sydney: AIRAANZ, 2005).

consider features of candidates that may broaden their appeal to voters, for example, ethnicity or religion. Cultivating working-class voters has the potential to both expand the party's appeal and to tap into one of the largest organized constituencies in Indonesia. Doing so can help to defeat other parties in the electoral arena.

In Thailand, Thaksin created a mass constituency through populist programs and has thrashed the competition ever since. Indonesia's parties have not made serious efforts to replicate this strategy. The courting of labor has not been accompanied by the development of a coherent policy platform that appealed to workers or to poor voters. Given that labor had not proven its ability to deliver votes, the tentativeness of party outreach to unions is understandable. Still, where parties anticipated tight races and where unions had significant membership, some party leaders believed that workers might deliver the small margins of victory necessary to win seats in local, provincial, and national races. Parties were therefore strategic and selectively placed union cadres on their lists in major industrial areas. Even PKS, the party that most assertively courted labor in the lead-up to the 2009 election, offered only a small number of spots on their slates to union candidates.

This reluctance reflects the thorny internal politics of candidate selection. Most union activists are not party cadres, so the decision to include them on a party ticket means fewer spots for loyal party members. Under a closed party list system, the order of candidates on the ballot paper determines which candidates receive seats in local and national legislative contest. Parties can thus accommodate the contending imperatives of broadening their appeal and rewarding loyal cadres by allocating lousy spots (*nomor sepatu*) on the party ticket to trade-union candidates. Under such a system, labor candidates can deliver votes to the party without themselves being elected. In Bekasi district, for example, the major parties only offered cadres from FSPMI what were expected to be losing slots on their tickets in 2009.[36] Even those with long associations with a party were treated in this way. Waras, a union activist and PDI-P cadre in Bekasi, stood for a seat in the provincial parliament; he was also allocated a losing slot on the ticket. The same pattern was evident in Tangerang, where the candidates from KSPSI, FSPMI, and SPN who ran at the district/municipality and provincial levels for PDI-P and PKS were all given *nomor sepatu*.[37]

This established strategy was put at risk in early 2009. Just before the legislative elections, the Constitutional Court overturned the closed-list system, ruling that the number of votes received by an individual candidate rather than his or her place on the ticket would determine the winners of electoral races.[38] Parties still controlled the lists, but their strategy of recruiting "vote-getters" and placing them below party cadres on the ticket was now fraught. Popular figures who attracted votes might be elected rather than party cadres. Although none of the union candidates won, in Tangerang some received substantial shares of the vote in their districts, and in

[36] It is for this reason that the branch decided to ignore the union's national-level push to mount candidates. Eight FSPMI members decided to run in Bekasi municipality despite this, but they ran for small parties.

[37] Elsewhere in Banten, a former high-level KSBSI official, Idin Rosidin, ran as a Gerindra candidate for a seat in the national legislature. In what was Gerindra's first national election, Idin nearly won a seat.

[38] Buehler, "Decentralisation and Local Democracy in Indonesia."

doing so jeopardized the chances of those higher up on the ticket.[39] Many union candidates suspected that the parties that had sponsored their candidacies responded to this unforeseen development by bribing electoral officials to reallocate some of their votes to candidates higher up on the list. For example, based on monitoring at the polling booths, an SPN candidate believes she had enough votes to win, but that votes were shifted to another PKS candidate at the regional electoral office, where she was not permitted to have her own monitors.[40]

The shift to an open-list system had potentially fundamental consequences for the ability of outsiders to be elected, and therefore may well alter the closed nature of Indonesia's political system. Its impact in 2009 was mediated by the extent to which parties were prepared to support their "external" candidates during the campaign phase and by the parties' apparent practice of illegally shifting votes between party candidates at the district electoral commission offices. Labor's inexperience in electoral politics, which requires a different sort of mobilization than mass protests, also contributed to its poor showing in 2009. Unions learned a great deal from that experience. Despite their massive losses, they were eager to give electoral politics another shot in 2014. And, once again, parties lined up to place union candidates on their slates.

CONCLUSION

Theorists of oligarchy have underestimated not only the labor movement's capacity to engage in effective and sustained collective action but also the links between collective action, policy outcomes, and the electoral strategies of Indonesia's power-holders. It is true that Indonesia's trade unions remain weak, fragmented, and divided in their views on the role organized labor should play in the political arena. But contrary to the expectations derived from oligarchic theory, trade unions have carved out a domain of influence in Indonesia's polity even in this weakened state. Mobilization in the streets—or a credible threat thereof—has forced politicians at the local and national level to make concessions to the labor agenda. Mass protests in union-dense districts have not only pushed local executives to support increases in the minimum wage but also thwarted employer efforts to challenge these increases in the courts. At the national level, the threat of sustained mass disruption in the capital has forced legislators and the government to concede to important policy demands put forth by labor.

The kind of mobilization needed in the streets is, of course, not the kind of mobilization required for electoral success. The individualizing logic of the ballot box demands a qualitatively different sort of mobilization, one that rests more on persuasion. In the Indonesian context, the importance of money politics, the varied political orientations of workers, and the absence of a significant party that advocates

---

[39] This development was not confined to the local level. The president of FSPMI, Said Iqbal, nearly won a seat for PKS in the national People's Representative Council despite resistance from local party cadres; he stood for election in the Riau Archipelago, the province where the Batam industrial zone is located. For a detailed discussion of FSPMI's engagement with the 2009 electoral campaign in Batam, see Michele Ford, "Learning by Doing: Trade Unions and Electoral Politics in Batam, 2004–2009," *South-East Asia Research* (in press).

[40] Party cadres admitted during interviews that "pendudukan'—the transfer of votes from candidates low down on the list to the party's preferred candidates—might have occurred in some 2009 races.

a social democratic agenda make this task extremely challenging for unions. Nevertheless, unions have experienced a degree of success in their attempts to influence local executive elections, which lend themselves to a combination of horse-trading and mass protest. As demonstrated in this essay, local executive candidates—many of them minor oligarchs in their own right—have proven keen to cultivate labor when facing tight electoral races, offering redistributive policies to unions in exchange for their political support. And even though parties have sought to use unionists as "vote-getters" and offered them little in return, the need for oligarchs to win elections has created new space for organized labor to begin to insert its agenda into the political realm. The incremental effects of these challenges to the distribution of resources are under-theorized in analyses of Indonesia's oligarchy, which mistakenly dismiss them as being inconsequential to the main game.

The critique presented here is not simply a matter of our saying that theorists of Indonesia's oligarchy "do not pay enough attention to the part [we] study" in "the division of labor that is academia."[41] These theorists assert that the political realm is an important realm of wealth defense—in the case of Hadiz and Robison, for instance, the authors assert that it is, in fact, integral to the construction of the oligarchy itself. It is thus incumbent on them to ensure that their theory is sufficiently robust to explain not just transitions *between* different modes of oligarchy, but the nuances *within* them, in this case the extent to which the inherent contradictions within the political system create fissures within the oligarchy that can be exploited by marginalized actors incrementally over time. Without such an engagement, oligarchic theory not only ignores important empirical developments in contemporary Indonesia—the emergence of a dynamic working-class movement—but also undercuts its capacity to account for forces that provoke transformations in oligarchic politics. Thus, just as we cannot understand contemporary labor politics without some engagement with oligarchic theory, oligarchic theorists cannot possibly fully understand the mechanics of wealth defense and the forces that might transform it without a more serious consideration of the opportunities that inter-oligarch conflict provide for working-class actors to claim a bigger share of the economic pie.

---

[41] Winters, "Oligarchy and Democracy in Indonesia," p. 30.

ELITE COMPETITION AND CHANGING STATE–SOCIETY RELATIONS: *SHARI'A* POLICYMAKING IN INDONESIA

Michael Buehler[1]

Since the New Order collapsed in 1998, scholars have tried to characterize the "deep architecture" of politics in Indonesia.[2] This search for patterns in the accumulation and exercise of power has centered around the question of whether *ancien régime* figures continue to dominate politics or whether groups that were marginalized during the dictatorship have gained influence. Vedi Hadiz, Richard Robison, and Jeffrey Winters, who argue that a small group of wealthy individuals rooted in the New Order regime continue to define politics in contemporary Indonesia, have made an important contribution to this debate.[3] This "oligarchy thesis" has been influential for many scholars of Indonesian democracy, yet its focus on wealth and material power has led it to neglect the fundamental role of the state in Indonesian politics.

This chapter challenges the oligarchy thesis, arguing that power continues to reside within Indonesia's state and political institutions in the post-New Order period. What is more, the overwhelming majority of figures populating these institutions represent "old interests," as the oligarchy thesis suggests. Yet, rather

[1] Thanks to Iqra Anugrah, Endah Asnari, Dani Muhtada, Ronnie Nataatmadja, Muhammad Said Mallari, and Ina Parenrengi for their research assistance; to the Equality Development and Globalization Studies (EDGS) Program at Northwestern University for providing a grant for me to conduct research in Indonesia; as well as to Michele Ford, Tom Pepinsky, Elizabeth Pisani, Danny Unger, and an anonymous reviewer for helpful comments on earlier drafts. All errors are my own.

[2] Edward Aspinall, "A Nation in Fragments: Patronage and Neoliberalism in Contemporary Indonesia," *Critical Asian Studies* 45,1 (2013): 27–54.

[3] Richard Robison and Vedi Hadiz, *Reorganising Power in Indonesia: The Politics of Oligarchy in an Age of Markets* (London: Routledge, 2004); Vedi R. Hadiz, *Localising Power in Post-Authoritarian Indonesia: A Southeast Asia Perspective* (Stanford, CA: Stanford University Press, 2010); Jeffrey A. Winters, *Oligarchy* (Cambridge: Cambridge University Press, 2011); Jeffrey A. Winters, "Oligarchy and Democracy in Indonesia," this volume, pp. 11–33.

than being "oligarchs," these figures are better described as "state elites."[4] Elite theory has shown that *some* elites are indeed defined by their relationship to the means of production. Others, however, have become elites as a result of their access to other power resources, such as official positions in the government.[5] In the Indonesian case, many figures consequential in politics, especially at the subnational level, are *political elites* rather than oligarchs. In other words, these figures resemble a Millsian "power elite" that derives strength from the commanding positions they hold within institutions rather than from material wealth.[6]

Drawing on insights from elite theory,[7] I argue that *changing relations among the elites that dominate the state apparatus* have *subsequently* altered state–society relations in contemporary Indonesia. Recruitment, promotion, and retirement mechanisms for state elites during the New Order were all oriented towards the central government and therefore ultimately regulated by President Suharto.[8] By controlling competition from within the regime (horizontal competition), as well as suppressing discontent and challenges from below (vertical competition), the New Order regime created and maintained a certain unity among state elites.[9] With their political survival at stake after the collapse of the dictatorship in 1998, state elites hastily adopted various institutional changes, such as the introduction of free elections, the decentralization of power, and reforms of the party system. These changes created competition *among* state elites. To find allies in their battles with one another, they subsequently started to "reach out" and "reach down" in the political arena.[10] As a result, state elites have become much more dependent upon "society" than during the New Order.[11] At the same time, state elites continue to *mediate* the influence of societal groups and

---

[4] I use the plural "state elites" to indicate the fractionalization of New Order elites since 1998 rather than to suggest diversity in the socio-economic backgrounds of these figures.

[5] Eric Carlton, *The Few and the Many: A Typology of Elites* (Brookfield, VT: Scolar Press 1996), pp. 4–21. Hadiz and Robison have repeatedly emphasized that they understand the Indonesian "politico–economic oligarchy" as a *distinct* class whose control over the means of production has social and political consequences. See Vedi Hadiz and Richard Robison, "The Political Economy of Oligarchy and the Reorganization of Power in Indonesia," this volume, pp. 35–56. In contrast, Winters has not only a more individualistic understanding of oligarchs, but, in his view, oligarchs derive their power simply from control over material sources and not because they control a certain mode of production. See Winters, *Oligarchy*, p. 12.

[6] See C. Wright Mills, *The Power Elite* (New York, NY: Oxford University Press, 1956), pp. 259–62. My understanding of elites is congruent with that of Winters, who says that elites emerge whenever coercive power, mobilizational power, official positions, and/or political rights are "…distributed in highly exclusive or concentrated ways." Winters, "Oligarchy and Democracy in Indonesia," p. 13.

[7] Richard Lachmann and Nelson Pichardo, "Making History from Above and Below: Elite and Popular Perspectives," *Social Science History* 18,4 (1994): 503.

[8] Ross McLeod, "The Struggle to Regain Effective Government under Democracy in Indonesia," *Bulletin of Indonesian Economic Studies* 43,1 (2005): 367–86.

[9] Michael Malley, "Resources Distribution, State Coherence, and the Changing Level of Political Centralization in Indonesia, 1950–1997" (PhD dissertation, University of Wisconsin-Madison, 1999), pp. 145–95.

[10] Michael Buehler, "Local Elite Reconfiguration in Post-New Order Indonesia: The 2005 Election of District Government Heads in South Sulawesi," *Review of Indonesian and Malaysian Affairs* 41,1 (2007): 119–47.

[11] Loren Ryter, "Their Moment in the Sun: The New Indonesian Parliamentarians from the Old OKP," in *State of Authority: The State in Society in Indonesia*, ed. Gerry van Klinken and Joshua Barker (Ithaca, NY: Cornell Southeast Asia Program Publications, 2009), p. 215.

interests as a consequence of their dominant position within the state and political institutions. I argue that the new dynamics among state elites have made them receptive to the demands of societal groups, *but only if* these groups provide resources that help those elites gain and maintain power in Indonesian politics. Resources that elites value include access to power brokers who can mobilize the electorate, the accumulation of financial means to pay for their political battles, and coercive power.

In order to illustrate this argument, I analyze the adoption of Islamic law (*shari'a*) in South Sulawesi since 1998. I operationalize "political influence" as influence over policymaking at the local level for two reasons. First, local politics are the "first frontier" for studying the concentration and dispersion of state power because the exchange between the state and society is more direct in this stratum than at the national level.[12] Hence, a focus on local politics can identify at an early stage the mechanisms through which boundaries between the state and society are created, sustained, and restructured. Second, some societal groups try to change the broad legal or institutional structures of a polity, such as the scope of participatory rights or the rules for party formation. However, societal groups are usually more effective at influencing politics at an intermediate level, namely by shaping public policy.[13]

I focus on *shari'a* policymaking because the adoption of Islamic law in Indonesia is one of the few tangible policy trends evident in a political system defined by clientelist rather than programmatic politics.[14] In addition, the discussion over the proper role of Islamic law in politics is one of the most enduring ideological fault lines in Indonesian politics. Dating back to the constitutional debates in 1945, the *shari'a* debate allows for a longitudinal comparison of the political influence of different groups before and after 1998. Moreover, the groups traditionally fighting over the adoption of Islamic law have always been rooted in a relatively clearly defined class of peasant entrepreneurs and traders of non-aristocratic origin situated outside the state.[15] Local *shari'a* policymaking is therefore a good indicator for how changing relations within the state subsequently shape relations between the state and society. Finally, South Sulawesi provides an excellent vantage point from which to examine my two arguments because the number of *shari'a* regulations adopted there is relatively high compared to other provinces.

The chapter begins with my analysis of the major themes within the oligarchy thesis and in the literature that has sought to challenge it, arguing that—just as the explanatory power of the oligarchy thesis is limited by its inattention to the power resources of New Order figures in the political arena—voluntarist and collectivist

---

[12] Daniel Elazar, "The Local Dimension in Israeli Government and Politics," in *Local Government in Israel*, ed. Daniel Elazar and Chaim Kalchheim (Lanham, MD: University of America Press, 1988), pp. 3–40.

[13] Edwin Amenta, Neal Caren, Elizabeth Chiarello, and Yang Su, "The Political Consequences of Social Movements," *Annual Review of Sociology* 36 (2010): 290.

[14] Islamic law has been described as a "total discourse" that includes religious, legal, moral, and economic rules and regulations. See Brinkley Messick, *The Calligraphic State* (Berkeley, CA, and London: University of California Press, 1993), p. 3. I confine my analysis to the local regulations (*peraturan daerah/ surat bupati*) with a religious connotation.

[15] Ruth McVey, "Review: Islam Explained," *Pacific Affairs* 54,2 (1981): 272; Christian Pelras, "Patron–Client Ties among the Bugis and Makassarese of South Sulawesi," in *Authority and Enterprise among the Peoples of South Sulawesi*, ed. Roger Tol, Kees van Dijk, and Greg Acciaioli (Leiden: KITLV Press, 2000), p. 38.

challenges to it lack the explanatory power of an approach that privileges the dynamics within the political elite. Turning to the case study, the chapter shows first how the power of political elites is determined by a concentration of non-economic power rather than of material wealth. It then provides evidence of the increasingly competitive nature of relations among state elites since 1998, and of how this heightened competition has *subsequently* allowed *some* societal groups that were politically impotent during the New Order to gain influence. The conclusion returns to the broader theme of changing state–society relations in post-New Order Indonesia.

OLIGARCHY AND BEYOND

If we are to engage with the oligarchy thesis, it is important to isolate its key questions, concepts, and hypotheses. There are important differences between the work of Hadiz and Robison and that of Winters, which makes a structured critique of the "oligarchy thesis" challenging. However, there are elements where their approaches clearly overlap. First, they agree that economic conditions have long defined politics in Indonesia. Winters argues that the New Order regime provided a formidable tool for a small number of individuals to protect (and expand) their wealth and income.[16] While defining the power base of these individuals in purely material terms, he acknowledges that strategies of wealth defense commonly include interventions in the political realm. In Hadiz and Robison's version of the oligarchy thesis, the accumulation of wealth in Indonesia occurs primarily through "control of public institutions."[17] As a consequence, "politico–economic oligarchs" directly occupy bureaucratic and political posts from where they control access to the state as well as nodal points in state–business relations.

Second, Hadiz and Robison argue that this constellation of power survived the end of the regime because the demise of the New Order resembled a palace revolt rather than a social revolution. According to these authors, since class relations established during the New Order were not affected by the collapse of the dictatorship, it was possible for the small group of people who had accumulated financial and political power to reconstitute their power within democratic institutions after 1998.[18] This also explains why the political forces of the preceding regime are able to define the way state authority and social power is transformed within the new institutions of democracy. Similarly, Winters argues that the end of the New Order regime marked a change from a sultanistic oligarchy to an untamed ruling oligarchy; in other words, a change only in how oligarchs relate to one another.

Third, new wealth and income defense strategies required in the post-1998 context have shaped politics. According to Winters, the demise of Suharto has forced oligarchs, in the name of wealth defense, to become more directly involved in

---

[16] Winters, *Oligarchy*, pp. 140–1.

[17] Hadiz and Robison, "The Political Economy of Oligarchy," p. 37. Boudreau also argues that New Order interests control access to the political system. However, he talks about "elites" rather than "oligarchs" and does not think that economic conditions define political dynamics. See Vincent Boudreau, "Elections, Repression and Authoritarian Survival in Post-transition Indonesia and the Philippines," *Pacific Review* 22,2 (2009): 233–53.

[18] Hadiz and Robison, "The Political Economy of Oligarchy."

politics. In a context where "being an oligarch is closely intertwined with governing," they have thus morphed into "electoral ruling" oligarchs.[19] In the electoral arena, their great wealth has allowed them to "play a central role in shaping who can contend for office."[20] As a consequence, "Indonesians get to choose among options that are strongly oligarchically determined."[21] Hadiz and Robison, meanwhile, argue that because the established fabric that had connected state authority, political power, and economic wealth remained largely intact, genuinely new parties are either absent or have been co-opted into the oligarchy.[22] And since oligarchs dominate the political arena, there is no room for a "progressive civil society," for Indonesian civil society is fragmented and lacks the mobilizational capacity to mount an effective challenge against oligarchic rule.[23] Hence, organizations and interests situated outside the state are unable to impose their will on the state and its officials and oligarchs are free to pursue a political agenda that is incompatible with truly democratic politics.[24]

Fourth, these modes of accumulation and exercise of power define both national and subnational politics. Although "reformers" may initially have introduced "some change" in several provinces and districts, they, too, have fallen victim to the logics of predatory politics defined by "the same kinds of social interests previously at the heart of Suharto's New Order," according to Hadiz and Robison.[25] In Hadiz's view, "little kings" (*raja kecil*) rig the rules of the game and form collusive networks that prevent social forces from gaining access to the local political system.[26] Winters does not explicitly mention subnational oligarchs, but his account of the Jakarta gubernatorial elections suggests that he agrees that oligarchs dominate both national and subnational politics.[27]

Fifth and finally, reflecting the classic Marxist argument that the democratization of economic relations ought to precede elections if the latter are to be meaningful,[28] Hadiz and Robison conclude that genuine democratization and political change will

---

[19] Winters , "Oligarchy and Democracy in Indonesia," pp. 15ff.

[20] Ibid., p. 22.

[21] Ibid.

[22] Hadiz and Robison, "The Political Economy of Oligarchy," p. 36.

[23] Ibid., p. 50.

[24] Hadiz and Robison backtrack from this view to some extent in their contribution to this volume (pp. 35–56). According to Winters's more nuanced theory, the presence of a democracy is perfectly compatible with the presence of an oligarchy as long as democratization and electoral politics do not interfere with the wealth-defense strategies of oligarchs. If this happens, however, oligarchs actively undermine democratic politics. See Winters, "Oligarchy and Democracy in Indonesia."

[25] Hadiz and Robison, "The Political Economy of Oligarchy," p. 53.

[26] Hadiz, *Localising Power*, p. 43. Some scholars have even argued that democratization and decentralization allowed New Order interests to *expand* and *strengthen* their influence. See Nankyung Choi, *Local Politics in Indonesia: Pathways to Power* (New York, NY: Routledge, 2011), p. 102.

[27] Hadiz and Robison see oligarchs dominating subnational politics while Winters sees national oligarchs at least influencing local politics through funding local elites. See Winters, "Oligarchy and Democracy in Indonesia," pp. 22–25.

[28] Benedict Anderson, "Elections and Participation in Three Southeast Asian Countries," in *The Politics of Elections in Southeast Asia*, ed. Robert H. Taylor (New York, NY: Cambridge University Press, 1998), p. 12.

occur if economic change determines "new forms of production and property [that] give rise to new forces and interests."[29] Similarly, Winters argues that oligarchy cannot be overcome through elections in the absence of a fairer distribution of wealth.[30] To summarize, there is broad agreement that, since the events of May 1998 did not democratize class relations, Indonesian politics may have changed in style but not in substance.[31]

There are many possible challenges to these premises. For instance, voluntarist approaches claim that state–society relations in Indonesia are changing. Individual "decision-makers" are the drivers of this change since classes "cannot overwhelm and deny the individual's capacity for autonomous choice."[32] These approaches claim that Indonesians have voted for "attractive leadership"[33] that is "both responsive and responsible" to citizens' demands at the national level.[34] At the subnational level, meanwhile, the decentralization of power facilitated the emergence of "reform-minded individuals."[35] While acknowledging that such leaders are rare, these scholars observe that provinces and districts that have been blessed with such "good leadership" have seen change ranging from the inclusion of hitherto marginalized groups in political deliberations[36] to the reform of tax codes in favor of private sector interests.[37]

But those who see "enlightened leadership" as the main catalyst for changing state–society relations struggle as much as do theorists of oligarchy when it comes to explaining power dynamics in post-1998 Indonesia. Key concepts such as "good leadership" are, if at all, poorly conceptualized, and the mechanisms and processes through which individual leaders change Indonesian politics are neither described nor explained. Hence, we learn neither how "reform-minded leaders" manage to bypass bureaucratic resistance and opposition within the state apparatus nor why only certain figures are able to act in new ways. Furthermore, the number of reform-minded individuals represented in formal politics is far too small to explain the fact that state–society relations have changed across the archipelago.

Meanwhile, scholars working within a pluralist theoretical framework have mounted two lines of attack against the oligarchy thesis. "Interest group pluralists" doubt that the oligarchs are as dominant in Indonesian politics as Hadiz and Robison

---

[29] Hadiz and Robison, "The Political Economy of Oligarchy," p. 41.

[30] Winters, "Oligarchy and Democracy in Indonesia," p. 12.

[31] Similar arguments are made by John Sidel, "The Changing Politics of Religious Knowledge in Asia: The Case of Indonesia," in *The Politics of Knowledge*, ed. Saw Swee-Hock and Danny Quah (Singapore: ISEAS, 2009), pp. 156–92; and Yuki Fukuoka, "Oligarchy and Democracy in Post-Suharto Indonesia," *Political Studies Review* 11,1 (2013): 52–64.

[32] R. Willam Liddle, "The Politics of Development Policy," *World Development* 20,6 (1992): 796.

[33] Saiful Mujani and R. William Liddle, "Leadership, Party, and Religion: Explaining Voting Behavior in Indonesia," *Comparative Political Studies* 40,7 (2007): 844.

[34] Saiful Mujani and R. William Liddle, "Personalities, Parties, and Voters," *Journal of Democracy* 21,2 (2010): 49.

[35] Arianto Patunru, Neil McCulloch, and Christian von Luebke, "A Tale of Two Cities: The Political Economy of Local Investment Climate in Solo and Manado, Indonesia," *IDS Working Papers* 228 (2009): 1–43.

[36] Sebastian Eckardt, *Accountability and Decentralized Service Delivery: Explaining Performance Variation across Local Governments in Indonesia* (Berlin: Nomos Verlag, 2009).

[37] Christian von Luebke, "The Political Economy of Local Governance: Findings from an Indonesian Field Study," *Bulletin of Indonesian Economic Studies* 45,2 (2009): 201–30.

and Winters claim. They argue that after 1998, representatives from a variety of interest groups, including entrepreneurs, politically ambitious newcomers, and civil society representatives, entered politics. There, they effectively counterbalance oligarchic dominance.[38] There are, however, several problems with this argument. Interest group pluralism somewhat naïvely assumes that the presence of interest groups in politics equates to political influence. In addition, there is only scant evidence that a broad range of societal interests is represented in formal Indonesian politics. Even if one believes that a broad range of interest groups have come to inhabit the legislative branch of government after 1998, many crucial decisions in Indonesian politics are not presented for legislative debate because the executive branch of government drives the policymaking process.[39] The powers assigned to the president, governors, and district heads since 1998 means that those who want to retain political prominence need to connect themselves to the executive branch of government. However, rather than being home to a "very heterogeneous class" of political actors,[40] the top posts of the executive branch are dominated by a single social type: a male bureaucrat who started his career during the New Order.[41]

Aware of these problems, "critical pluralists" have mounted a second line of attack against the oligarchy thesis, which no longer focuses on the "social foundations" of political conflict but on "policy outcomes."[42] The explanatory power of the "oligarchy thesis" is weak, according to this argument, because it is unable to account for the kind of policy outcomes that have been evident in both national and local politics after 1998. Examples of policies that have undergone change include those associated with women's affairs, labor issues,[43] and human rights, as well as predatory taxes and levies. While there is no space here for an in-depth analysis of concrete policies in these (and other) areas, it is clear that many of them could be interpreted as a sign of continuing oligarchic dominance.[44] Even if one agrees that many policy outcomes in contemporary Indonesia cannot be explained within an

---

[38] Marcus Mietzner, "Fighting the Hellhounds: Pro-democracy Activists and Party Politics in Post-Suharto Indonesia," *Journal of Contemporary Asia* 43,1 (2013): 28–50.

[39] Anis Ibrahim, S. H. Sirajuddin, Nuruddin Hady, dan Umar Sholahuddin, *Parlemen Lokal DPRD: Peran dan Fungsi dalam Dinamika Otonomi Daerah,* (Malang: Setara Press, 2008), p. 27.

[40] Marcus Mietzner, "Oligarchs, Politicians, and Activists: Contesting Party Politics in Post-Suharto Indonesia," this volume, pp. 99–116.

[41] Michael Buehler, "Married with Children: The Second Round of Direct Elections for Governors and District Heads Shows that Democratisation is Allowing Powerful Families to Entrench Themselves in Local Politics," *Inside Indonesia* 112 (April–June 2013).

[42] Thomas Pepinsky, "Pluralism and Political Conflict in Indonesia," this volume, p. 88.

[43] Teri L. Caraway and Michele Ford, "Labor and Politics under Oligarchy," this volume, pp. 139–55.

[44] For instance, one may argue that the higher number of women in parliament in 2009 compared to 2004 has not resulted from the struggle of women's organizations for gender parity through the introduction of a quota system, but was due to a shift from a closed- to an open-party list system in 2008. The open-party list system created disincentives for candidates to run under a party label and therefore placed a premium on "face recognition." Hence, many of the new female legislators are softcore-porn starlets, soap opera actresses, and singers. In addition, many female parliamentarians belong to families that managed to entrench themselves in politics after 1998. See Michael Buehler, "Married with Children." The higher number of female representatives in the 2009 parliament compared to previous parliaments could therefore be interpreted as indicative of the *growing* power of oligarchic interests in Indonesian politics.

oligarchic framework, the explanatory power of a critical pluralism is hardly any stronger. Stripping pluralist theory of its core idea that governments are responding to the concerns of organized interest groups from *all* levels of society, critical pluralism shifts its focus to the very top of the political pecking order. The language used to describe the players shaping policymaking at both the national and local level in post-1998 Indonesia is revealing. "Allies of the regime" and "Indonesia's most extremely wealthy … citizens"[45] fight it out against one another.

Against this backdrop, critical pluralism looks in many ways more like an elite competition model of the kind I suggested earlier. However, it lacks important components, which an elite competition model incorporates. For instance, its focus on policy outcomes neglects a thorough analysis of power constellations at the beginning of the policymaking process. This not only poses the danger of producing *ex post facto* explanations of policies,[46] but, more important, it risks ignoring important players altogether. For instance, Thomas Pepinsky's take on pluralism leaves the state entirely untheorized, and fails to deal with such important issues as the background of figures inhabiting the government, dynamics between them, and the sequence in which change unfolds.

Finally, proponents of state-in-society approaches argue that change in Indonesia is unfolding from the bottom up through collective action and "popular agency."[47] These scholars see the state as a relatively limited actor that competes with groups in society for influence and political hegemony.[48] They argue that societal groups have reclaimed authority at the "street level"[49] by holding demonstrations and protests.[50] Like interest group pluralists, many of these scholars also claim that the demise of the New Order has allowed "new men" to occupy state office.[51] Yet, in fact, civil society is fragmented,[52] and many nongovernmental organizations remain poorly organized.[53] Moreover, many of these early studies did not specify the mechanisms through which this weak and fragmented civil society imposes its agenda onto the

---

[45] Pepinsky, "Pluralism and Political Conflict in Indonesia," pp. 91, 92.

[46] See, for instance, Ryan Tans, "Mobilizing Resources, Building Coalitions: Local Power in Indonesia," *Policy Studies* 64 (Honolulu, HI: East–West Center, 2012), pp. 1–17.

[47] Danielle N. Lussier and M. Steven Fish, "Indonesia: The Benefits of Civic Engagement," *Journal of Democracy* 23,1 (2012): 70–84; Gerry van Klinken, "The Maluku Wars: Bringing Society Back In," *Indonesia* 71 (April 2001): 1–26; Marcus Mietzner, "Indonesia's Democratic Stagnation: Anti-reformist Elites and Resilient Civil Society," *Democratization* 19,2 (2012): 209–29; Edward Aspinall, "Popular Agency and Interests in Indonesia's Democratic Transition and Consolidation," this volume, pp. 117–37.

[48] Joel Migdal, *State in Society: Studying How States and Societies Transform and Constitute One Another* (Cambridge: Cambridge University Press, 2001).

[49] Joshua Barker, "*Negara Beling*: Street-Level Authority in an Indonesian Slum," in *State of Authority: The State in Society in Indonesia*, ed. van Klinken and Barker, pp. 47–72.

[50] Caraway and Ford, "Labor and Politics under Oligarchy."

[51] Syarif Hidayat and Gerry van Klinken, "Provincial Business and Politics," in *State of Authority: The State in Society in Indonesia*, ed. van Klinken and Barker, pp. 149–62; Jacqueline Vel, "Pilkada in East Sumba: An Old Rivalry in a New Democratic Setting," *Indonesia* 80 (October 2009): 80–107.

[52] Aspinall, "A Nation in Fragments," pp. 27–54.

[53] Hans Antlov, Derick W. Brinkerhoff, and Elke Rapp, "Civil Society Capacity Building for Democratic Reform: Experience and Lessons from Indonesia," *Voluntas* 21,3 (2010): 417–39.

state to effect change from below.[54] Finally, "civil society" is not broadly represented in Indonesian formal politics, a fact some state-in-society scholars readily admit.[55]

Addressing such flaws in earlier research, more recent studies have argued that subaltern groups, despite their fragmentation and their lack of representation in formal politics, have nevertheless changed politics from below. For instance, Edward Aspinall argues that a fragmented civil society has become influential in politics because "[p]olitical pressure exerted … through mobilization …" shaped policymaking in the context of "the rise of competitive elections."[56] These dynamics result in policy outcomes the oligarchy theory cannot explain.[57]

Such an interpretation of change in Indonesian politics is problematic for several reasons. Most important, the influence of groups from below is contingent on elite conflict. In other words, the "networks and clusters of actors that connect [the] ruling elite with activist groups and coalitions, providing … conduits for policy influence from below"[58] have emerged and gained importance *as a consequence* of heightened competition among state elites. Only an elite competition model that locates the trigger for social change at the apex of the political structure can explain, for instance, why organized labor "has not seen a radical expansion of … political power [after 1998]"[59] but has nevertheless gained some influence over policymaking. If elite competition were absent, labor would have been unlikely to have gained more influence.

An elite competition model not only better explains the sequence in which change unfolds and why societal actors have gained influence without commensurate improvements in capacity compared to the New Order, but also illuminates the specificities of policymaking in contemporary Indonesia. For instance, the elite competition model reveals that Indonesia's many local healthcare schemes are driven by incumbents rather than class mobilization, as collectivist approaches have acknowledged.[60] An elite competition model can also explain better than collectivist approaches why the influence of most societal groups is confined to the agenda-setting stage of the policy cycle.[61]

To summarize, an approach that sees changing relations among state elites as explaining changes in state–society relations thus both challenges the oligarchy thesis and better explains why and in what order change has occurred than either the voluntarist or collectivist approach do. In contrast to oligarchy theory, such an approach acknowledges that many players who influence policymaking do so based

---

[54] Mietzner, "Indonesia's Democratic Stagnation," pp. 9–14; Lussier and Fish, "Indonesia," pp. 70–84.

[55] For example, Aspinall, "Popular Agency and Interests," shows that sixteen years after the demise of the New Order, there is no "embedded institutional power for labor … " (p. 128).

[56] Ibid., p. 119.

[57] Caraway and Ford, "Labor and Politics under Oligarchy," make a similar argument.

[58] Aspinall, "Popular Agency and Interests," p. 124.

[59] Ibid., p. 129.

[60] Ibid., p. 130.

[61] Aspinall, "Popular Agency and Interests," and Caraway and Ford, "Labor and Politics under Oligarchy," mention on several occasions that services are promised but rarely delivered, while policies are often adopted but patchily implemented. Overall, societal groups seem to have become most influential at the agenda-setting stage of the policy cycle, which is what we would expect according to the elite competition model as outlined at the beginning of this chapter.

on their political rather than economic power. Change in state–society relations has therefore been possible without change in broader economic structures. An elite competition model also addresses the failure of voluntarist accounts to acknowledge that it is not "new men" but, in fact, "old elites" socialized and politicized during the authoritarian New Order who for the first time in their careers are conducting surveys to sound out their popularity, employing new campaign tactics, and spending months on dusty roads campaigning in remote villages. Likewise, the acknowledgement that change began at the top and radiated downward explains better than collectivist approaches the timing and extent of influence from below. Political change is contingent on elite conflict since societal groups became more influential *after* competition among state elites had increased. Furthermore, an elite competition model explains why some groups but not others have managed to take advantage of elite competition, thereby revealing the limits of "pressure from below." Since state elites continue to dominate formal politics, they mediate the influence of societal groups. Groups gain influence only if they provide state elites with resources the latter deem useful for accumulating and maintaining power. Those that do not provide such resources may *mobilize* but are unlikely to gain political *influence*.

SHARI'A POLICYMAKING IN SOUTH SULAWESI

The case study of subnational *shari'a* policymaking illustrates the distinctiveness of an approach that centers on dynamics among state elites and how these dynamics subsequently affect state–society relations. Moreover, by stepping outside of the Jakarta-centric study of Indonesia that has so preoccupied the analysis of oligarchy, this approach reveals where most important changes in post-Suharto Indonesian politics are occurring.

A close-knit aristocracy has long dominated politics in South Sulawesi province. While mythical conceptions of the hierarchical order of society, control over syncretist forms of Islam, and intermarriage among the noble families of South Sulawesi strengthened the position of the aristocracy *vis-à-vis* commoners, it was mainly economic conditions that determined the political power of the aristocracy over ordinary people. For centuries, the main source of aristocratic political power was an appanage system of landownership that became increasingly exploitative after the Kingdom of Bone, a land-based court without much stake in sea-trade activities, rose to power in 1667.[62] The aristocracy's economic dominance came under pressure after the Dutch colonial government took control of "a large part of the 'regalia lands' (*tanah arajang*) and 'privileged lands' (*tanah ongko*)."[63] The income the nobility obtained from their landholdings was successively reduced in the following decades so that, by the 1920s, accountability reports submitted by outgoing Dutch officials to the colonial government, the *memories van overgave*, stressed that the local aristocracy had only a few large landholdings left and that only a few peasants in South Sulawesi were actually landless.[64]

---

[62] Burhan Djaber Magenda, "The Surviving Aristocracy in Indonesia: Politics in Three Provinces of the Outer Islands" (PhD dissertation, Cornell University, 1989), pp. 548–55; Pelras, "Patron–Client Ties," p. 38.

[63] Pelras, "Patron–Client Ties," p. 38.

[64] Ibid., p. 36.

The economic decline of the local aristocracy worked to the advantage of a commercial class of rich peasants and rice traders of non-aristocratic background. Over time, many of these commoners replaced the nobles as agricultural patrons (*punggawa allaonrumang),* and from this situation, they branched out into other sectors of the economy.[65] Many of these new-wealth elites organized under the banner of religious organizations such as the modernist Muhammadiyah. Opening its first branch in the provincial capital Makassar in 1926, Muhammadiyah's decisive anti-aristocratic tone and its message of upward social mobility based on merit and personal achievements made the organization an ideal vehicle for these rice traders and landowners to seek more influence in the rigidly structured society of South Sulawesi.

The cleavage between the ruling aristocracy, members of which practiced mixed forms of Islam, and non-aristocratic landowners and rice traders attracted to more purist strains of Islam became even more pronounced after the outbreak of a rebellion. Guerrilla units that had fought for Indonesia's independence in South Sulawesi demanded their incorporation into the army after 1949. After the national government refused to accommodate these guerrilla groups, their leaders revolted. Initially, the rebellion in South Sulawesi attracted many aristocrats who had fought for independence and now wanted to be rewarded with positions in the Indonesian army and bureaucracy. However, the rebel movement split in 1953 after leader Kahar Muzakkar pledged allegiance to the Darul Islam rebellion, which had been fighting for a state based on Islamic law in West Java since 1948. After 1953, the national government provided most aristocrats with local government positions, thereby effectively terminating their resistance to the republic.

The Darul Islam rebellion under the Muzakkar leadership, however, continued for another decade, weakening the economic position of the aristocracy further. Most noblemen fled to the cities of South Sulawesi, which isolated them from their landholdings and trading points. Without access to these assets, they were forced to sustain the followers that had come with them to the cities from funds they had accumulated before the rebellion. After the Indonesian army had killed Muzakkar in 1965, the aristocrats realized that "[t]he establishment of security was ... of no assistance to them, since the traditional forms of government, as well as the incomes attached to them, had been abolished in the meantime."[66] Their economic situation worsened further when the national government distributed land to poor peasants across the province under the Land Reform Act, which had been adopted nationwide in 1960 but was implemented in the province only after 1965 due to the rebellion. By the 1970s, 60 percent of the peasants in South Sulawesi owned the land on which they worked, while 40 percent were share tenants, approximately only a quarter of whom cultivated land owned by the local nobility.[67]

Although reliable data on landownership patterns in post-1998 South Sulawesi are not available, it is clear that the majority of people continue to work as relatively independent subsistence farmers.[68] Yet, despite material resources becoming more evenly spread across the population in the province, the local aristocracy was able to

---

[65] Ibid., p. 37.

[66] Ibid., p. 38.

[67] Makaliwe, "An Economic Survey of South Sulawesi," *Bulletin of Indonesian Economic Studies* 5,2 (1969): 18–20.

[68] Badan Pusat Statistik, *Sulawesi Selatan Dalam Angka* (BPS: Makassar 2004), pp. 42–43.

retain its *political* dominance under Suharto's regime because the end of the Darul Islam rebellion in 1965 coincided with the rise of the New Order. Suharto continued to reward the aristocrats who had abandoned Muzakkar with positions in the local army and the bureaucracy.[69] Hence, aristocrats occupied most of the governor and district head posts in South Sulawesi throughout the New Order period.[70] Since the national government appointed subnational government heads, local aristocrats understood that tight connections to Jakarta were necessary to maintain power. Having links to the local population was simply not important in the advancement of one's career.

Increased Elite Competition after 1998

As a consequence of the hierarchical nature of the New Order regime, open competition among state elites in South Sulawesi was minimal between 1965 and 1998. This changed after the fall of Suharto, when new rules were adopted that introduced elections for governors and district heads via local parliaments until 2005, and through direct elections since. Despite these institutional changes, state elites continue to dominate South Sulawesi politics. At least 45 percent of candidates competing in local elections in South Sulawesi, and at least 42 percent of the winners, are New Order academics, bureaucrats, and military personnel who had joined the state apparatus during the Suharto years (see Table 1).[71]

At first glance, this data seem to confirm Hadiz' reading of the continuing political dominance of New Order "interests" in local politics.[72] There were very few representatives of mass organizations or other society based groups participating in these local elections, and even fewer newcomers succeeded in entering the formal political system as a member of a local legislature or a district head. Where the oligarchy thesis breaks down is in its reading of the power resources of these elites, as shown above, and how dynamics among these elites shape state–society relations. Both the indirect elections between 1998 and 2005 and the direct elections since 2005 triggered fierce competition among state elites. In South Sulawesi, there were two indirect and two direct gubernatorial elections as well as thirty-two indirect and forty-seven direct district head elections between 1998 and 2013. Almost all these elections were fiercely contested. In most elections, there were at least two viable candidates with a good chance of winning and relatively equal strength with regard to the number of votes they obtained (see Table 2).[73]

---

[69] Ichlasul Amal, *Regional and Central Government in Indonesian Politics: West Sumatra and South Sulawesi, 1949–1979* (Yogyakarta: Gadjah Mada University Press, 1992).

[70] District heads control rural district governments, and mayors control municipalities. Both these entities are situated below the province in Indonesia's institutional hierarchy. For brevity's sake, I refer to district heads and districts only, unless there are dynamics distinct to mayors and municipalities.

[71] At least 567 candidates have been competing in South Sulawesi local government head elections since 1998. I obtained the data on the career trajectory of candidates between 1998 and 2005 from local newspaper archives. The curriculum vitae of candidates for direct elections I collected at local election commissions.

[72] Hadiz, "Localising Power," pp. 88–119.

[73] Using election data from archival research and local election commissions, I calculated the number of "effective candidates" for all the races in South Sulawesi since 1998 based on Laakso, Markku, and Rein Taagepera, "Effective Number of Parties: A Measure with Application to West Europe," *Comparative Political Studies* 12,1 (1979): 3–27.

Table 1: Background of District Head and Deputy District Head Candidates, 1998-2013

		South Sulawesi						
		Governor	Deputy Governor	District Head	Deputy District Head	Mayor	Deputy Mayor	Total
Academic	Winner	0	0	0	2	0	0	**2**
	Loser	0	0	2	9	2	4	**17**
Bureaucrat	Winner	2	0	27	21	3	2	**55**
	Loser	0	2	76	66	11	5	**160**
Military/ Police	Winner	0	0	3	0	0	1	**4**
	Loser	1	0	8	5	1	0	**15**
Politician	Winner	0	2	1	5	0	0	**8**
	Loser	1	1	8	17	3	5	**35**
Politician/ Private Sector	Winner	0	0	7	4	0	0	**11**
	Loser	0	0	5	3	1	1	**10**
Private Sector	Winner	0	0	6	2	6	2	**16**
	Loser	2	1	21	23	9	9	**65**
Other	Winner	0	0	0	0	0	0	**0**
	Loser	0	0	0	1	0	0	**1**
Missing	Winner	0	0	17	25	2	6	**50**
	Loser	0	0	47	44	13	14	**118**
Total		**6**	**6**	**228**	**227**	**51**	**49**	**567**

This newly competitive environment has shifted the focus of state elites downward and outward in the political arena: instead of lobbying superiors and pulling strings in Jakarta, state elites are now dependent on the support of ordinary people. South Sulawesi's population may be poor, but because many residents own the land on which they live, they are relatively independent compared to "locked-in" electorates in other parts of Southeast Asia, such as voters in parts of the Philippines under the control of land-based oligarchs.[74] Since it is impossible to lobby every citizen individually, candidates running for local elections have had to find ways to mobilize and structure the electorate. There are many challenges that candidates must overcome to achieve these two goals, especially because many avenues available to politicians in consolidated democracies do not exist in Indonesia. Most

---

[74] James C. Scott, "Corruption, Machine Politics, and Political Change," *American Political Science Review* 63,4 (1969): 1146, ftn. 16.

important, Indonesian political parties are weakly institutionalized and lack stable constituencies. Parties also have no comprehensive and well-formulated party platforms, and no money to appeal to voters. As a consequence, Indonesian politicians need to establish *personal* political machines to mobilize and structure the masses.[75] It is against this backdrop that linkages to local power brokers and their networks have acquired new importance.

Growing Interdependence between State Elites and Islamist Groups

The three gubernatorial campaigns in South Sulawesi after 1998 exemplify the increased competition among state elites, and the growing links between candidates and Islamist groups that have emerged as a consequence of that competition. In the first gubernatorial election in South Sulawesi in 2003, the provincial parliament elected Amin Syam as governor. Syam was born in Bone district in South Sulawesi in 1945 and joined the military in 1960. He was initially stationed in West Java, but transferred to South Sulawesi a few years later to fight against the Darul Islam. Over the following decades, Syam rose through the ranks of the local military command and eventually became a major-general. He also occupied civilian posts like many military men during the New Order. He was the district head of Enrekang between 1988 and 1993 and became the head of the South Sulawesi parliament as a member of the Golkar party (Partai Golongan Karya, Party of the Functional Groups) in the final years of the New Order.

Syam announced in 2005 that he would seek reelection in 2007. In anticipation of the first *direct* gubernatorial election to be held in South Sulawesi province, he started to establish campaign structures across South Sulawesi.[76] Syam mobilized the bureaucracy, courted the Golkar party, and established a campaign team consisting of relatives and supporters. To increase his electability, he also approached various groups with extensive networks in South Sulawesi society. In this context, Syam began to visit religious boarding schools across South Sulawesi, and also to mingle with figures from Islamist networks in 2006.[77]

A year before the gubernatorial elections, for instance, Syam visited the grave of Ahmad Marzuki Hasan, the founder of a radical *pesantren* called Darul Istiqamah. The visit was clearly a campaign event, as a large entourage of local politicians and journalists accompanied him on the visit.[78] In July 2006, Syam visited the Islamist Darul Ulum Pesantren in Maros, where he praised the important contributions the school had made in the fight for the adoption of Islamic law in South Sulawesi. Syam

---

[75] Michael Buehler, "The Rising Importance of Personal Networks in Indonesian Local Politics: An Analysis of District Government Head Elections in South Sulawesi in 2005," in *Deepening Democracy in Indonesia? Direct Elections for Local Leaders (Pilkada)*, ed. Maribeth Erb and Priyambudi Sulistiyanto (Singapore: ISEAS 2009), pp. 101–24.

[76] For instance, Syam hired many candidates from the 2005 *district* head elections to form an "expert team." He hoped to have these local notables at his disposal during the elections, according to his campaign manager. Rauf, personal communication, March 27, 2006.

[77] Many of these Islamist groups have direct links to the Darul Islam. After 1965, the remaining rebels established a clandestine but densely knit network of schools, foundations, and nongovernmental organizations across the province. This network survived throughout the New Order.

[78] Anonymous, "Pendiri Pesantren Darul Istiqamah Berpulang," *Fajar*, June 28, 2006, p. 26.

Table 2: Number of Effective Candidates in South Sulawesi Government Head Elections, 1998–2013

Locality	1998	1999	2000	2003	2004	2005	2007	2008	2010	2011	2012	2013
S. Sulawesi	NA			2.59 (3)			2.86 (3)##					2.2 (3)#
Bantaeng	NA			NA#				3.25 (4)				1.4 (5)#
Barru			2.1 (13)			2.59 (3)			2.95 (4)			
Bone		NA#		1.08 (3)				2.18 (3)#				3.2 (6)
Bulukumba			1.95 (4)			4.24 (5)			1.98 (2) [6]##			
Enrekang	2.4 (3)			NA				2.8 (3)#				2.3 (4)
Gowa		NA				3.73 (4)			2.05 (4)#			
Jeneponto		1.9 (3)			NA			2.43 (6)#				2.1 (3)
Makassar		NA			1.99 (2) [3]			2.04 (7)#				5.2 (10)
Maros		NA				3.01 (4)#			4.02 (6)			
Palopo				NA				2.31 (4)#				2 (2) [9]
Pangkep		NA (5)				2.3 (3)			3.48 (6)			
Pare-Pare	2.2 (3)			NA				3.4 (5)#				2.9 (5)
Pinrang		NA		NA				1.99 (2) [7]				4.3 (6)#
Selayar		NA				4.02 (5)			2.62 (3)#			
Sidrap		†		NA				3.8 (6)				2.7 (7)#
Sinjai	NA#			NA				1.94 (2)#				4.2 (9)
Soppeng		NA				3.16 (4)			3.52 (7)#			
Takalar							3.32 (4)#				4.7 (7)	
Tanah Toraja		NA (5)				4.28 (6)#			4.41 (6)			
Tanah Toraja Utara*										2 (7)		
Luwu		NA		NA				2.83 (4)				2.4 (3)#
Luwu Timur**						2.96 (4)			2.4 (4)#			
Luwu Utara***		NA				2.7 (3)#			2 (2) [9]			
Wajo		NA		NA				3.34 (4)				3.5 (6)#

The total number of candidates appears in parentheses and the total number of candidates participating prior to second-round elections appears in square brackets. There were no local government head elections in South Sulawesi in 2001, '02, '06, and '09.

* Established in 2008; ** Established in 2003; *** Established in 1999
† Appointed; # Incumbent won; ## Incumbent lost; NA = Data not available

also made a significant cash donation to the school.[79] Only a few weeks later, Syam, as governor, adopted *shari'a* regulation No. 4/2006 to improve Quran reading skills across the province.

Syam's interest in these networks marked a clear change in political strategy. In 2001, as the head of the provincial parliament (and facing no immediate elections), Syam had refused to embrace the agenda of Islamist groups. At that time, he told the local press that as a private citizen he was sympathetic to the cause of Islamist groups, but as the head of the provincial parliament, he was against adopting *shari'a*.[80] On the eve of Election Day in 2007, he told me: "Yes, if people reelect me, I will continue to adopt *shari'a* regulations in South Sulawesi province."[81]

Despite Syam's efforts to embrace local policy demands, it was his deputy, Syahrul Yasin Limpo, who eventually won the first direct gubernatorial election. Limpo's background and political trajectory show interesting parallels to Syam's. Limpo belongs to a military family that rose to power during the New Order. He entered the bureaucracy in Gowa district in 1980 and steadily rose through the ranks of the New Order civilian apparatus until he was appointed district head in Gowa in 1994. A member of the Golkar party since the early 1980s, and with good connections to the local parliamentarians, Limpo was elected by the local legislature for a second term in 1999. Although known for his involvement in various drug and sex scandals,[82] rather than for his piety, Limpo adopted his first *shari'a* regulation as Gowa district head in 2001. Soon after he became governor in 2007, Limpo announced his plans to run for reelection in 2013. In the following years, Limpo frequently socialized with Islamist groups across the province. In 2011, he adopted a *shari'a* regulation that prohibited the activities of Ahmadiyah, a heterodox Islamic group, in South Sulawesi province.

Limpo's main competitor in the 2013 gubernatorial race was the mayor of Makassar, Ilham Arief Sirajuddin. Son of Arief Sirajuddin, a New Order police lieutenant-colonel who had been district head in Gowa between 1976 and 1984, Ilham Arief Sirajuddin used his father's affiliation with the New Order state to establish various businesses, which he then managed between 1992 and 2004. The younger Sirajuddin also led various associations linked to the New Order, including the Communication Forum for the Daughters and Sons of Retired Military and Police Officers, the Association of Young Indonesian Businessmen, and South Sulawesi's Chamber of Commerce. A Golkar member since 1992, he had occupied a seat in the 1999–2004 provincial parliament for Golkar. In 2004, the parliament elected him as mayor of Makassar. In his campaign to become governor, Sirajuddin, too, approached Islamist networks. For the 2013 election campaign, he chose Aziz Kahar Muzakkar, the son of the former Darul Islam leader, as his running mate. Sirajuddin also adopted various *shari'a* regulations as mayor of Makassar, including the collection of religious taxes and rules concerning dress codes for schoolgirls.

---

[79] Anonymous, "Amin Syam Bantu Pesantren Rp 50 Juta," *Tribun Timur*, July 27, 2006, p. 22.

[80] Juhannis Hamdan, "The Struggle for Formalist Islam in South Sulawesi: From Darul Islam (DI) to Komite Persiapan Penegakan Syariat Islam (KPPSI)" (PhD dissertation, Australian National University, 2006), p. 190.

[81] Amin Syam, personal communication, October 31, 2007.

[82] For instance, Limpo was arrested in the company of a female "entertainer" at the Aryaduta hotel in Makassar in 2002. The police also found a bag of *shabu-shabu*, a methamphetamine, in the hotel room, local newspapers reported.

This brief sketch of the gubernatorial elections in South Sulawesi province after 1998 shows that they almost exclusively involved state elites, who competed against one another. It also shows that these figures, some of whom fought against Islamist groups before 1998, are now collaborating with Islamist networks because they believe that Islamist networks can provide mobilizational, financial, and coercive resources important to entice voters. Candidates have tried to gain access to *pesantren* networks, prayer groups, and Qur'an recitation circles in which hundreds of thousands of people meet daily across South Sulawesi. Islamist groups are gatekeepers to some of the largest of these networks. In addition, many boarding schools have mobilized their students to support the candidate endorsed by the school owner. Often, *shari'a* regulations have also served as a means to accumulate capital. Many *shari'a* regulations on religious alms have been adopted, allowing local government heads to collect considerable amounts of money they have later used for political ends. Finally, Islamist groups have provided candidates with coercive power. Local Islamist paramilitaries, many consisting of local thugs and petty criminals, frequently serve as election witnesses, intimidate voters, and act as "enforcers" for local government heads.[83]

The provincial patterns sketched here are mirrored at the district level. There, state elites with similar backgrounds to the candidates described above have sought to develop links to Islamist groups as a way of gaining an advantage in their competition against one another. The outcome of this growing interconnectedness parallels that at the provincial level. During the New Order, not a single *shari'a* regulation was in force in the province. Between 1998 and 2013, almost all districts in South Sulawesi adopted at least one *shari'a* regulation, amounting to forty-four such regulations in total. There have been similar developments in a number of other provinces in Indonesia. Since 1998, local state elites have adopted at least 420 *shari'a* regulations.[84] These *shari'a* regulations cluster in former Darul Islam areas. There, Islamist pressure groups similar to those found in South Sulawesi have gained influence over the policymaking process as a consequence of heightened competition among state elites.[85]

I argued earlier that state elites mediate the influence of societal groups. In other words, state elites have only become more receptive to pressures from societal groups in places and situations where such players can provide them with resources they deem important to gain and maintain power. Groups that cannot offer such information and resources remain unable to influence local politics through state elites. This point can be demonstrated by comparing the Islamist movements described here with the Prosperous Justice Party (Partai Keadilan Sejahtera, PKS), the country's strongest and most successful Islamist party. In the late New Order, a *dakwah* movement emerged among the pious urban middle class. Members of this movement used the political opening in 1998 to mobilize and establish PKS, much like the local Islamist groups mentioned above that also established organizations

---

[83] For details, see Michael Buehler, "*Shari'a* By-Laws in Indonesian Districts: An Indication for Changing Patterns of Power Accumulation and Political Corruption," *Southeast Asia Research* 16,2 (2008): 165–95.

[84] Michael Buehler and Dani Muhtada, "The Diffusion of *Shari'a* Policies across Indonesia," unpublished manuscript, 2014.

[85] Michael Buehler, "Subnational Islamization through Secular Parties: Comparing *Shari'a* Politics in Two Indonesian Provinces," *Comparative Politics* 46,1 (2013): 63–82.

after the fall of Suharto. However, due to PKS's roots in urban areas, its networks are of no use to state elites in need of clientelistic networks that are—in Indonesia as in most other Asian countries—largely a rural phenomenon.[86] Consequently, local state elites have not reached out to PKS. And since PKS cannot provide state elites with resources the latter deem necessary to win elections, the party's influence over *shari'a* policymaking remains negligible. Immediately after 1998, PKS, too, pushed for the adoption of Islamic law at both the national and local level. Realizing its political impotence, however, the party leadership decided to abandon its *shari'a* platform and to adjust to the political mainstream.[87] This pattern reinforces the conclusion that increased visibility and assertiveness of interest groups should not automatically be taken as a sign of their growing influence.

run/

CONCLUSION

New Order elites continue to dominate the state, and representatives of hitherto excluded groups are rarely running in and almost never winning South Sulawesi elections (or elections in any other province). However, local politics in Indonesia is not produced by "oligarchs." It is produced by state elites who have adapted to the changing nature of post-New Order Indonesian politics by selectively reaching out to societal groups that can provide them with the resources they need to win elections.

In provinces with strong Islamist networks, the rapprochement between "the state" and "society" finds its expression in the adoption of *shari'a* regulations. The politics of *shari'a* policymaking shows that, rather than the structure of economic relations defining the possibilities for change in contemporary Indonesian politics, such opportunities are found in the interstices created by *changing* relations among state elites. For both Hadiz and Robison and for Winters, the fact that candidates endowed with bureaucratic power are winning most Indonesian elections is indicative of how the state continues to serve the interests of that class. However, most candidates losing elections are bureaucrats, too. This fact implies a sociology of the state that goes beyond an image of "the state" as the champion of unified class interests. The Indonesian state is not merely a condensation of existing class relations, and the nature of the state cannot be uncovered by analyzing the interests of some "dominant class" *as a whole* vis-à-vis society. The key explanatory variable behind changing state–society relations in Indonesia after 1998 is a political, not economic, one: the relationship among state elites.

The finding that political dynamics are now different, since the collapse of the New Order, even though economic structures have not changed significantly, is not immediately incompatible with Winters's observation that oligarchs define politics only in areas from where potential threats to their wealth and income may arise.[88] The adoption of Islamic law, one could argue, is simply not of any interest to oligarchs. At the same time, however, the struggle over Islamic law in South Sulawesi (as in other parts of Indonesia) was always a proxy for a more deep-

---

[86] Dan Slater, *Ordering Power: Contentious Politics and Authoritarian Leviathans in Southeast Asia* (Cambridge: Cambridge University Press, 2010), p. 42.

[87] Michael Buehler, "Revisiting the Inclusion-Moderation Thesis in the Context of Decentralized Institutions: The Behavior of Indonesia's Prosperous Justice Party in National and Local Politics," *Party Politics* 19,2 (2012): 210–29.

[88] Winters, *Oligarchy*, p. 31.

reaching conflict over control of resources between state elites and economic elites situated in society. The adoption of *shari'a* regulations thus reflects the strengthening of groups with the potential to threaten the wealth and income of current state elites. It is not a peripheral interest to those elites who control state power.

The elite competition model suggested in this chapter also better explains the contours of state–society relations in post-1998 Indonesian than do voluntarist and collectivist approaches. A focus on changing relations among "old" elites inhabiting the state explains why state–society relations are changing across the archipelago despite the lack of comprehensive elite turnover after the demise of Suharto. Rather than the presence of "reform champions," it is the competition among "old" elites that has pushed the interaction between the state and society in new directions. At the same time, the elite competition model shows that change in state–society relations occurs in a top-down rather than bottom-up manner. Societal groups have become more influential in politics only *after* competition between elites increased. A view of Indonesian politics that centers on the relations among state elites not only reveals the opportunities for change in state–society relations, but also its limits. State elites are primarily motivated to adopt policies to attract the support of groups they need to gain and maintain power in Indonesia's electoral democracy. Whether these policies are actually implemented is of secondary importance. Hence, groups situated in society seem to have, at best, won influence over agenda-setting and policy adoption, but lack influence over the implementation stage of the policy cycle. So long as these groups have no representatives in the formal political arena, this situation is unlikely to change, and this fact has important consequences for the quality of democracy in Indonesia.[89] Moreover, due to the causal primacy of elite relations, and the dependency of these elites on the state, institutional change may quickly close the interstices through which some societal groups have managed to gain and exert political influence.[90] In other words, the "deep architecture" of post-1998 Indonesian politics may, in fact, not be all that deep after all.

---

[89] Buehler, "Decentralisation and Local Democracy in Indonesia," pp. 267–85.

[90] At the time of writing, the national parliament was discussing abolishing direct elections for governors and district heads.

CONTRIBUTORS

EDITORS

Michele Ford is Professor of Southeast Asian Studies and Director of the Sydney Southeast Asia Centre at the University of Sydney, where she holds an Australian Research Council Future Fellowship. Michele's research focuses on the Indonesian labor movement, trade union aid, and trade union responses to labor migration in East and Southeast Asia. She has edited several volumes and is the author of *Workers and Intellectuals: NGOs, Trade Unions and the Indonesian Labour Movement* (NUS/Hawaii/KITLV, 2009).

Thomas B. Pepinsky is Associate Professor in the Department of Government and Associate Director of the Modern Indonesia Project at Cornell University. His research lies at the intersection of comparative politics and international political economy, with a focus on emerging markets in Southeast Asia. He is the author of *Economic Crises and the Breakdown of Authoritarian Regimes: Indonesia and Malaysia in Comparative Perspective* (Cambridge University Press, 2009).

CONTRIBUTORS

Edward Aspinall is Professor of Political Science in the Department of Political and Social Change in the School of International, Political, and Strategic Studies at the Australian National University. He is the author of *Opposing Suharto: Compromise, Resistance and Regime Change in Indonesia* (Stanford University Press, 2005) and *Islam and Nation: Separatist Rebellion in Aceh, Indonesia* (Stanford University Press, 2009). He has also written many shorter pieces about Indonesian politics, and has edited seven volumes. His research focuses on democracy, social movements, and social change in Indonesia.

Michael Buehler is a Lecturer in Comparative Politics in the Department of Politics and International Studies at the University of London's School of Oriental and African Studies (SOAS). His teaching and research interests are in local politics with a focus on Indonesia. Michael has published on local politics in Indonesia in journals such as *Comparative Politics, Party Politics, Indonesia*, and the *Bulletin of Indonesian Economic Studies*.

Teri L. Caraway is Associate Professor of Political Science at the University of Minnesota, Twin Cities. Her research focuses on comparative labor politics, international political economy, and the Indonesian labor movement. She is author of *Assembling Women: The Feminization of Global Manufacturing* (Cornell University ILR Press, 2007) and numerous peer-reviewed articles. She holds, with Michele Ford, an

Australian Research Council Discovery Project grant entitled "The Re-emergence of Political Labor in Indonesia."

Vedi R. Hadiz is Professor of Asian Societies and Politics at the Asia Research Centre, Murdoch University. He is the author of *Localising Power in Post-Authoritarian Indonesia: A Southeast Asia Perspective* (Stanford University Press, 2010) and co-author (with Richard Robison) of *Reorganising Power in Indonesia: The Politics of Oligarchy in an Age of Markets* (RoutledgeCurzon, 2004). As an Australian Research Council Future Fellow, he is currently conducting research on state, class, and Islamic populism in Indonesia and the Middle East.

R. William Liddle is Professor Emeritus of political science and research associate at the Mershon Center, Ohio State University. His research focuses on Indonesian political leadership and voting behavior. Recent publications include *Memperbaiki Mutu Demokrasi di Indonesia: Sebuah Perdebatan* (Yayasan Paramadina, 2012) and *Kuasa Rakyat* (Mizan 2012), with Saiful Mujani and Kuskridho Ambardi.

Marcus Mietzner is Senior Lecturer and Fellow at the Department of Political and Social Change in the School of International, Political, and Strategic Studies at the Australian National University. His research focuses on the political role of the military, political parties, and electoral politics in Southeast Asia, particularly Indonesia. Marcus is the author of *Money, Power, and Ideology: Political Parties in Post-Authoritarian Indonesia* (NUS/Hawaii/NIAS, 2013). He has edited a number of volumes, including *The Political Resurgence of the Military in Southeast Asia* (Routledge, 2011).

Richard Robison is Professor Emeritus at Murdoch University and a former Director of its Asia Research Centre. His research is focused on the political economy of Indonesia and, more generally, the politics of markets and ideologies of neoliberalism. Among his publications are *Indonesia: The Rise of Capital* (Allen and Unwin, 1986) and *Reorganising Power in Indonesia: The Politics of Oligarchy in an Age of Markets* (Routledge, 2004, with Vedi Hadiz). He has published widely in leading journals, including *World Politics, World Development, New Political Economy, Pacific Review, Journal of Development Studies,* and *Indonesia.*

Jeffrey A. Winters is a Professor in the Department of Politics and the founding Director of the Equality Development and Globalization Studies (EDGS) program at Northwestern University. He is also the founder and chair of the Board of Trustees of the Indonesian Scholarship and Research Support Foundation (ISRSF) in Jakarta. Winters studies oligarchs and elites in comparative perspective. His most recent book, *Oligarchy* (Cambridge, 2011), received the 2012 APSA Luebbert Award for the best book in comparative politics.

SOUTHEAST ASIA PROGRAM PUBLICATIONS
Cornell University

Studies on Southeast Asia

Number 64　*Slow Anthropology: Negotiating Difference with the Iu Mien*, Hjorleifur Jonsson. 2014. ISBN 978-0-87727-764-4 (pb.)

Number 63　*Exploration and Irony in Studies of Siam over Forty Years*, Benedict R. O'G. Anderson. 2014. ISBN 978-0-87727-763-7 (pb.)

Number 62　*Ties that Bind: Cultural Identity, Class, and Law in Vietnam's Labor Resistance*, Trần Ngọc Angie. 2013. ISBN 978-0-87727-762-0 (pb.)

Number 61　*A Mountain of Difference: The Lumad in Early Colonial Mindanao*, Oona Paredes. 2013. ISBN 978-0-87727-761-3 (pb.)

Number 60　*The* Kim Vân Kieu *of Nguyen Du (1765–1820)*, trans. Vladislav Zhukov. 2013. ISBN 978-0-87727-760-6 (pb.)

Number 59　*The Politics of Timor-Leste: Democratic Consolidation after Intervention*, ed. Michael Leach and Damien Kingsbury. 2013. ISBN 978-0-87727-759-0 (pb.)

Number 58　*The Spirit of Things: Materiality and Religious Diversity in Southeast Asia*, ed. Julius Bautista. 2012. ISBN 970-0-87727-758-3 (pb.)

Number 57　*Demographic Change in Southeast Asia: Recent Histories and Future Directions*, ed. Lindy Williams and Michael Philip Guest. 2012. ISBN 978-0-87727-757-6 (pb.)

Number 56　*Modern and Contemporary Southeast Asian Art: An Anthology*, ed. Nora A. Taylor and Boreth Ly. 2012. ISBN 978-0-87727-756-9 (pb.)

Number 55　*Glimpses of Freedom: Independent Cinema in Southeast Asia*, ed. May Adadol Ingawanij and Benjamin McKay. 2012. ISBN 978-0-87727-755-2 (pb.)

Number 54　*Student Activism in Malaysia: Crucible, Mirror, Sideshow*, Meredith L. Weiss. 2011. ISBN 978-0-87727-754-5 (pb.)

Number 53　*Political Authority and Provincial Identity in Thailand: The Making of Banharn-buri*, Yoshinori Nishizaki. 2011. ISBN 978-0-87727-753-8 (pb.)

Number 52　*Vietnam and the West: New Approaches*, ed. Wynn Wilcox. 2010. ISBN 978-0-87727-752-1 (pb.)

Number 51　*Cultures at War: The Cold War and Cultural Expression in Southeast Asia*, ed. Tony Day and Maya H. T. Liem. 2010. ISBN 978-0-87727-751-4 (pb.)

Number 50　*State of Authority: The State in Society in Indonesia*, ed. Gerry van Klinken and Joshua Barker. 2009. ISBN 978-0-87727-750-7 (pb.)

Number 49　*Phan Châu Trinh and His Political Writings*, Phan Châu Trinh, ed. and trans. Vinh Sinh. 2009. ISBN 978-0-87727-749-1 (pb.)

Number 48　*Dependent Communities: Aid and Politics in Cambodia and East Timor*, Caroline Hughes. 2009. ISBN 978-0-87727-748-4 (pb.)

Number 47　*A Man Like Him: Portrait of the Burmese Journalist, Journal Kyaw U Chit Maung*, Journal Kyaw Ma Ma Lay, trans. Ma Thanegi, 2008. ISBN 978-0-87727-747-7 (pb.)

Number 46   *At the Edge of the Forest: Essays on Cambodia, History, and Narrative in Honor of David Chandler*, ed. Anne Ruth Hansen and Judy Ledgerwood. 2008. ISBN 978-0-87727-746-0 (pb).

Number 45   *Conflict, Violence, and Displacement in Indonesia*, ed. Eva-Lotta E. Hedman. 2008. ISBN 978-0-87727-745-3 (pb).

Number 44   *Friends and Exiles: A Memoir of the Nutmeg Isles and the Indonesian Nationalist Movement*, Des Alwi, ed. Barbara S. Harvey. 2008. ISBN 978-0-877277-44-6 (pb).

Number 43   *Early Southeast Asia: Selected Essays*, O. W. Wolters, ed. Craig J. Reynolds. 2008. 255 pp. ISBN 978-0-877277-43-9 (pb).

Number 42   *Thailand: The Politics of Despotic Paternalism* (revised edition), Thak Chaloemtiarana. 2007. 284 pp. ISBN 0-8772-7742-7 (pb).

Number 41   *Views of Seventeenth-Century Vietnam: Christoforo Borri on Cochinchina and Samuel Baron on Tonkin*, ed. Olga Dror and K. W. Taylor. 2006. 290 pp. ISBN 0-8772-7741-9 (pb).

Number 40   *Laskar Jihad: Islam, Militancy, and the Quest for Identity in Post-New Order Indonesia*, Noorhaidi Hasan. 2006. 266 pp. ISBN 0-877277-40-0 (pb).

Number 39   *The Indonesian Supreme Court: A Study of Institutional Collapse*, Sebastiaan Pompe. 2005. 494 pp. ISBN 0-877277-38-9 (pb).

Number 38   *Spirited Politics: Religion and Public Life in Contemporary Southeast Asia*, ed. Andrew C. Willford and Kenneth M. George. 2005. 210 pp. ISBN 0-87727-737-0.

Number 37   *Sumatran Sultanate and Colonial State: Jambi and the Rise of Dutch Imperialism, 1830-1907*, Elsbeth Locher-Scholten, trans. Beverley Jackson. 2004. 332 pp. ISBN 0-87727-736-2.

Number 36   *Southeast Asia over Three Generations: Essays Presented to Benedict R. O'G. Anderson*, ed. James T. Siegel and Audrey R. Kahin. 2003. 398 pp. ISBN 0-87727-735-4.

Number 35   *Nationalism and Revolution in Indonesia*, George McTurnan Kahin, intro. Benedict R. O'G. Anderson (reprinted from 1952 edition, Cornell University Press, with permission). 2003. 530 pp. ISBN 0-87727-734-6.

Number 34   *Golddiggers, Farmers, and Traders in the "Chinese Districts" of West Kalimantan, Indonesia*, Mary Somers Heidhues. 2003. 316 pp. ISBN 0-87727-733-8.

Number 33   *Opusculum de Sectis apud Sinenses et Tunkinenses (A Small Treatise on the Sects among the Chinese and Tonkinese): A Study of Religion in China and North Vietnam in the Eighteenth Century*, Father Adriano de St. Thecla, trans. Olga Dror, with Mariya Berezovska. 2002. 363 pp. ISBN 0-87727-732-X.

Number 32   *Fear and Sanctuary: Burmese Refugees in Thailand*, Hazel J. Lang. 2002. 204 pp. ISBN 0-87727-731-1.

Number 31   *Modern Dreams: An Inquiry into Power, Cultural Production, and the Cityscape in Contemporary Urban Penang, Malaysia*, Beng-Lan Goh. 2002. 225 pp. ISBN 0-87727-730-3.

Number 30   *Violence and the State in Suharto's Indonesia*, ed. Benedict R. O'G. Anderson. 2001. Second printing, 2002. 247 pp. ISBN 0-87727-729-X.

Number 29   *Studies in Southeast Asian Art: Essays in Honor of Stanley J. O'Connor*, ed. Nora A. Taylor. 2000. 243 pp. Illustrations. ISBN 0-87727-728-1.

Number 28   *The Hadrami Awakening: Community and Identity in the Netherlands East Indies, 1900-1942*, Natalie Mobini-Kesheh. 1999. 174 pp. ISBN 0-87727-727-3.

Number 27   *Tales from Djakarta: Caricatures of Circumstances and their Human Beings*, Pramoedya Ananta Toer. 1999. 145 pp. ISBN 0-87727-726-5.

Number 26   *History, Culture, and Region in Southeast Asian Perspectives*, rev. ed., O. W. Wolters. 1999. Second printing, 2004. 275 pp. ISBN 0-87727-725-7.

Number 25   *Figures of Criminality in Indonesia, the Philippines, and Colonial Vietnam*, ed. Vicente L. Rafael. 1999. 259 pp. ISBN 0-87727-724-9.

Number 24   *Paths to Conflagration: Fifty Years of Diplomacy and Warfare in Laos, Thailand, and Vietnam, 1778-1828*, Mayoury Ngaosyvathn and Pheuiphanh Ngaosyvathn. 1998. 268 pp. ISBN 0-87727-723-0.

Number 23   *Nguyễn Cochinchina: Southern Vietnam in the Seventeenth and Eighteenth Centuries*, Li Tana. 1998. Second printing, 2002. 194 pp. ISBN 0-87727-722-2.

Number 22   *Young Heroes: The Indonesian Family in Politics*, Saya S. Shiraishi. 1997. 183 pp. ISBN 0-87727-721-4.

Number 21   *Interpreting Development: Capitalism, Democracy, and the Middle Class in Thailand*, John Girling. 1996. 95 pp. ISBN 0-87727-720-6.

Number 20   *Making Indonesia*, ed. Daniel S. Lev, Ruth McVey. 1996. 201 pp. ISBN 0-87727-719-2.

Number 19   *Essays into Vietnamese Pasts*, ed. K. W. Taylor, John K. Whitmore. 1995. 288 pp. ISBN 0-87727-718-4.

Number 18   *In the Land of Lady White Blood: Southern Thailand and the Meaning of History*, Lorraine M. Gesick. 1995. 106 pp. ISBN 0-87727-717-6.

Number 17   *The Vernacular Press and the Emergence of Modern Indonesian Consciousness*, Ahmat Adam. 1995. 220 pp. ISBN 0-87727-716-8.

Number 16   *The Nan Chronicle*, trans., ed. David K. Wyatt. 1994. 158 pp. ISBN 0-87727-715-X.

Number 15   *Selective Judicial Competence: The Cirebon-Priangan Legal Administration, 1680–1792*, Mason C. Hoadley. 1994. 185 pp. ISBN 0-87727-714-1.

Number 14   *Sjahrir: Politics and Exile in Indonesia*, Rudolf Mrázek. 1994. 536 pp. ISBN 0-87727-713-3.

Number 13   *Fair Land Sarawak: Some Recollections of an Expatriate Officer*, Alastair Morrison. 1993. 196 pp. ISBN 0-87727-712-5.

Number 12   *Fields from the Sea: Chinese Junk Trade with Siam during the Late Eighteenth and Early Nineteenth Centuries*, Jennifer Cushman. 1993. 206 pp. ISBN 0-87727-711-7.

Number 11   *Money, Markets, and Trade in Early Southeast Asia: The Development of Indigenous Monetary Systems to AD 1400*, Robert S. Wicks. 1992. 2nd printing 1996. 354 pp., 78 tables, illus., maps. ISBN 0-87727-710-9.

Number 10   *Tai Ahoms and the Stars: Three Ritual Texts to Ward Off Danger*, trans., ed. B. J. Terwiel, Ranoo Wichasin. 1992. 170 pp. ISBN 0-87727-709-5.

Number 9	*Southeast Asian Capitalists,* ed. Ruth McVey. 1992. 2nd printing 1993. 220 pp. ISBN 0-87727-708-7.
Number 8	*The Politics of Colonial Exploitation: Java, the Dutch, and the Cultivation System,* Cornelis Fasseur, ed. R. E. Elson, trans. R. E. Elson, Ary Kraal. 1992. 2nd printing 1994. 266 pp. ISBN 0-87727-707-9.
Number 7	*A Malay Frontier: Unity and Duality in a Sumatran Kingdom,* Jane Drakard. 1990. 2nd printing 2003. 215 pp. ISBN 0-87727-706-0.
Number 6	*Trends in Khmer Art,* Jean Boisselier, ed. Natasha Eilenberg, trans. Natasha Eilenberg, Melvin Elliott. 1989. 124 pp., 24 plates. ISBN 0-87727-705-2.
Number 5	*Southeast Asian Ephemeris: Solar and Planetary Positions, A.D. 638–2000,* J. C. Eade. 1989. 175 pp. ISBN 0-87727-704-4.
Number 3	*Thai Radical Discourse: The Real Face of Thai Feudalism Today,* Craig J. Reynolds. 1987. 2nd printing 1994. 186 pp. ISBN 0-87727-702-8.
Number 1	*The Symbolism of the Stupa,* Adrian Snodgrass. 1985. Revised with index, 1988. 3rd printing 1998. 469 pp. ISBN 0-87727-700-1.

SEAP Series

Number 23	*Possessed by the Spirits: Mediumship in Contemporary Vietnamese Communities.* 2006. 186 pp. ISBN 0-877271-41-0 (pb).
Number 22	*The Industry of Marrying Europeans,* Vũ Trọng Phụng, trans. Thúy Tranviet. 2006. 66 pp. ISBN 0-877271-40-2 (pb).
Number 21	*Securing a Place: Small-Scale Artisans in Modern Indonesia,* Elizabeth Morrell. 2005. 220 pp. ISBN 0-877271-39-9.
Number 20	*Southern Vietnam under the Reign of Minh Mạng (1820-1841): Central Policies and Local Response,* Choi Byung Wook. 2004. 226pp. ISBN 0-0-877271-40-2.
Number 19	*Gender, Household, State: Đổi Mới in Việt Nam,* ed. Jayne Werner and Danièle Bélanger. 2002. 151 pp. ISBN 0-87727-137-2.
Number 18	*Culture and Power in Traditional Siamese Government,* Neil A. Englehart. 2001. 130 pp. ISBN 0-87727-135-6.
Number 17	*Gangsters, Democracy, and the State,* ed. Carl A. Trocki. 1998. Second printing, 2002. 94 pp. ISBN 0-87727-134-8.
Number 16	*Cutting across the Lands: An Annotated Bibliography on Natural Resource Management and Community Development in Indonesia, the Philippines, and Malaysia,* ed. Eveline Ferretti. 1997. 329 pp. ISBN 0-87727-133-X.
Number 15	*The Revolution Falters: The Left in Philippine Politics after 1986,* ed. Patricio N. Abinales. 1996. Second printing, 2002. 182 pp. ISBN 0-87727-132-1.
Number 14	*Being Kammu: My Village, My Life,* Damrong Tayanin. 1994. 138 pp., 22 tables, illus., maps. ISBN 0-87727-130-5.
Number 13	*The American War in Vietnam,* ed. Jayne Werner, David Hunt. 1993. 132 pp. ISBN 0-87727-131-3.
Number 12	*The Voice of Young Burma,* Aye Kyaw. 1993. 92 pp. ISBN 0-87727-129-1.

Number 11   *The Political Legacy of Aung San,* ed. Josef Silverstein. Revised edition
              1993. 169 pp. ISBN 0-87727-128-3.

Number 10   *Studies on Vietnamese Language and Literature: A Preliminary
              Bibliography,* Nguyen Dinh Tham. 1992. 227 pp. ISBN 0-87727-127-5.

Number 8   *From PKI to the Comintern, 1924–1941: The Apprenticeship of the Malayan
              Communist Party,* Cheah Boon Kheng. 1992. 147 pp. ISBN 0-87727-125-9.

Number 7   *Intellectual Property and US Relations with Indonesia, Malaysia, Singapore,
              and Thailand,* Elisabeth Uphoff. 1991. 67 pp. ISBN 0-87727-124-0.

Number 6   *The Rise and Fall of the Communist Party of Burma (CPB),* Bertil Lintner.
              1990. 124 pp. 26 illus., 14 maps. ISBN 0-87727-123-2.

Number 5   *Japanese Relations with Vietnam: 1951–1987,* Masaya Shiraishi. 1990.
              174 pp. ISBN 0-87727-122-4.

Number 3   *Postwar Vietnam: Dilemmas in Socialist Development,* ed. Christine White,
              David Marr. 1988. 2nd printing 1993. 260 pp. ISBN 0-87727-120-8.

Number 2   *The Dobama Movement in Burma (1930–1938),* Khin Yi. 1988. 160 pp.
              ISBN 0-87727-118-6.

Cornell Modern Indonesia Project Publications

Number 77   *Beyond Oligarchy: Wealth, Power, and Contemporary Indonesian Politics,*
              ed. Michele Ford and Thomas B. Pepinsky. 2014. ISBN 978-0-87727-
              303-5 (pb.)

Number 76   *Producing Indonesia: The State of the Field of Indonesian Studies,* ed. Eric
              Tagliacozzo. 2014. ISBN 978-0-87727-302-8 (pb.)

All Following CMIP titles available at http://cmip.library.cornell.edu

Number 75   *A Tour of Duty: Changing Patterns of Military Politics in Indonesia in the
              1990s.* Douglas Kammen and Siddharth Chandra. 1999. 99 pp.
              ISBN 0-87763-049-6.

Number 74   *The Roots of Acehnese Rebellion 1989–1992,* Tim Kell. 1995. 103 pp.
              ISBN 0-87763-040-2.

Number 72   *Popular Indonesian Literature of the Qur'an,* Howard M. Federspiel. 1994.
              170 pp. ISBN 0-87763-038-0.

Number 71   *A Javanese Memoir of Sumatra, 1945–1946: Love and Hatred in the
              Liberation War,* Takao Fusayama. 1993. 150 pp. ISBN 0-87763-037-2.

Number 69   *The Road to Madiun: The Indonesian Communist Uprising of 1948,*
              Elizabeth Ann Swift. 1989. 120 pp. ISBN 0-87763-035-6.

Number 68   *Intellectuals and Nationalism in Indonesia: A Study of the Following
              Recruited by Sutan Sjahrir in Occupation Jakarta,* J. D. Legge. 1988.
              159 pp. ISBN 0-87763-034-8.

Number 67   *Indonesia Free: A Biography of Mohammad Hatta,* Mavis Rose. 1987.
              252 pp. ISBN 0-87763-033-X.

Number 66   *Prisoners at Kota Cane,* Leon Salim, trans. Audrey Kahin. 1986. 112 pp.
              ISBN 0-87763-032-1.

Number 64	*Suharto and His Generals: Indonesia's Military Politics, 1975–1983*, David Jenkins. 1984. 4th printing 1997. 300 pp. ISBN 0-87763-030-5.
Number 62	*Interpreting Indonesian Politics: Thirteen Contributions to the Debate, 1964–1981*, ed. Benedict Anderson, Audrey Kahin, intro. Daniel S. Lev. 1982. 3rd printing 1991. 172 pp. ISBN 0-87763-028-3.
Number 60	*The Minangkabau Response to Dutch Colonial Rule in the Nineteenth Century*, Elizabeth E. Graves. 1981. 157 pp. ISBN 0-87763-000-3.
Number 57	*Permesta: Half a Rebellion*, Barbara S. Harvey. 1977. 174 pp. ISBN 0-87763-003-8.
Number 52	*A Preliminary Analysis of the October 1 1965, Coup in Indonesia (Prepared in January 1966)*, Benedict R. Anderson, Ruth T. McVey, assist. Frederick P. Bunnell. 1971. 3rd printing 1990. 174 pp. ISBN 0-87763-008-9.
Number 48	*Nationalism, Islam and Marxism*, Soekarno, intro. Ruth T. McVey. 1970.
Number 37	*Mythology and the Tolerance of the Javanese*, Benedict R. O'G. Anderson. 2nd edition, 1996. Reprinted 2004. 104 pp., 65 illus. ISBN 0-87763-041-0.

Copublished Titles

The Ambiguous Allure of the West: Traces of the Colonial in Thailand, ed. Rachel V. Harrison and Peter A. Jackson. Copublished with Hong Kong University Press. 2010. ISBN 978-0-87727-608-1 (pb.)

The Many Ways of Being Muslim: Fiction by Muslim Filipinos, ed. Coeli Barry. Copublished with Anvil Publishing, Inc., the Philippines. 2008. ISBN 978-0-87727-605-0 (pb.)

Language Texts

INDONESIAN

Beginning Indonesian through Self-Instruction, John U. Wolff, Dédé Oetomo, Daniel Fietkiewicz. 3rd revised edition 1992. Vol. 1. 115 pp. ISBN 0-87727-529-7. Vol. 2. 434 pp. ISBN 0-87727-530-0. Vol. 3. 473 pp. ISBN 0-87727-531-9.

Indonesian Readings, John U. Wolff. 1978. 4th printing 1992. 480 pp. ISBN 0-87727-517-3

Indonesian Conversations, John U. Wolff. 1978. 3rd printing 1991. 297 pp. ISBN 0-87727-516-5

Formal Indonesian, John U. Wolff. 2nd revised edition 1986. 446 pp. ISBN 0-87727-515-7

TAGALOG

Pilipino through Self-Instruction, John U. Wolff, Maria Theresa C. Centeno, Der-Hwa V. Rau. 1991. Vol. 1. 342 pp. ISBN 0-87727—525-4. Vol. 2., revised 2005, 378 pp. ISBN 0-87727-526-2. Vol 3., revised 2005, 431 pp. ISBN 0-87727-527-0. Vol. 4. 306 pp. ISBN 0-87727-528-9.

THAI

A. U. A. Language Center Thai Course, J. Marvin Brown. Originally published by the American University Alumni Association Language Center, 1974. Reissued by Cornell Southeast Asia Program, 1991, 1992. Book 1. 267 pp. ISBN 0-87727-506-8. Book 2. 288 pp. ISBN 0-87727-507-6. Book 3. 247 pp. ISBN 0-87727-508-4.

A. U. A. Language Center Thai Course, Reading and Writing Text (mostly reading), 1979. Reissued 1997. 164 pp. ISBN 0-87727-511-4.

A. U. A. Language Center Thai Course, Reading and Writing Workbook (mostly writing), 1979. Reissued 1997. 99 pp. ISBN 0-87727-512-2.

KHMER

Cambodian System of Writing and Beginning Reader, Franklin E. Huffman. Originally published by Yale University Press, 1970. Reissued by Cornell Southeast Asia Program, 4th printing 2002. 365 pp. ISBN 0-300-01314-0.

Modern Spoken Cambodian, Franklin E. Huffman, assist. Charan Promchan, Chhom-Rak Thong Lambert. Originally published by Yale University Press, 1970. Reissued by Cornell Southeast Asia Program, 3rd printing 1991. 451 pp. ISBN 0-300-01316-7.

Intermediate Cambodian Reader, ed. Franklin E. Huffman, assist. Im Proum. Originally published by Yale University Press, 1972. Reissued by Cornell Southeast Asia Program, 1988. 499 pp. ISBN 0-300-01552-6.

Cambodian Literary Reader and Glossary, Franklin E. Huffman, Im Proum. Originally published by Yale University Press, 1977. Reissued by Cornell Southeast Asia Program, 1988. 494 pp. ISBN 0-300-02069-4.

HMONG

White Hmong-English Dictionary, Ernest E. Heimbach. 1969. 8th printing, 2002. 523 pp. ISBN 0-87727-075-9.

VIETNAMESE

Intermediate Spoken Vietnamese, Franklin E. Huffman, Tran Trong Hai. 1980. 3rd printing 1994. ISBN 0-87727-500-9.

Proto-Austronesian Phonology with Glossary, John U. Wolff, 2 volumes, 2011. ISBN vol. I, 978-0-87727-532-9. ISBN vol. II, 978-0-87727-533-6.

To order, please contact:
Mail:
Cornell University Press Services
750 Cascadilla Street
PO Box 6525
Ithaca, NY 14851 USA

E-mail: orderbook@cupserv.org

Phone/Fax, Monday–Friday, 8 am – 5 pm (Eastern US):
Phone: 607 277 2211 or 800 666 2211 (US, Canada)
Fax: 607 277 6292 or 800 688 2877 (US, Canada)

Order through our online bookstore at:
SEAP.einaudi.cornell.edu/publications